Gospel Truth

VOLUME 2

Gospel Truth

DISCOURSES AND WRITINGS

OF

President George Q. Cannon

FIRST COUNSELOR TO PRESIDENTS
JOHN TAYLOR, WILFORD WOODRUFF, AND LORENZO SNOW

VOLUME 2

Selected, Arranged, and Edited
by
JERRELD L. NEWQUIST

PUBLISHED BY DESERET BOOK COMPANY
SALT LAKE CITY, UTAH
1974

Library of Congress Number 57-35445

ISBN Number 0-87747-520-2

GOSPEL TRUTH

VOLUME 2

Unquestionably the grand design of the Gospel may be summed up in one word —salvation. . . . The Gospel is the plan which our merciful and all-wise Father has devised for the redemption of the world and its inhabitants, not merely from the effects of sin but from sin itself, so that by removing the cause we may be forever freed from its effects. To sum the matter up in a few words, the design of the Gospel is to make men and women perfectly happy.

—GEORGE Q. CANNON
Millennial Star 24:601
(September 20, 1862)

Never at any previous time in the world's history has a Prophet come forth having stronger evidence to support him in claiming to be a servant of God in possession of the Spirit of the Lord than has this Prophet [Joseph Smith]. It was necessary that it should be so that this generation might be left without excuse. The work was to be a great and mighty one; and though in the commencement the means seemed inadequate to produce it, yet, like the tree grown from the mustard seed, of which Jesus spoke, it is destined eventually to overshadow the earth and afford shelter to all who are willing to accept it.

—George Q. Cannon
Liahona 30:543

No man ever calmly sat down with a prayerful heart to examine the claims of this work, popularly termed "Mormonism," who did not rise from the investigation convinced that there was a power, an influence and a spirit accompanying this work that he had never met with before. . . . But the difficulty now is, as it has been in every age when God has attempted to establish his work upon the earth—men in general are blinded by the traditions of their fathers. This, and the love of ease, and popularity, and other worldly objects that surrounded them, prevents men from seeing the work of God in its true light, and blinds them to their highest interests.

—George Q. Cannon
Journal of Discourses 19:199-200
(July 21, 1867)

CONTENTS

Section 3: ASSORTED GOSPEL THEMES

VOLUME 1 CONTAINS THE FOLLOWING:

PREFACE

"No man in Utah, after the passing of President Brigham Young, wielded with all classes so great an influence as President George Q. Cannon, and this influence was felt up to the very close of his life," wrote the historian Elder Orson F. Whitney.

President Cannon was a man of varied gifts and wide experience. He was a natural counselor, and his eminence and influence as such were great. As a speaker, he shone among the brightest, and probably equal to his powers as a speaker were his abilities as a writer. As President Heber J. Grant observed, "There has been no other man in Utah who has shown such marked ability in so many different ways as has he."

President George Q. Cannon certainly can be regarded as one of the greatest authorities on gospel doctrine and principles found in the restored Church. His answers to the gospel questions of his day are well worth the study of Church members of any day. There were few gospel truths not discussed by him at one time or another.

This volume is a continuation of the attempt in Volume 1 to make available to the Church membership of today some of the choicest material taken from his hundreds of discourses and editorials covering a wide variety of gospel subjects. Most of this material is not otherwise available to the Latter-day Saint today. It is my hope that many others will also benefit from the wisdom and inspiration of this great man, as I have done in preparing these volumes.

Jerreld L. Newquist

Seattle, Washington
June 1974

KEY TO ABBREVIATIONS

CF—*Conference Report,* annual and semiannual (1897- .).

DEN—*Deseret Evening News* (1867-).

DNW—*Weekly Deseret News* (1850-88).

DW—*Deseret Weekly* (1888-98).

Era—*Improvement Era* (1897-1970).

JD—*Journal of Discourses* (26 volumes, 1851-86).

JH—"Journal History" (mss.) of The Church of Jesus Christ of Latter-day Saints.

JI—*Juvenile Instructor* (later known as *Instructor*) (1866-1970). A magazine published and edited by George Q. Cannon during his lifetime.

LJS—*Life of Joseph Smith, the Prophet.* A book of 512 pages written and published by George Q. Cannon in 1888.

MS—*Millennial Star* (1840-1970). A periodical published in Great Britain.

Review—A Review of the Decision of the Supreme Court of the United States in the Case of Geo. Reynolds vs. the United States. A booklet of 57 pages written by George Q. Cannon and published in 1879.

WS—*Writings from the Western Standard* (Liverpool, 1864). A compilation of editorials written for the newspaper *Western Standard,* which George Q. Cannon published in San Francisco, 1856-57.

Titles of other sources are written out in full. The abbreviated references are preceded by a day, which is the date the speech was given or the date the article was published. All references are verbatim quotations except where ellipsis points (. . .) indicate that some material has been left out. In a few cases, corrections have also been made in spelling.

SECTION 1

THE CHURCH AND THE WORLD

No man ever calmly sat down with a prayerful heart to examine the claims of this work, popularly termed Mormonism, who did not rise from the investigation convinced that there was a power, an influence and a spirit accompanying this work, that he had never met with before. . . . If mankind loved the truth and would examine these things, they would see something desirable about this work, and they would be prompted to investigate. . . . An honest man cannot go to the Lord in the name of Jesus Christ, and ask Him respecting this Gospel without receiving a knowledge for himself that it is true.

—GEORGE Q. CANNON
Journal of Discourses 19:199
July 21, 1867

Chapter 1

Truth—The Only Anchor

TRUTH A SURE FOUNDATION. Men of understanding have left on record, as the fruit of their experience and their observation of mankind, that "the fear of the Lord is the beginning of wisdom." [Psalms 111:10.] It is the sure foundation upon which all true knowledge is based. Men may acquire extensive information and learning; but unless accompanied by faith in and fear of God such acquirements are not so profitable unto them as they might be. A knowledge of the truth as revealed by the Lord furnishes men who obtain it a sure foundation on which to stand; it is also a standard by which all man-made systems, theories and opinions can be measured.

A most excellent illustration of its value for this purpose can be found in judging what is known as the Darwinian theory. According to this theory, man has gradually ascended, through a process of evolution covering ages of time, from some low form of animal life; he stands today as the product of a long period of development. . . .

But to the Latter-day Saints who understand the principles of truth, it is the greatest absurdity and folly to state that man has been evolved from an inferior form of animal life, and has progressed step by step through the ages until he has reached his present stage of development. They do not need to spend any time to examine such a proposition for they know better.

God has revealed in these last days, as well as in former times, that He is the Father of mankind, that we are descended from Him, that He "created man in his own image, in the image of God created he him; male and female created he them." [Genesis 1:27.] The theories of all the philosophers in the world, however cunningly framed or speciously argued, cannot shake the faith of a man or woman of God in this immutable truth.

Here, then, is seen the value of the fear of God. It "is the beginning of knowledge." [Proverbs 1:7.] He who fears God and receives the truths He reveals can safely trust them; he can test men's opinions and systems by them without a doubt as to the result. Building upon these truths, he can go on from knowledge to knowledge until he enters into possession of a fullness.

But "the fool has said in his heart, there is no God." [Psalms

14:1; 53:1.] He seeks no light from heaven. He gropes in search of it by his own wisdom. He builds theories and systems of philosophy which only exhibit his own folly. Calling himself wise, and proud of his acquirements, he fails to recognize the truths of heaven and measures Divinity by his miserable little yardstick.

Man by his own wisdom cannot know God. To know Him man must go to Him in the way he has appointed, or he cannot find him. (June 11, 1888, MS 50:371-72)

THE VALUE OF TRUTH. Too great a value cannot be placed upon the possession of the truth. It is indeed beyond estimate. For its sake men have died and gone to their fate with gladness. Latter-day Saints have endured all manner of afflictions and privations and hardships and in many instances have risked and even suffered death for the sake of truth. Yet, the thought sometimes occurs that we do not sufficiently value this precious knowledge.

Everything untrue, no matter how widely believed and advocated, must sooner or later perish. This huge structure which has grown up in the earth since the withdrawal of the Priesthood from men after the death of the Apostles, which is called Babylon by sacred writers, must at some time not far distant topple over and be broken to pieces, because it is not founded upon the truth. It has grown, and its roots have spread in every direction and have sought to fasten themselves in the earth never to be destroyed; yet, sooner or later it will undoubtedly perish. The truth, though it may have but a slight foothold and be believed by few, will endure forever. . . .

TRUTH TO PREVAIL. The Prophet Joseph Smith received the truth. God gave it to him. He stood alone. But he and the truth he represented were mightier than the whole world. He taught the true knowledge of God. The opposition of the whole world could not affect this; it could not change it, for the truth concerning God is eternal. Joseph received the true Priesthood. He received the true ordinances of salvation. He received the true Gospel. He was empowered to organize the true Church. By the introduction and teaching of these truths a power that cannot be overcome was brought among men.

If the enemies of the Prophet Joseph had succeeded in killing him before anyone else received from him the truths that he had received, would that have changed or destroyed the truth? Not in the least. Truth cannot be changed. It cannot be altered. It is eternal. All other things may perish; the heavens and the earth may pass away; but the truth cannot be destroyed. Wicked men may succeed in hiding the truth; they may make lies take the place of truth; they may kill men for believing and practicing the truth and may appear very successful in their operations, but their success is false; it has no real foundation.

The man that dies for the truth will live, and the truth that he believes in will live when falsehood and lies will be swept away. The triumph of error and falsehood and the believers therein over truth and its believers is very shortlived. It is only a temporary victory. It must in the very nature of things be made apparent that it is not a victory. It is those who cling to the truth who become victors in every conflict, either in a small circle or upon a large scale. False gods, false religion, false worship, false doctrine, false conduct cannot save the least human being. Error may triumph for a while, but its triumph is only temporary. The man who possesses the truth and will abide by it and cling to it will most assuredly, whatever conflicts he may have and evil influences to contend with, be ultimately victorious.

LOVE THE TRUTH. As a people and as individuals we should love the truth. Our hearts should be filled with gratitude to God for having revealed it. It will endure forever. It will triumph. Nothing can hinder it. We shall triumph with it if we are true to it. No one who has the truth need fear falsehood. No one who has the true doctrine need fear error. The contest between error and truth may sometimes involve serious consequences to the individual or the people who possess truth; but there can be no question nor the shadow of a doubt concerning the result. This is true of us as a people. We have only to be patient in the midst of our trials and difficulties, and we shall emerge into the glorious light of truth from the darkness which those who practice falsehood endeavor to surround us with.

A man whose life is truthful need not fear slander and misrepresentation. All that is necessary is for him to patiently endure, and whether in this life or in the life to come he is sure to be vindicated and sustained. That which is true in him, whether in his belief, in his worship, in his words, in his actions and conduct, will live, and no amount of falsehood and misrepresentation can submerge it. It will come forth shining, bright and lustrous and will never perish. . . .

How necessary is it, then, that we should love the truth, that we should cherish it with all our hearts, that we should teach it and endeavor to obtain a foothold for it in the earth, that we should impress upon our children its value, even in the smallest details of life. Our children should be taught to always shun everything that is false, whether in belief, in word or in act. Every falsehood must perish. Truth alone will survive and triumph. (May 1, 1895, JI 30:273-75)

LOVE OF TRUTH THE ONLY ANCHOR. That which has influenced men and women to join this Church has been their desire to embrace the truth. The truth—God's truth—has appealed to them and for that they have been willing to forsake their homes, their country, their kindred and all earthly ties and in many cases to go to a far distant land, among a strange people, whose language perhaps was unknown to them and who had been represented to them as such wicked, unprincipled characters. . . .

There is no inducement for men and women to remain Latter-day Saints, only the love of the truth. . . . Therefore, when the love of truth dies out of any Latter-day Saint, you find them ready to leave the Church . . . because when that which caused them to join the Church—the love of the truth—has gone from their hearts, there is no inducement for them to remain associated with the people.

Now, experience has proved that the love of truth can be extinguished in the hearts of men. It will not live under circumstances adverse to purity and to truth itself. Men must be pure to have the love of the truth remain with them. Do you know why men and women leave this Church? They leave it because the love of the truth dies out in their hearts. The love of the truth is the only anchor that will save them amid the storms that beat upon them. It is that which prompted them to embrace the

Gospel when they heard it declared by a servant of the Lord; it is that which holds them secure and safe when they are in the Church. When that is gone, all that ties them to the work of God and makes them secure in the midst of trials and difficulties is gone too. The anchor which held them fast is broken, and they drift away. But remember, this love does not die without cause. . . .

OPPOSITION TO TRUTH. I expect if we could get a glimpse of heaven we would find many things there that would be so contrary to our ideas and traditions that we might revolt in our feelings against them. I heard the Prophet Joseph Smith make a remark at one time which, though I was but a boy, made a deep impression upon me. Said he, "If I were to reveal what the Lord has revealed to me there are men on this stand, sitting beside me, (and he mentioned two of them by name, one of them being an Apostle) who would go around the streets of Nauvoo seeking to take my life." I wondered what there could be that he knew that would produce such a result. One of those men did apostatize and join the murderers of Joseph Smith. (DEN, September 15, 1900)

Truth has ever met with opposition; but that opposition is intensified when the principles of truth are embodied in a system of salvation such as was taught by Jesus when he was upon the earth and as revealed by Him from the heavens in these last days.

Jesus knew perfectly well what effect the rejection of truth would have on the human mind. He knew that if obedience to the Gospel would produce love, peace and good will to all, its rejection must leave the person rejecting it a prey to hatred, strife and bloodthirstiness. He knew that obedience to the Gospel would implant in the human breast a desire to save, while its rejection would produce the opposite feeling—a desire to destroy. He perfectly understood the operations of the two spirits—the spirit of light and the spirit of darkness—and that the rejection and decrease of one was sure to be accompanied by the encouragement and increase of the other, and, therefore, he could with perfect assurance say that his teachings would be followed by variance and division.

Men imagine that because these effects follow the preaching of the Gospel by the Latter-day Saints they must of necessity be deceivers; whereas, instead of such things being an evidence of an incorrect doctrine, they are a strong evidence to the contrary. While the Gospel of Jesus causes variance to spring up between those who reject and those who obey it, yet it causes peace, unity and every good feeling to increase in the breasts of those who listen to its precepts. (September 6, 1856, WS 198-99)

TRUTH WILL TRIUMPH. Nothing can be done against the truth but for it. Circumstances of an opposing nature may apparently overwhelm it temporally, but by and by the storm subsides, the clouds disperse, the sun breaks forth as brightly as before and the rock of truth is seen again firm and enduring as ever. It is the same with principles. There never was a new and needed principle promulgated, or an old and needed one restored to notice and new development, that was not met by storm after storm of opposition and abuse, and followed up and relentlessly pursued thereby, until it was manifest that the new or newly presented principle had obtained such influence that it would no longer pay to oppose it. Then is the time the abuse and the opposition cease, or become so weak and local as to be no longer worthy of notice. But at all other times the opposition and the abuse ebb and flow like the tide.

Thus it is in regard to what the world knows as "Mormonism." It is a system of needed truths, some new, some old, but which had become practically obsolete. From the beginning unmeasured opposition and abuse have met and followed and sought to overwhelm it, but in vain. Though sometimes struck at fiercely and apparently near utter destruction, yet, in one way or another, it has invariably triumphed over its enemies, and has advanced with mighty strides while they have retrograded.

Opposition to the principles of "Mormonism" now and henceforth will have the same results—the truth, though overshadowed for a time, will ultimately triumph. This is just as sure as that the sun will shine again after it sets or is obscured by clouds. Storms and clouds, physical, religious, social or political, do not endure forever; they are only temporary and often evanescent, while the truth does and will endure unimpaired and immutable through all eternity, and those who abide by it will partake of its character and share in its triumphs. (1873, MS 33:700-701)

MISCONCEPTIONS OF TRUTH. I do not believe that, taking the human family generally, there could be many found who would hesitate concerning this matter if they could be convinced of its truth. But, the difficulty is to get men and women to comprehend the truth, to recognize it, to understand it when they hear it, to be able to separate the truth from error, for the reason that in the human mind there are certain conceptions of truth. We entertain certain ideas as to what the truth should be, how it should come to us and also as to who its teachers should be, the kind of men they should be. And this is the difficulty that is all the time in the way of preaching the Gospel. There is an arch enemy of mankind who is constantly laboring to blind the eyes, to darken the understanding and to harden the hearts of the children of men and to prevent them from receiving the truth when they hear it. (May 15, 1881, JD 22: 369)

ALL TRUTH NOT REVEALED. All truth has not been revealed. Paul said once he knew a man who had ascended into the third heaven, and he had heard things that were not lawful for man to utter. That has been a good deal the case with us. Many things have been revealed to us which, if we had taught, men would have sought to kill us, so entirely opposed would they have been to the prevailing religious sentiment. This has been the case even with the small amount of truth which we have taught. We dare not tell all the truth we know, because it would not be lawful to utter some things that God has revealed. That which we do teach and which has enabled us to progress to our present condition sometimes gets us into trouble when we attempt to tell it. It arouses hatred and prejudice. . . .

New truths are unwelcome, and you have to lead mankind along by degrees to comprehend truth. . . . Will there be more truth revealed? Why, yes, the heavens are full of truth, and the Lord desires to communicate it to His children when they are ready to receive it. Things which, as I have said, are not lawful for man to utter at the present time will be revealed, and God will continue giving revelation if we will prepare our hearts for it. (January 28, 1900, MS 62:163-64)

The possession and complete understanding of one truth or principle in the system is but the stepping-stone to the complete and perfect comprehension of its adjacent truth; and thus the investigator is gradually led on from one truth to another, until the mind is fully developed, and he beholds a grand and beautiful system, perfect in all its parts, and every truth having such an intimate relationship with its fellow-truth, that to believe and fully grasp one with the mind is to believe and grasp the other. (April 12, 1856, WS 67)

VOICE OF PEOPLE NOT VOICE OF GOD. Some assert that "what everybody says must be true." We confess we see no must in the case. What everybody says is as likely to be false as true. Truth does not depend on what is said of it or what anybody knows about it. Truth is independent of anybody and everybody and still remains the same however much it may be praised or blamed. Yet, we hope to see the day when ignorance, error and sin will be swept away, and the knowledge of God and truth will be universal. When that day comes, "what everybody says will be true."

Vox Populi vox Dei, that is, "The voice of the people is the voice of God," is a favorite saying with many in this land who believe in the "sovereignty of the people." It is true that the voice of the people may be very powerful, but it is very changeable and very liable to err and, moreover, often very unjust, especially when the wicked rule. How different from the voice of God. . . .

Sometimes we hear it said, "One might as well be out of the world as out of the fashion." Why so? Is fashion more valuable than life? Does fashion add one virtue to that which is vicious or make a folly wise? . . . If we have no excuse but fashion for doing any certain thing, we have the poorest of excuses, the weakest of all crutches. Remember that "fashion is the plague of wise men and the idol of fools." Let none of us make it our idol. (April 25, 1874, JI 9:102)

POPULAR OPINION UNRELIABLE. One of the most unreliable things connected with mankind is popular opinion. So far as God's dealings with the children of men are concerned and the sending of Prophets and Apostles to them, those who have been guided by popular opinion have always erred. The opinions of the great majority concerning the truth have in almost every instance been unreliable. . . .

The more wicked the generation, the harder they were to convince of the truth of the predictions that were uttered among them by the servants of God; and so much was this the case that it became almost an infallible rule that when a majority of the people decided against a man he was sure to be a servant of God. . . .

GOD'S WAYS HIGHER THAN MAN'S. There is one saying written in ancient days that is as true today as when it was written, that is, "For as the heavens are higher than the earth, so are my [God's] ways higher than your ways, and my thoughts than your thoughts." [Isaiah 55:9.] In our degradation and ignorance we cannot comprehend the purposes and plans of our Heavenly Father. No man can do this. If any man were capable of doing this, he would be unfit to dwell on earth, and he might perhaps be translated, as Enoch was anciently.

No man can rise to the wisdom of Deity and comprehend the purposes and designs of Him who created the earth and placed us upon it and Who regulates the movements of the universe of which we form a part; and when we try to do it, it is like a child just beginning to talk, seeking to dictate and comprehend the movements, actions and thoughts of men who are in possession of the wisdom and experience of mature age. In fact, the difference is greater. (March 23, 1873, JD 15:368-69)

SCIENTIFIC RESEARCH AND SKEPTICISM. Fortunately for the Latter-day Saints, the Lord has not left us to be carried about by every wind of doctrine or the cunning craftiness of men. He has given unto us a sure word, upon which we can rely, and from which, if we are faithful, we cannot be moved. There are certain immutable truths which the Lord has revealed in our day to His Church and to every member of it, if they will seek for them. First, that God our Eternal Father is a personal Being. Second, that man was created in His image and likeness. Third, that we are His offspring, and that we have not been evolved from some low order of creation.

These are important truths. No amount of scientific assertion or argument can disturb these. Therefore, we can permit people to go on with their theories, and publish volume after volume in support of them, and pay no attention to them, because if they attempt to attack these truths, we know that their arguments are not worth listening to or spending time upon. We know, too, that while it may be an ancient Chaldean belief, that which is contained in the books of Moses, those books nevertheless were written by Moses, and that they are not what those who indulge in the higher criticism endeavor to prove them to be. (1867, MS 60:13)

Chapter 2

The Gospel—A Practical Religion

SUPERIORITY OF GOSPEL. The Gospel of the Son of God is superior to every system known among men. It feeds the soul with knowledge. It points out with exceeding plainness the path which leads to God. It teaches man his duty to his fellow-man and to his Maker. It gives him understanding concerning the nature of God and the character of the Godhead.

Through the Gospel man learns why he is here, why he is in ignorance, why exposed to temptation, and what is expected from him. Who can place a proper estimate upon this knowledge? In value it is beyond price. . . .

With the promises before us which the Gospel brings, what a boundless career of glory is opened before the Saints of God! The kingly dignity is promised—not a toy crown and a bauble throne, but an actual dominion, a fruitful sceptre, an extensive realm—to all who honor the laws of God. They are promised increase—perpetual, eternal increase—and through that increase they will have that employment which the cares of royalty or, more properly speaking, government always demand. Every power inherited from our Father, the Almighty Ruler of heaven and earth, and which is now latent and undeveloped within us, will then find room for its exercise; and with the exercise these powers will expand and develop from eternity to eternity. . . .

How glorious is the Gospel when compared with the systems of men! How full of intelligence, light and happiness! It is the only philosophical system on the earth . . . which answers questions to the immortal soul of man, and satisfies the longing of his divine nature. Before its grand truths sectarianism flees away and skepticism becomes abhorrent. (1888, MS 50:786-87)

THE GOSPEL—A PRACTICAL RELIGION. The Gospel of the Lord Jesus Christ as taught in our day by His servants is a practical, every-day religion. This constitutes its chief beauty and chief strength. . . . Our religion is not a holiday or Sunday religion—a religion to be assumed on the Sabbath day—but a religion that enters into all the affairs of our lives, that which accompanies us in our fields, in our gardens, in our workshops, in our offices, in our households, in our schools, in every vocation and calling and in every direction. (July 5, 1891, MS 53: 481)

THE OBJECT OF THE GOSPEL. The Gospel has been revealed for the purpose of enabling mankind to comprehend saving truths. It contains the laws which men and women must obey to prepare them for that higher society which exists in heaven. It is by observing these laws and precepts that angels have attained to their glory and by which also He who is greater than the angels has reached His high and exalted position—our beloved Savior and Redeemer, Jesus Christ.

If we would have our children attain to heavenly glory, it must be by obeying these same laws. Nor can we who are adults reach that blissful condition except by the same power and conforming to the same requirements. (November 1, 1894, JI 29:680)

Jesus, the Son of God, has attained to His exalted station by obeying the very principles that constitute our religion. The angels that surround the throne of our Almighty Father have received their exaltation and glory by obeying these principles, observing one law after another until the whole character is transformed and becomes Godlike. (DEN, June 30, 1900)

HAPPINESS THE OBJECT. When men or women become acquainted with the principles of the Gospel, as they are revealed for the salvation of mankind, they have had a treasure revealed unto them of priceless worth—a mine of endless riches opened up before them, the proper appreciation of which will lead them to seek after the acquisition of those truths which will bring salvation to them and affect for good all their temporal and spiritual interests. This is the object for which the Gospel was revealed to man. It was revealed in ancient days for the purpose of making men and women happy, and a proper cultivation of its principles will make them happy now, even as it did then. (November 10, 1861, MS 23:795)

SALVATION—BOTH BODY AND SPIRIT. The Gospel when thoroughly and effectively preached will not only improve a man's spiritual being and reveal unto him new and pleasing spiritual truths but will also improve his physical being and teach him the necessity of taking proper care of his body—the tabernacle of his spirit—and of adopting such principles as will tend to improve and develop, to its utmost extent, every faculty of the mind and body. When this is the case, then and only then is the Gospel a system of salvation—salvation in the broadest sense of the term, saving and redeeming both body and spirit from the evils to which they may have been subjected. A system that is not capable of this, we can not recognize as the fullness of the Gospel of Christ. (March 8, 1856, WS 25)

MUST CONQUER OURSELVES. There is a work developing upon every son and daughter of Adam; there is a fight that we have to fight against—the evils of our own natures, for the heart of man is deceitful and desperately wicked. . . . We may be heralded through the earth as famous; but unless we conquer ourselves, it is in vain that our names are known and that our deeds resound through the earth. . . .

That which is applicable to the individual is applicable to us as a people. Our fame may go forth for great works and mighty things that we have done; but unless we ourselves bring forth the fruits of righteousness in our lives, unless we conquer our evil passions, our evil habits, our evil inclinations, our evil desires, and bring them under complete subjection to the Spirit of God, our labor is comparatively profitless for that is the object of preaching the Gospel to us. (October 5, 1879, JD 21:79)

SAVED FROM CONSEQUENCES OF FALL. In the prayer of the brother of Jared to the Lord . . . the Prophet used this language:

> . . . because of the fall our natures have become evil continually; nevertheless, O Lord, thou hast given us a commandment that we must call upon thee, that from thee we may receive according to our desires. [Ether 3:2.]

The fall that was here referred to by the brother of Jared took place when Adam and Eve disobeyed the command of God and partook of the forbidden fruit and were driven out of Eden. Through that act the natures of man and his posterity became, as the Prophet said, subject to evil continually. . . .

The Gospel has been revealed to save man from all the consequences of the fall. . . . While here in this probation, we have to struggle to overcome our fallen natures and to bring them in subjection to the holy principles which we call the Gospel of Jesus Christ. It requires a constant struggle for all human beings to resist the temptations of Satan who appeals to us and tries to obtain power over us through our fallen natures. (May 15, 1900, JI 35:312)

THE GOSPEL ALWAYS INTERESTING. It is a characteristic of the Gospel of Jesus Christ to not be easily exhausted; on the contrary, it is always attractive. You hear it to-day as you heard it thirty years or thirty-five years ago, and it possesses as many charms and as many attractions now as then; repeating it does not wear it out—does not make the subject threadbare—does not deprive it of its interest; but, on the contrary, its interest increases as years roll over our heads; as they pass by, our interest in the work of God and our love for it and our appreciation of its greatness increase. In this respect it differs from everything else we know of; it satisfies every want of man's nature. (October 8, 1865, JD 11:169)

A COMPREHENSIVE RELIGION. Everything . . . is so intimately blended in the work in which we are engaged that it is an exceedingly difficult thing to draw the line of distinction between the temporal and the spiritual, between that which pertains to the body and that which pertains to the spirit, or which pertains to the dissemination of the Gospel and the welfare of the people in political matters. . . . Our religion extends its ramifications into every department of our lives, leaving nothing untouched, nothing connected with our earthly existence uninfluenced by its power and its teaching. . . .

Our God is not a religious God alone. The God we worship does not confine himself to religious matters, so-called, in contradistinction from those that are secular. He is not a God that concerns himself alone with the spirit of man, but He is a God of science; He is a God of mechanism; He is a God of creative power, a God of government, a God who attends to all the departments of human life and progress, as we see them exemplified here upon the earth. . . .

There was no principle connected with man's existence upon the earth that is not a part and parcel of that Gospel which God has revealed unto us and commanded us to obey; that which the world call "Mormonism" embraces within its scope every good thing upon the face of the earth, leaving nothing outside. Every true principle of science, everything connected with the cultivation of the earth, with the government of cities and of nations, with the management of all the multiplied affairs of men in their great and varied diversity—everything of this character comes within the scope of the Gospel which God has revealed, in the system of salvation that He has commanded us to receive. (March 18, 1883, JD 24:57-58)

FALSE TRADITIONS AND THEIR EFFECTS. The greatest obstacle that has ever opposed the spread of truth and the diffusion of correct principles is the traditions of the people. So potent is their influence and so much importance is there attached to them that truth is but seldom received, even when supported by the best of reasons and evidence, if it comes in contact with them. They are set up as a standard or criterion by which every new principle or idea must be measured and judged; and whether they be true or false, correct or incorrect, by its agreement or disagreement with them must it be accepted or rejected. Every advocate of truth, whether religious or scientific, has experienced this. . . .

But the people who have not received "Mormonism" are not the only people who have to contend with these things. The Latter-day Saints themselves have not progressed as they might have done had they been free from traditions which induce unbelief. . . .

The people have not yet learned the lessons which the experience of the past should have taught them. They have not yet learned that every tradition must be uprooted and that when God speaks and commands, even if it should be contrary to everything that tradition may make dear, there is no other course but to obey. They are too apt to set up their traditions (which their experience has repeatedly proved to be unreliable) as a standard or criterion. Everything that agrees with them is readily gulped down—it is all right—but every truth that does not is viewed with distrust and unbelief.

Mankind will yet learn that they cannot by their wisdom know God; to know Him they will have to strip themselves of the multitudinous notions and opinions which they have imbibed and come before Him humbly, realizing their own lack of knowledge, and submit to be taught by His Spirit and by those to whom He has delegated a portion of His authority on the earth. This they will have to learn before they can make any progress. (March 27, 1857, WS 370-74)

TENDENCIES TOWARD WORLDLINESS. There are many, perhaps all of us, that have more or less of a desire to conform to the ideas which prevail in the world. These ideas we have inherited, and they come natural to us; and not having progressed sufficiently to overcome them, we naturally lean toward them. . . .

If we could have a glimpse of heaven and understand things as they are, we might be able to do better; but this is not God's way of doing things. He wants us to work out our own development and to exert the powers we have inherited from Him in conquering the wrong tendencies we have inherited from our fathers. He gives us line upon line, precept upon precept, here a little and there a little; but He does not reveal it all at once. At the same time He would like us to comprehend more than we do.

OUR LEADERS FAR AHEAD OF US. I have sometimes thought that the Prophet Joseph, with the knowledge he possessed and the progress he had made, could not stay with the people, so slow were we to comprehend things and so enshrouded in our ignorant traditions. The Saints could not comprehend Joseph Smith; the Elders could not; the Apostles could not. They did do a little towards the close of his life; but his knowledge was so extensive and his comprehension so great they could not rise to it. It was so with President Young; and I may say it is so with the leaders of the Church now. It is a continual labor on their part to lift the people up to the comprehension of the will of God and His purposes connected with this work. The people are bound down by their traditions, and because of this it is rarely that you can get even the Elders to see the propriety of certain things. . . .

God is lifting this people, and He will do it faster and faster if we will obey His counsels and seek to free ourselves from these miserable traditions that we have inherited from our fathers. . . . Men have strayed from God and adopted systems of their own; and the difficulty with us is to comprehend the truth so that we may know how to emancipate ourselves from this condition. (April 16, 1899, MS 61:629-30)

PLAN OF SALVATION BROAD AS ETERNITY. The work of God is not confined to this little earth of ours; but it embraces within it all the eternities of God. It embraces the work that took place before the earth was created, and it brings within its pale that which will take place thousands of centuries hereafter. The plan of salvation is as broad as eternity and is as eternal as its Great Author. (March 28, 1869, DNW 18:103)

The Church of Christ among the Jews at Jerusalem, among the Nephites in South America and among the people who now live is the same Church in every minute particular. The organization is alike, the officers are alike, the ordinances are alike and the doctrines are alike. The truths of God are eternal. They do not wear out or become changed by the lapse of time. (March 1, 1883, JI 18:72)

God has revealed unto us that Adam himself was taught the Gospel in the same purity and with the same power and gifts that it was taught to the Twelve Apostles whom the Lord chose as His disciples. We have been taught that Jesus Himself was the Revelator, so to speak. He was the Being who revealed to Adam and to his children, to Abraham, to Moses, and to the Prophets, the plan of salvation and gave them the laws which they practiced. . . .

ANCIENTS HAD SAME GOSPEL. In that early day God sent His angels to Adam; he repented of his sins and was baptized in water by an angel, and he received the Holy Ghost, just as much as we who live now do, and probably in greater power. These are the principles of the Gospel, and this was in the beginning. Every principle that was taught to men by the Savior in His day, so far as pertaineth to the Gospel, was taught in those early days.

It is the height of folly, it is a libel on our Father in heaven, to say that those men who lived in those days walked in ignorance or that the revelations of God to them were imperfect or that God has improved since their day. He was perfect then; He knew all things then; and He taught that which was necessary then for man's salvation.

The name of Jesus is the only name given under heaven whereby man can be saved. No man could be saved in the beginning without that name, and if he did not hear it on the earth, he would have to hear it somewhere else, or he could not be saved. . . . (September 24, 1893, DW 47:506-507)

GOSPEL PRINCIPLES TO SAVE MANKIND. The Church of Jesus Christ of Latter-day Saints has been built up by the revelations of God for the purpose of correcting the evils that exist in society, as well as to save the inhabitants of the earth from their sins; not only to prepare them for the life to come, but to qualify them to enjoy the life that now is. Its mission is to save the people spiritually and temporally. (March 11, 1894, DW 48:477)

Its principles alone will save mankind; there is no other plan of salvation, either temporal or spiritual, than that which is found in the Gospel, and there is no salvation, temporal or spiritual, excepting that resulting from obedience to it. Its principles are from God; by its principles God is what He is today. By observance of its principles heaven is made heaven and is peopled by beings who have obeyed the Gospel, and through their practical obedience to the Gospel have produced heaven, or rather made themselves fit to dwell in heaven. And through those glorious principles, which we have received to some extent at least, and through obedience to them, carrying them out practically in our lives, the children of men can be elevated into the region of God and angels, and heaven can be brought about, to a certain extent at least, upon the earth, thus fulfilling the prayer of the Savior when He commanded His disciples to pray, "Thy kingdom come. Thy will be done in earth, as it is in heaven." [Matthew 6:10.] (February 23, 1890, DW 40:378)

MORMONISM EITHER TRUE OR FALSE. "Mormonism" is advocated before mankind on the testimony of God's word. To this its advocates appeal to substantiate its truth. By this it should be judged. If it be untrue and contrary to the revealed will and laws of God, the proof should be produced from His accredited records. It is time that men should think calmly, considerately and impartially on this subject. Every man should thoroughly satisfy himself as to the truth or falsity of this system. It is a question of momentous importance, upon the correct decision of which eternal destinies hang. To trust to another's opinion, to another's judgment, to another's convictions, and be guided by them, in an affair of so much importance, is folly.

"Mormonism" . . . is either true or false; if true, it is every man's duty to obey it; if false, it is every man's prerogative to know its falsity. We say it is true. . . . We say it will have to be believed and obeyed by all men, or they will be condemned. (September 27, 1856, WS 205)

DOCTRINES ARE IMPREGNABLE. Our doctrines are impregnable, so far as the Bible is concerned. No man can successfully meet the Latter-day Saints on the Bible. It is our Bible. We need not talk about "Joseph Smith's Bible"; King James' translation of the Bible is sufficient for us to prove the doctrines we teach to be from God, for they are precisely similar to the doctrines taught in the ancient days. It is our Bible more than any other people's, because we live nearer to it; we practice its principles; we teach its ordinances, and we do everything for man's salvation that it teaches us is necessary.

Men have ceased long ago to endeavor to disprove our doctrine from the Bible, and in place of that they have had recourse to falsehood, to maligning us and telling all manner of stories concerning us to prejudice the minds of those who would listen to them. That is now their only refuge. (September 23, 1900, MS 62:771)

It is astonishing that "Mormonism," or the "Mormons," cannot be assailed by any other weapons than ridicule and falsehood—that their system present no vulnerable spot for them to be attacked reasonably and logically. One would think that after making such bold pretensions and laying so broad a foundation there would be some point that would be sufficiently unguarded to afford the assailants an opportunity to overturn their position with advantage. But it is not the case. (June 21, 1856, WS 137)

The religion of the Latter-day Saints is the only religion that will bear the test of philosophical investigation and that will meet the burning questions of the day. I believe that it is the only religion that will satisfy the yearnings of the human heart and that will give light upon points that are considered mysterious by the religious world. I believe that the religion of the Latter-day Saints shows in the plainest, in the simplest and in the most conclusive manner the relation of man to God. (October 9, 1892, DW 45:617)

AN INFALLIBLE RELIGION. Who is there that can recall a single instance of recantation of any of its [the Church's] principles? Has there ever been a doctrine declared by the authorities of this Church, as a part of the Gospel of Jesus Christ, that they have had to take back or modify? Not one. Has there been anything in the organization that has had to be perfected? No. The organization was as perfect in theory—being revealed of God—50 years ago as it is today. . . .

That constitutes the strength of this work. It is its infallibility. Not that man connected with it is infallible, for he is fallible; but the work itself, its principles and everything connected with it, is infallible, having a divine origin, being revealed of God. (July 15, 1883, JD 24:184)

EVIDENCE OF THE TRUE GOSPEL. Many people ask for signs to prove that this is the work of the Lord and they close their eyes to the evidence which is before them. It is a great evidence of the truth of the Gospel to see the change that takes place in the people who join the Church; they are born again; they become new creatures in the Lord; a love takes possession of them which they never knew before. They love their brothers and sisters in the Church with an affection entirely new to them. . . . The great evidence of its being the work of the Lord is seen in the fruits which the people bring forth. Union, love and peace prevail among all genuine Latter-day Saints. Where they live as they should do, we can see the beginning of that spirit and feeling which will prevail during the millennium. (February 15, 1898, JI 33:150-51)

THE GOSPEL OUR GREATEST LOVE. If we cannot sacrifice everything there is upon the face of the earth that men hold dear to them, then we are unworthy of that great salvation that God has promised unto the faithful. The man that cannot bring every appetite into subjection to the mind and will of God, that cannot forgo everything of this kind and that is not willing to sacrifice houses and lands and father and mother, wives and children and everything that men hold dear to them, is unworthy that great salvation that God has in store for His faithful children. . . .

If we value this salvation as we should, there is nothing that will stand between us and it. . . . We must love the Gospel of the Lord Jesus Christ, and the cause that He established, better than we do our wives and our children, better than we do our own lives. There is nothing upon the face of the earth that we should love as we do the Gospel. God requires this of us. (November 20, 1881, JD 23:100)

THE LOVE OF THE GOSPEL. When men receive the everlasting Gospel and the Priesthood, there is a love begotten in their hearts for their fellowmen such as they never have felt before. Like the love of Jonathan for David, it is "Passing the love of women." It is stronger than the love of women. It overpowers it. Not that it quenches the love of women or makes it improper; but it is a greater love; it surpasses it. This is the love that enters into the hearts of women who embrace the Gospel and causes them to love the Elders of this Church as they never loved any one before. And it is a pure love. They love them as they would angels from heaven.

It is not an unvirtuous love. It is a love that comes from God. It is the love of the Holy Ghost, the love of purity, the love of truth, the love that we would have for holy beings—a part of the love that we have for God Himself and for our Lord and Savior Jesus. This love unites them together with a bond and strength of affection that was never known before. (August 3, 1890, DW 41:486)

What are its fruits? Precisely the same as the gospel brought forth anciently. Men are no longer Americans, British, French, Scandinavians, Germans, Swiss or any other nation; they are Latter-day Saints. Differences of language, of education, of race and of nationality all disappear. Under its influence, prejudices and animosities vanish. Union and love prevail. Its power in blending people together and making them one is marvelous. (January 1, 1884, JI 19:8)

GOSPEL ELEVATES MANKIND. The Gospel lifts the poorest, the humblest, the most obscure and places him on the level with the most intelligent, the most exalted man in the Church, in that every man and every woman is exhorted and pleaded with to seek to God for himself and for herself, that he and she may know . . . whether that is the word of God or not. (September 19, 1897, DW 55:483)

It is said that in the old countries it takes three generations to make a gentleman. The Gospel of Jesus Christ will make a man a gentleman in one generation. . . . The poor, the lowly and the obscure who have obeyed and carried out in their lives the principles of the Gospel have been elevated and polished. This work is not for the abasement but the elevation of mankind. It is a work of evolution. Out of this people God will evolve a nation that will excel in everything. (September 18, 1898, DW 57:514)

ONLY GOSPEL CAN CURE WORLD'S ILLS. Apart from religion no schemes or plans for the amelioration of the condition of mankind can hope to be successful; relief can only be found in the teachings of the Son of God. Men must learn to carry into practical effect His precepts; they must learn to love their neighbor as they do themselves.

If ever the time shall come, such as has been described by Prophets and Apostles—that millennium era to which the righteous of all ages have looked forward—it will only be brought about by the practical adoption and application in every-day life of those principles that the Savior inculcated and which He commanded His followers to observe and practice. This cannot be done without His aid; there must be divine power brought into operation and made to bear upon mankind. Man of himself is incapable of effecting the needed reforms; he must have God's help. (June 1, 1896, JI 31:333-34)

Chapter 3

Temptations, Trials, and Persecutions

TRIALS—A NECESSARY EXPERIENCE. What a variety of circumstances the Latter-day Saints have had to contend with from the organization of the Church up to the present time. No people of modern times have had such a variety of trials by which their faith, their constancy and their devotion have been tested. The persecutions which the people have endured and the wrongs which have been practiced upon them have furnished excellent opportunities for the exhibition of the qualities they possess, and they have shown their greatness and strength and nobility of character to the world in a very convincing manner. Step by step, from the very outset, they have had the most serious and forbidding obstacles to encounter and overcome. Their pathway has been beset with difficulties. Yet, in the great majority of cases, they have never wavered but pressed steadily onward, bearing patiently and heroically their afflictions and surmounting all difficulties.

In the providence of the Almighty it is undoubtedly necessary that we should have such a schooling as we have received. It is scarcely possible that we could fill the destiny that lies before us without this severe training. It is not pleasant to have to pass through these ordeals; but after we have emerged from them, we look back at them with satisfaction, and do not regret that we had to grapple with them. In fact, the most bitter and painful experience, after it has once been gained, is appreciated as most valuable; and no man who has endured such, regrets after he has passed through it that he had it to encounter. (August 15, 1890, JI 25:503-504)

The experience of the Latter-day Saints has taught one important lesson which everyone should endeavor to make profitable. It is that it is not a wise thing for men to define the lines which the work of God shall pursue, or to set stakes concerning results that will be brought about.

Though the Church has been favored with the spirit of prophecy and revelation, and those who have borne the Priesthood have been inspired to counsel the people according to the mind and will of the Lord, still there are many details connected with the work of God which have not been fully made known. The reason for this is obvious. We must be a tried people. We must walk by faith, putting our trust in the Lord and not, at present, by sight. In this way the leaders of the people of God, as well as the people themselves, have their faith tested. . . .

THIS IS GOD'S WORK. One thing, however, has been clearly made manifest, and that is that this is God's work. He is shaping its destinies. He is permitting events to occur which, from a human standpoint, may not be viewed as favorable to the accomplishment of the destiny predicted. But knowing all things, the end from the beginning, He, in His infinite wisdom, can perceive plainly how His purposes shall be accomplished in ways that are strange to men.

It is natural for men to expect, in connection with a work like this in which we are engaged, success to attend every step of its progress. When what men call success is wanting, then fears come in, and doubts are apt to intrude; and yet how often it has been the case, as we have proved by our experience, that that which we have viewed as a disaster has been overruled and made a cause of triumph.

We are apt to mark out in our feelings certain lines that the work of God should pursue. . . . But how different has been the result. We have been thrown into the arena. We have been like a city set upon a hill that cannot be hid. The eyes of all nations have been drawn toward us. The power of Babylon has been leveled against us, with a view of our overthrow and destruction. . . .

It should be the aim of all to exercise faith, so that whatever the trials may be we may stand firm, steadfast and immovable in the truth, cherishing within us the testimony which God has given, and relying on His promises. Depend on it, He is able to fulfill every word that He has spoken. He will not leave His people to themselves. He will sustain those who put their trust in Him, and they will be brought off victorious. (August 1, 1890, JI 25:470-72)

ALL TO BE TESTED TO UTTERMOST. If we will be faithful to our God, He will redeem us, no matter what the circumstances may be through which we may be called to pass. We may wade through sorrow. We may have to endure persecution. We may have to meet with death. We may have to endure imprisonment and many other things that our predecessors had to endure. God may test us in this manner.

Every human being that is connected with this work will have to be tested before he can enter into the Celestial Kingdom of our God. He will try us to the uttermost. If we have any spot more tender than another, He will feel after it. He will test all in some way or other. But like the promises that have been made in regard to the work as a work, so are the promises made to us as individual members of the Church. (October 5, 1884, JD 25: 326)

We have learned that there are plenty of trials and difficulties for all, if they will live faithful, to have their full share and all that are necessary to test them and their faith and integrity to the fullest extent. Each generation may not have to pass through exactly the same scenes. They are apt to vary as the circumstances which surround each vary; but they will, nevertheless, accomplish the desired end. There is one thing certain, every Latter-day Saint who is faithful to the truth and who lives to the ordinary age of man will have all the opportunities of this kind he or she can desire to gain experience and to have his or her zeal, integrity, courage and devotion to the truth fully exhibited. (May 1, 1885, JI 20:136)

DIFFERENT KINDS OF TRIALS. If trials do not come to the Latter-day Saints in one shape, they will in another. The Lord has said that He will have a tried people. Trials must, therefore, come. In the early days of the Church there were mobs and persecutions to test the faith and constancy of the people. The Saints were driven by the wicked from place to place, and those who did not love the Lord and His truth better than all else were apt to have their faith and fortitude fail them.

But since the people came to these valleys, mobs have not had power to afflict them. . . . Not having the trials of mobs and persecutions to endure, there have been trials of a different character to overcome. They have had the effect to test the people in a different direction, but probably as effectually as the old trials did. In the providence of the Lord this is all right. (September 15, 1876, JI 11:210)

Satan will let no opportunity of tormenting the people of God, or of throwing obstacles in the way of the work of God, pass by without being used. His weapons are falsehood and violence. He uses falsehood in the most cunning manner, filling the hearts of the people with hatred and anger against the truth. . . .

THE FURNACE OF AFFLICTION. In the future trials may not be exactly of the same kind in all respects as they have been up to the present time; but, nevertheless, they will give the strong and the reliable, the faithful and the zealous every necessary opportunity to show the stuff they are made of and the faith which God has given them. So also with the impure and the weak, the hypocrite and the unbelieving; under the pressure of circumstances which will surround them they will exhibit the defects in their lives and characters, for God will have a tried people. He will bring us through the furnace of affliction, and if we endure the fiery trial, the dross of our natures will be burned out and the gold will appear the brighter and the purer. (January 1, 1887, JI 22:3)

MUST MEET AND RESIST TEMPTATIONS. It is liquor shops today, gambling saloons today, houses of ill-fame today. These are the evils which confront us and which furnish allurements for vice to our children. But we will overcome them and will cope with greater evils and will overcome them; and we will show the world that we have principles that can stand the test of time and can withstand all the evil influences that can be brought against us.

If we must rear our children in the midst of these, then let them rise superior to them. We cannot enclose our children in glass houses. We cannot exempt our children . . . from the temptations of the world. . . . They have to rise above them. . . .

I am looking forward for such a development of wisdom, strength and skill . . . and power that the development and training of our children will be a matter almost of perfect safety in the midst of all hostile influences. Still, we have to contend against these wicked things, the literature of the age and all the evils that abound—we have to contend against these and to teach our children to shun them. (April 8, 1883, DNW 32:258)

ON THE WATCH-TOWER. Do not expect there will ever be a time when we can listlessly fold our arms and still progress with the truth. Every one who desires to be saved must be on the watch-tower and be prepared for the events that will transpire. . . .

We may as well make up our minds to be faithful at once and prepare ourselves for the trials that we shall have to meet, for we may rest assured that everything that can be shaken will be shaken. To avoid being shaken we must seek for and obtain the Spirit of God and gain favor with God through the practice of the principles of truth; and our prayers should be continually ascending to Him to aid us in attaining to glory with him in the eternal world. (December 31, 1863, MS 26:83-84)

It should be remembered that the evils which are seeking to obtain a foothold among us are the products of Babylon. Babylon reigns. Its fashions are popular in our nation. The determination is to make us conform to them—to make us drink of the cup of her fornications. . . . While Babylon has dominion it will have more or less influence among us; and it will require all the power we can muster to counteract its example and have the rising generation understand the disastrous consequences of adopting its follies and sins. (November 1, 1889, JI 24:516)

DISOBEDIENCE OUR GREATEST DANGER. There is only one thing that we, as a people, have to dread and that is our own weaknesses and our failure to keep the commandments of God. This alone can do us injury. If all the hosts of earth were to band together, with their wealth, their influence, and with all the power at their control, and they were to unitedly oppose this work of our God, and the Latter-day Saints were united and full of faith and integrity and determined to keep the commandments of God, I say to you this day . . . that there is no power upon earth that can injure or in any manner retard the advancement of this cause and the deliverance of this people from every peril to which they may be exposed. . . .

The only cause that will create fear in my mind—and that feeling does sometimes assail me—is the knowledge that the Latter-day Saints are not living as they should do, that there is division among them, that they are loving the world and the things of the world and that they are placing their affections upon something else more than upon the building up of the Kingdom of God. When I witness such a spirit, I confess that I am assailed with fear, not that the work of God will be endangered, not that the purposes of God will be turned aside, but I fear lest the Latter-day Saints, as a people, will be scourged because of the conduct of those who profess to be Saints and bear the name of the Lord Jesus Christ. If, however, we are living as we should do, keeping the commandments of God and walking in the straight and narrow path, then we have no need for fear. . . .

We will find as we grow in strength, as we gain influence and power, the opposing forces will also increase until . . . it will not only be a nation, but it will be the whole world that will fight against Zion and will seek her destruction. And under those circumstances what will save us? Nothing will save us but the righteousness of the Latter-day Saints and the power of God which that righteousness will bring forth. . . . (July 21, 1889, DW 39:194-95)

KEEPING COVENANTS THE SAFE COURSE. Whatever fate may threaten us, there is but one course for men of God to take, that is, to keep inviolate the holy covenants they have made in the presence of God and angels. For the remainder, whether it be life or death, freedom or imprisonment, prosperity or adversity, we must trust in God. We may say, however, if any man or woman expects to enter into the Celestial Kingdom of our God without making sacrifices and without being tested to the very utmost, they have not understood the Gospel. If there is a weak spot in our nature, or if there is a fiber that can be made to quiver or to shrink, we may rest assured that it will be tested. Our own weaknesses will be brought fully to light, and in seeking for help the strength of our God will also be made manifest to us. (October 6, 1885, MS 47:708)

In regard to our religion, or our eternal covenants, we

have no compromise to make, nor principles to barter away; they emanate from God and are founded upon the rock of eternal ages; they will live and exist when empires, powers and nations shall crumble and decay; and with the help of the Almighty we will guard sacredly our covenants and maintain our interests and be true to our God while time exists or eternity endures. (August 29, 1882, MS 44:613)

BLESSINGS FOLLOW TRIALS. After the trials there cometh the blessing. We have never yet passed through severe afflictions without there being compensation in the shape of great blessings bestowed upon us. And so it will be. Trial will follow trial; but blessings will follow trial also. Blessing will follow blessing; and the cause of truth will spread; the honest in heart will be gathered out; and the great work of God go forth, notwithstanding every effort to oppose it and to thwart it. (October 5, 1890, DW 41:651)

BENEFITS OF CONFLICT WITH WORLD. Contact with the world, while it is attended with many evils, is also attended with much good. The danger of isolation and exclusiveness is that men become narrow and prejudiced, opinionated and somewhat self-righteous. Contact with the world removes much of this feeling and teaches men that there are others who are also the children of God, who are the objects of His care and who possess many admirable qualities and many grand truths; and though they may not be open to receive the principles of the Gospel, and may have many erroneous ideas concerning the plan of salvation, they are, nevertheless, the objects of the Great Creator's care. He is their Father, and He intends to save them if they will only permit Him to do so. (August 15, 1891, JI 26:510)

PRAISE OF WORLD A BAD SIGN. It is no good sign for us to be beloved by the world, and to be spoken kindly of by the world, however pleasant it may be to us, and however much we may shrink from the opposite condition of affairs, and dread its manifestation, and wish that it could be otherwise—and it is natural to human nature to shrink from these trials—nevertheless, it is one of the worst signs for us as a people to be spoken well of by the world, and to be free from threatenings, from opposition and from hatred. It is not the true condition for the Church of Jesus Christ of Latter-day Saints to be in, to be petted by the world, to be fostered by the world, to be spoken well of by the world, to be welcomed by the world, to have favor showered upon it by the world, because we ought not to be of the world, God having chosen us out of the world. . . . (December 2, 1883, JD 24:360)

GODLY TO SUFFER PERSECUTION. At no time has the Lord led His people to expect that they would not have to endure trials, or not have their faith fully tested. . . .

In the providence of the Almighty persecution serves a most useful purpose. Every faithful Saint must perceive and acknowledge this. Each one feels its effect upon himself; he sees its effects upon his friends and neighbors. Persecution develops character. Under its influence we all know ourselves better than we did before we felt its pressure: and we discover traits in our brethren and sisters of the existence of which, perhaps, we were in entire ignorance. (April 6, 1886, MS 48: 307)

The hatred and opposition of the wicked may be considered as a compliment rather than otherwise. The Saints have no favors to ask at their hands; they do not seek their love. When they embraced the Gospel, they enlisted to forsake the ways of the world. They understood, too, what that implied—the severing in some instances of the dearest ties of kindred and affection. But they were prepared for it. They knew the Savior had said, "He that loveth father or mother more than me is not worthy of me: and he that loveth son or daughter more than me is not worthy of me." [Matthew 10:37.]

So long as our actions are such that our enemies cannot say anything against our characters without speaking falsely, we have nothing to fear. We can afford to do our duty and leave the result with the Lord. (February 1, 1882, JI 17:40)

APOSTASY WOULD END PERSECUTION. There is nothing short of complete apostasy, a complete denial of every principle we have received, a throwing away of the Holy Priesthood, that can save us from persecution. When this takes place, when all the chief features of the Gospel are obliterated, when we can float along the stream and do as the world does, then and not till then will persecution cease, or until the adversary is bound, for the day will come when Satan will be bound and then persecution will cease, but until then there will be no cessation; until then persecution will always exist in some form or other, and we shall have to meet it so that we may as well make up our minds on the subject. (May 15, 1881, JD 22:374)

GOSPEL CAUSES FAMILY STRIFE. Luke informs us that the Savior said:

> Suppose ye that I am come to give peace on earth? I tell you, Nay; but rather division. . . . The father shall be divided against the son, and the son against the father; the mother against the daughter, and the daughter against the mother; the mother in law against her daughter in law, and the daughter in law against her mother in law. [Luke 12:51, 53.] . . .

This sounds very strange, coming, as it does, from Him who is called the Prince of Peace, and whose mission was to save mankind. No one but a Latter-day Saint can understand the meaning of this language, for no one but Saints have the experience necessary to make it plain. In the days of the Savior upon the earth His doctrine brought a division between those who were obedient to it and those who were not. Instead of peace, strife, hatred and opposition were brought to the surface by it, not in the hearts of those who received His doctrine, but in the hearts of those who fought it.

This is also a most remarkable peculiarity of the Gospel of Jesus Christ as we see it preached in our day. The nearer the relatives are who fight against the work and refuse to receive the Gospel, the more bitter appears to be the hostility which they manifest. They divide themselves from their obedient kindred, become their enemies and literally fulfill the words of the Savior, that "a man's foes shall be they of his own household." (February 15, 1885, JI 20:56)

HATED FOR JESUS' NAME'S SAKE. We are hated of all men and of all nations for Christ's sake. It is because of our religion. If we discarded the forms of religion, if we did not attach importance to the solemnization of the marriage ordinance, if it were done in any other name, or in any other form, or for any other purpose, it would pass, doubtless, as it does in other society without being challenged or receiving particular condemnation. . . .

Because we make this the religion of Jesus, because we profess to be the followers of Jesus, and because of being His followers, therefore, as Jesus said, "ye shall be hated of all nations for my name's sake" [Matthew 24:9], not for anything else, but for the sake of the name of our Lord and Savior Jesus Christ, whose religion we have espoused, whose followers we claim to be, and because of being his followers we do as we are doing. Most signally, then, has this prediction been fulfilled in our sight and hearing. (December 7, 1884, JD 26:43-44)

WORLD WILL NOT LOVE US. If we would be like the rest of the world, we would have no opposition from the world. Jesus said to His disciples, "If ye were of the world, the world would love his own: but because ye are not of the world, but I have chosen you out of the world, therefore the world hateth you." [John 15:19.]

It is just the same today. If we were like the world, the world would love us; but because God has chosen us out of the world, therefore the world hates us; and we shall be hated as long as we preserve these virtues and contend for them, as long as we refuse to partake of the cup of fornications which the mother of abominations holds out to us; as long as we refuse to have the mark of the beast upon us, so long shall we have this opposition to contend with, until Babylon is overthrown and destroyed from the face of the earth—a consummation that is not very far distant.

If we would drink of that cup which that great mother of abominations holds in her hands, opposition would cease, for we would then be like them; we would be of them. But while we stand firm and steadfast, maintaining the principles which God has taught us, and seeking to carry out the glorious Gospel of His Son which He Himself taught when upon the earth—as long as we do this, you may depend upon it, the world will have no love for us. I am speaking now in general terms. There are men and women, not very numerous, that do have kindly feelings for us, who would not do us wrong, but their voices are unheard amid the general clamor that is raised against us. (February 23, 1890, DW 40:379)

TRUTHFULNESS OF BIBLE PROVEN. Let a man commence to investigate the principles of the Gospel as they are taught by the servants of God—I care not what his position may be, how good a reputation he may have, what his standing in society may be—if he will turn his attention to the investigation of the principles of the Gospel of Jesus Christ as they are taught by His servants, he will suddenly awaken to the consciousness of the existence of a spirit in the world that is precisely like the spirit that was manifested in ancient days against Jesus and His Apostles. He will be astonished, if he has had no experience in this matter, at the spirit of persecution and opposition that will be aroused by his action in this direction, and how quickly his good name will be lost, and how quickly, also, he will be shunned and avoided by his late companions and associates and friends. . . .

Now, this treatment which Latter-day Saints have received has been confined to them. Men and women may espouse other forms of religion and not experience such consequences as these. . . . Let one who has passed through this experience read the New Testament and the treatment which the people of God received in those days, and he will see how similar is the treatment extended unto him to that which the disciples of Jesus received when He was upon the earth. If any evidence were wanted by such a person of the truth of the Bible, his own experience would furnish it to him. . . .

TRUE SAINTS NEVER PERSECUTE. You will never find a people of God who have the truth persecuting another people. If they were to do so, they would cease to be the people of God. It is the characteristic of the Church of God always that it never condescends to persecution. It does not fear the announcement of any doctrine, or any principle, or any form of belief, or any so-called revelation. Strong in the knowledge that they have the truth and that God is with them, such a people can afford to let false doctrine, when it manifests itself, have the freedom of action, the right of agency which God has given to every human being and which every human being has a right to exercise undisturbed by his fellow man so long as he does not interfere with the happiness and the lives and the liberties of his fellow man. (DEN, July 11, 1885)

PERSECUTION AN INFALLIBLE EVIDENCE OF TRUTH. It is an evidence, an infallible evidence, of truth to have persecution accompany it. It is not that every one who is reviled and who is persecuted possesses the truth. That does not always follow. But there never was a Prophet of whom we have any account, raised up in the midst of the children of men to proclaim unto them divine truths, who did not receive in his life and experience these very things of which Jesus has spoken. They were hated; they were separated from the company of their fellows; they were reproached; their names were cast out as evil; they were reviled; their lives were sought. . . .

One of the greatest evidences of the bad condition of affairs now existing in Christendom is the popularity that attends what is called the preaching of the Gospel of the Lord Jesus Christ. Whenever a preacher is popular in the midst of a wicked generation, or a man is popular who professes to be a minister of truth, you may set it down as a certain fact that that man does not preach the truth as it exists in Christ. . . .

PROFESSED MINISTERS AS PERSECUTORS. There is this remarkable fact connected with the persecution of the people called Latter-day Saints—and it is the same characteristic that attended the preaching of the Gospel of the Son of God by Himself and His Apostles—the chief persecutors, and those who have stirred up strife in the hearts of the people, have been popular preachers, have been themselves, in too many instances, the professed ministers of Jesus Christ. It was the High Priests, it was the Pharisees, it was the religious people in the days of the Savior who were His chief persecutors, and I am sorry to say the chief persecutions which we as a people have had to endure have had their origin with the same class. (October 6, 1879, JD 20:333-35)

PERSECUTION OUR NECESSARY DISCIPLINE. Persecution! Who cares for it? Who fears it? What is there connected with it to make us tremble or to weaken us in the least degree if we are possessed of the knowledge which God has restored. . . ? That which we term persecution is only the discipline necessary for our development. There is a great destiny in store for this people, and they never can attain unto it unless they pass through just such scenes as they have passed through in the past, and such scenes as they doubtless will have to pass through of a more trying character in the future. This is the discipline that is necessary to purify us, to prepare us in every respect for the fulfilling of that high destiny that awaits us. . . .

PERSECUTION CAUSES GREATER UNITY. Hostile legislation and opposition have but one tendency as a rule, that is, to drive us closer together, to make the cause a common one, to cause us to feel united. . . . The more they are driven the tighter it brings the people together, solidifies them, makes them one, and it gives them a consciousness of strength because when they emerge from these trials victorious, they feel better able to cope with greater difficulties and greater and greater oppression when they are brought to bear upon them. And they are necessary, as I have said, for our development.

WORLDLY FAVOR OUR GREATEST DANGER. But let us have ease, let us prosper in worldly things, let the world smile upon us and bid us welcome and treat us as they treat those whom they love, let the world do this, and how long should we be united? Why, the influence would be towards disintegration. Worldly influence would creep in. That is more to be dreaded than persecution. Prosperity is far more to be dreaded under circumstances such as we are placed in—what I mean by prosperity, I mean worldly prosperity, worldly sympathy, worldly favor—these are more to be dreaded than the disfavor of the world and the tyranny that may be brought to bear upon us because of our being obnoxious to them. (June 22, 1884, JD 25: 239-42)

PERSECUTION CAUSES GREATER DILIGENCE. As a people, in times past we have been careless and indifferent in many directions. Neglect of duties has been too common everywhere. Hypocrisy has been indulged in to some extent, and a laxity has prevailed in many quarters concerning the keeping of the laws of God which is not in accord with the spirit of the Gospel. Under these circumstances the Lord has permitted persecutions and trials to come upon His people that have had the effect of stirring them up to greater diligence. When the Lord, for any reason, turns His face away from His people, and is slow to hear their cries, thorough repentance on their part, and a complete abandonment of their evil ways, are sure to bring back His favor, and to cause His countenance to shine upon them.

This has been the case in every age when God has had a people upon the earth. In our own day we have seen frequent illustrations of this. We have never feared for the people, nor for the prosperity of the work, when the Latter-day Saints have been fully alive to the duties and requirements of their religion. But when they have been careless and neglectful, or disobedient and hard in their hearts, then we have trembled; for when the Saints are in such a condition the displeasure of the Lord is sure to be awakened against them, and His scourges are likely to fall upon them.

The Lord does not permit his enemies, nor the enemies of His people, to prevail over them for any length of time when they are living near unto Him and complying strictly with His will. All His promises, of the brightest and most glorious character, encouraging and hopeful, are given to those who keep His commandments, and who seek earnestly to carry out in their lives the principles of salvation which He has revealed. When a people are in this condition their enemies cannot have much power over them. (April 8, 1887, MS 49:290)

PERSECUTION STRENGTHENS FAITH. The faith of the Latter-day Saints seems to grow stronger from these efforts to destroy it; and men, women and children who have been living in the practice of the requirements of their religion feel more determined than ever to maintain their integrity, and to do all that the Lord requires at their hands with cheerful willingness, whatever may be the consequences from a worldly point of view.

This persecution is not without its effects upon those who have made a pretense of being faithful members of the Church. Iniquity is being brought to light. The wrongdoer is being made to feel, in a most remarkable manner, that his sin will find him out; and the evidence that God is pleading with and awakening the consciences of those who have been living in sin is frequently furnished to us.

There have been many violations of the law of God practiced among us which have been hidden from the public gaze. The trials through which we are passing have the effect of causing these evils to be brought to light. It seems as though the Lord is tearing the covering, not only from the nations of the earth, but from the Latter-day Saints; and the time is not far distant—in fact, it has reached us already in part—when the sinner in Zion shall tremble, and fear shall seize upon the hypocrite. (October 6, 1886, MS 704-705)

GOD'S PURPOSES FULFILLED. The Lord has numberless ways of effecting His purposes, and the slanderers of His people He uses as instruments to warn mankind. Were there no slanderers of "Mormonism", there would be nothing to attract the attention of the people. If our enemies had not reported that we were murderers, adulterers, thieves, impostors, disloyal, etc., etc., there would be no contrast; but, having heard these lies, their falsity, when they come in contact with "Mormonism", is demonstrated.

Coming in contact with "Mormonism" has different effects upon different people; but with the honest-hearted lover of truth it has but one effect, and that is to convince him that it is the system of salvation designed by the Lord for his benefit. He may not arrive at this conclusion at once, but, if he cherishes a love and regard for the principles of truth, he will be convinced of it sooner or later. (August 23, 1856, WS 190)

REVELATION CAUSES PERSECUTION. It was the fact that the Prophet Joseph Smith and the Elders of this Church declared that revelation had been received from God that excited animosity in the first place. The Elders of this Church might have preached any doctrines they pleased and not said they had been taught them by revelation, nor by special divine assistance, nor by angels having come from heaven, but preached them as the speculations of men, as doctrines discovered, framed and arranged by men, by some theologians of eminent ability, and they would have had no particular difficulty. In preaching precisely the same doctrines we now preach —that is, the first principles of the Gospel—a church might have been made one of the most popular churches upon the face of the earth.

But what was it that excited animosity? It was the declaration that God had spoken from the heavens and had restored the primitive Gospel in its original purity and power, and that we had the power and authority to administer in the ordinances of the Gospel through which had been restored the gifts and blessings and powers that pertained to the Gospel in the days of Jesus. It was this declaration that excited animosity throughout the religious world against the Latter-day Saints in the beginning.

Every preacher felt that he was condemned by this declaration. If we had stood upon the same platform as they, saying that our organization was the result of man's wisdom, we should then have had some sympathy from them. But because our Elders declared that God had spoken, and that we preached that which had been revealed to us, animosity was excited and mobs rose against us, entertaining the most bitter feelings and committing the most terrible outrages. . . . The cry against us . . . was that we believed that God was a God of revelation as He was in ancient days, that He was the same God in this the 19th century that He was in the first century of the Christian era, when Jesus and the Apostles ministered among men. This was considered sufficient cause for mobs to organize themselves and drive our people from their homes and lands and to kill some of them. (June 25, 1882, JD 24:41-42)

Had Joseph Smith confined himself to the proclamation of his doctrines and views as he deduced them from the Scriptures, and had made no mention of intercourse with angels and the aid which he obtained through revelation, he would have been venerated as a great reformer, a real benefactor to his fellowmen, and his name would have been lauded to the skies as the founder of the best system of religion of the age. (April 12, 1856, WS 67)

BELIEF IN RESTORED PRIESTHOOD CAUSES OPPOSITION. It is because the Latter-day Saints believe that God has restored from the heavens the everlasting Priesthood—that eternal authority by which man acts upon the earth as the ambassador of God. It is because we have testified that God has restored this once more to earth and we have received it, and that by virtue of it we act as Apostles, members of the Seventies, High Priests, Elders, Priests, Teachers and Deacons and in the several offices God has placed in his Church. This is the secret of the opposition that is and has been waged against the Church of God. . . . If we did not have the right to exercise heaven-bestowed authority, there would be no particular opposition to us.

Of course, the nearer a man draws to God and the more he lives according to the plan which God has prescribed, the more opposition he meets with. Satan will stir up strife, animosity and hatred against him. On this account Luther, Calvin, John Wesley and other reformers have been persecuted. The nearer they came to the truth, and the more zealous they were in proclaiming it, the more opposition they met with.

Men, in reasoning upon this subject, say that every sect, at the commencement of its career, is persecuted because men are not familiar with its doctrines; but, when they become known, opposition and persecution cease. They predict this about the Latter-day Saints; but the truth of the matter is this: if every new sect is persecuted, it is because it fearlessly denounces the sins, follies and vices of the age, and so long as they continue this, so long are they persecuted; but the moment they assimilate to the world, gloss over its follies and go with the stream and float with the popular current, opposition cease. (June 11, 1871, JD 14:165-67)

ADVERSARY INDIFFERENT TO PARTAKERS OF ERROR. For generations there has been an indifference manifested by the adversary of truth to the systems of religion which have prevailed among men. When men partake of error, when they are not accompanied by the Spirit of God, when the power and authority which God imparts to fulfill his great purposes are not in existence among them, then there is an indifference manifested by the adversary; religious organizations and religious movements are regarded by him with unconcern, because the necessity does not exist, under those circumstances, for vigilant exertion on his part.

But the moment the Holy Priesthood of God is restored, being the power and authority imparted by heaven to men, which gives them capacity to go forth and administer in the things of God, then all hell is moved; all who are under the influence of the adversary are at once in commotion, and they seek to destroy all those who have the temerity to stand up in the defence of the truth and righteousness in the power of the Holy Priesthood of the Son of God. This has been the case from the beginning until now, from the shedding of the blood of righteous Abel down to the time that the last Apostle was slain. . . .

GREATEST OF ALL WARFARES. It may be truthfully said respecting the warfare in which we are engaged that it is irrepressible, and it will not terminate until one power or the other succumbs to the other. Which power shall succumb? There will be no cessation to this strife and contest. One or the other has to ride triumphant and hold dominion over this earth. Truth must prevail, or error must hold sway. . . .

The contest is not with cannon or with rifles and swords and weapons of this description; but it is, nevertheless, a warfare —a warfare between the spirit of darkness and that of light— between he who attempts to usurp the dominion of this earth and the God of heaven. The war which was waged in heaven has been transferred to the earth, and it is now being waged by the hosts of error and darkness against God and truth; and the conflict will not cease until sin is vanquished and this earth is fully redeemed from the power of the adversary and from the misrule and oppression which have so long exercised power over the earth. (May 6, 1866, JD 11:227-29)

SUPREMACY OF EARTH CONTENDED FOR. It is the supremacy of this earth that is being contended for. Satan is determined that God shall not have this earth and that He shall not reign here; he is determined in this, and if he could he would shed the blood of every man and woman on the face of the earth rather than it should go into the hands of God. All those who are connected with him would, if they could, slay every man that stands in their pathway.

The more faithful a man is in the cause of God the more the hatred of the wicked is manifested against him. . . . Hence, a people who seek to establish the cause of righteousness, to build temples, to restore the authority of God, will be hated to the death, and thus the prophecy will be fulfilled concerning them. . . .

NO PEACE ON SATAN'S TERMS. This warfare will not cease. . . . God forbid that there should be peace on such terms as our enemies would have us make; for peace means surrendering the Kingdom of God, surrendering and giving up by the servants of God that which they have undertaken to do, namely, to restore the reign of righteousness and truth upon the earth, the reign of God and of heaven. . . . When we are ready to surrender these things, then there will be peace, but it will be the peace of hell, it will be the triumph of Satan and the destruction of everything that is pure and holy and godlike upon the face of the earth. (September 2, 1883, JD 24:375-76)

SATAN TO HAVE GREATER POWER OVER WORLD. As the nations grow harder in their hearts, persistently rejecting the message of mercy which God has sent unto them by his servants, Satan will have more power over them, because the Spirit of God will not always strive with man; and he will endeavor to rouse them to more terrible acts of violence and to the manifestation of more malignant and devilish hatred of the Work of God and those who are connected with it than he has ever done before.

The fires of persecution are now smouldering and seem to the inexperienced as though they were all but extinguished, but a blast from the foul fiend who has sought from the beginning to destroy the righteous can enkindle them again, and they would burn as fiercely as ever. For this, as Latter-day Saints and as servants of God, we must be prepared. Our only safety lies in diligently keeping the commandments of Him who has hitherto been our protector and in living such a life of holiness as will meet with His favour and approbation. (January 3, 1863, MS 25:9)

POWER OF SATAN RESTRAINED. In the very beginning of this work Joseph told the Saints, left on record the statement, as to how it would be received by the children of men—the hatred with which it would be met, the violence that would be manifested towards it, the various troubles through which it would have to pass. All these things he told, by his prophetic voice, as though their history had been written, as though they had taken place. . . .

Wonderfully has the providence of our God been exhibited in the care exercised over His growing Church and His increasing people. . . . Had Satan been permitted to wreak his vengeance upon the Church in the commencement, it could easily have been extinguished in blood. Had the same power that was exercised against the Church in the days of Nauvoo, when the blood of our Prophet and Patriarch, and our present President, drenched the soil of Illinois, had that same spirit been permitted to have wreaked its vengeance upon the Church in the early days, it could, with no more excitement than was then raised, have completely extirpated the Priesthood from the face of the earth.

But God, as I have said, in His wonderful providence, restrained the wrath of the wicked in the early days of the Church. . . .

OPPOSITION IN PROPORTION TO GROWTH OF CHURCH. There was a limit to its exercise over the Church in its weak condition. But as power increased, as the gifts of God were manifested, as the keys of the Priesthood were revealed unto the children of men, so did the wrath of the wicked, so did the violence of mobs, so did the combinations that were formed with the object of destroying the work of God increase in their strength and in their numbers.

As the work progressed, so did the spirit of opposition progress, one keeping pace, apparently, with the other, and there is a wise purpose in this when we contemplate the great destiny that awaits this people. We can see the wisdom and the purpose of our God in permitting persecution to keep pace with the growth and the advancement of the work. It is just as necessary that we should be developed in our faith as anything else connected with the work of our God. If it were not for this, we could not become the people that God designs; we could not fulfill the destiny that He has in store for us. . . .

ALL NATIONS TO BE ARRAYED AGAINST SAINTS. As the Church increases, so will the opposition to its increase, until it will extend itself beyond the confines of our own nation to other lands and to other nations until, in fact, the whole earth that has not received or will not receive the Gospel of the Son of God, the message of salvation, of which we are the unworthy bearers . . . will array themselves against the work of our God and exert their power to destroy it, as a township did, as a county did, as a state did, as the United States are now doing, and then the work of our God will rise in its sublimity, in its strength, in its God-like power and assume its place, its rightful position among the nations of the earth. (October 5, 1884, JD 25:320-22)

PERSECUTION RETARDS GROWTH OF CHURCH. The writer remembers hearing the Prophet Joseph speak upon the subject of religious liberty. He did not agree with the view which some entertain that the Church of Christ would thrive best in the midst of persecution. His view, as he expressed it, was that if the Church could be favored with full religious liberty and have a fair field for the spread of its principles, it would grow much faster than it would where severe measures were used against it and mobocracy waged war against it. (May 1, 1896, JI 31:273)

It is true that the persecutions we have endured have given us a world-wide name and have been overruled by the Almighty for our good. They have been productive of invaluable experience to the people who have endured them; but have they made a single individual love the truth and embrace it who would not have loved it without them? Has truth been rendered more attractive, or found a lodgment more willingly in the hearts of the people, because of the persecutions its adherents have endured?

Persecution, so far as the Latter-day Saints are concerned, has been attended with some good results; a more rapid spread of our principles, however, is not one of them. Had mankind been willing to have received the Gospel as it has been revealed by the Lord, without manifesting an opposition and hatred thereto, it would long ere this have covered the earth. But men choose not to have it so, and they have opposed and persecuted. This action of theirs the Lord has overruled for the benefit of those who have embraced the Gospel. (October 19, 1861, MS 23:676)

THE FATE OF OUR PERSECUTORS. One of the most remarkable facts connected with the history of the Latter-day Saints is the fate of those who have pitted themselves against the work and have sought to destroy the people. We have had presidents, governors, judges, and other prominent and noted men, who have undertaken the task of "solving the Mormon problem" by violence, and the framing of various devices and schemes, having in view the overthrow of the liberties of the people. But which of them has prospered? Which has achieved fame or credit? It is true that some have obtained some notoriety for the time being. This was not because of any superior merit which they possessed, but because their names have been connected with that of the Mormons. This notoriety has of course been only temporary. Everyone has sunk into dishonor and oblivion. (February 17, 1890, MS 52:98-99)

Chapter 4

Mormonism—The Leaven of the Earth

THE SPIRIT OF GOD BEARS WITNESS. The Spirit of God bears testimony to the things of God, and there would be no difficulty in convincing the inhabitants of the earth of the truth of the principles believed in by the Latter-day Saints were it not for tradition and the prejudices which exist in men's minds in relation to the truth. . . .

When men hear it proclaimed that God has restored the everlasting Gospel and they have a desire in their hearts to comprehend the truth, there is a spirit accompanies the testimony of the servants of God which bears witness to their spirit that these things are true. But immediately another spirit steps in, and the reflection arises in the minds of many: "What will my parents, relatives or friends say? What will the world say if I believe this doctrine? There is ignominy associated with belief in these doctrines. There is shame to be encountered if I go forward and join a people so despised as these. What will men say of me? In what light shall I be viewed?" These reflections arise, and the testimony of the truth is extinguished in the hearts of many.

GREAT MORAL COURAGE REQUIRED. It requires, therefore, on the part of people now, as in ancient days, great strength of mind, great moral courage, and great love of the truth, an overpowering desire to obtain salvation, and the Spirit of God to aid them, in order to enable people to receive the Gospel of the Lord Jesus Christ. Hence it is that so few, comparatively speaking, in every age have received the truth. . . .

It has been so easy for men to reject the truth and flow with the current; it has been so easy for men to spread their sails, catch the popular breeze and glide before it; and it has been so difficult for men to stem the tide of opposition which they have always had to contend with when they have embraced the truth. (October 6, 1873, JD 16:242-43)

A REQUEST FOR FAIRNESS. We do not expect that all men will view our faith and formulae through our eyes. Neither do we condemn or anathematize those who honestly differ with us or actively oppose our doctrines and practices. We claim religious liberty, the freedom of speech and of the press, and the right to combat what we believe to be error by all legitimate means, and we frankly accord this freedom to others. But we do object to misrepresentation and defamation of our principles and character and the lives and objects of our leading men. We do object to articles and sermons against certain views and actions attributed to us without any reason in truth. . . .

We are anxious to have "Mormonism" exposed. . . . We only ask that what they hold up to the world as our doctrines really are our doctrines, and not some ridiculous fabrication designed to deceive the public and injure us. (May 31, 1879, MS 41:387)

A SOCIAL PHENOMENON. Our acts show that there is a power and an influence with us that the inhabitants of the earth elsewhere do not possess. We are looked upon as a social phenomenon in the earth; we are diverse from every other people; and our community is the object of attention and I may say of respect that its numbers do not entitle it to. Men from afar cannot cross the continent without coming to visit the Latter-day Saints. . . . What is it that distinguishes us from our fellows? . . . That distinction is, we believe in revelation. We profess to be guided by revelation. We are peculiar, when compared with the rest of the world, because all our movements are under divine guidance. . . .

GOSPEL TO SPREAD WITH INCREASED RAPIDITY. The hardest thing in building up a people is to gain a foothold. We have gained this. . . . We have achieved a position that will render our future progress more rapid than in years past and gone. I fully expect to see the progress of this work in the future more rapid than it has been in the past. I see the providence of God laboring to bring this about. Not to build up a people distinct from all the rest of the earth, not to build up some little, narrow sect or denomination, but this work and Gospel is to embrace within its fold all earth's children, every son and daughter of God on the earth. That is its mission, and it will accomplish it. But it will spread with increased rapidity from this time forth.

The foundation and corner-stones have been laid in tears,

blood and in much sorrow, but they are laid firmly, cemented by the sufferings, toils, faith and endurance of this people . . . ; and I trust that they are laid so deep that they will never be torn up, shaken or disturbed, and that upon them will a superstructure be reared of such strength, beauty and symmetry that it will be the joy and pride of the whole earth. . . .

A WORLDWIDE INFLUENCE. God has given to this people qualities which, in the contest of races, must tell. There are qualities connected with the Latter-day Saints, and principles connected with their system that, persecute and crush them out as you may, as long as the men live who bear the authority, and so long as the principles have a believer and practicer in the world, must live, survive and have influence in the midst of the earth and upon the populations thereof. . . .

The people . . . will continue to rise and increase in strength and power by the practice of those qualities which God has given unto us through revelation, until their influence will be felt . . . throughout the length and breadth of the earth, and thus will the sayings of the Prophets be fulfilled. . . .

WORLD ATTRACTED TO THE SAINTS. Do you think we could live in any spot on the earth without attracting attention? Do you think that a people such as we are could go to any land, or into the greatest desert on the earth, and live there any length of time without attracting the attention of the world as much as we do now? Why, the thing is impossible. When we came to this region, it was as much out of the way as any place on the earth could be. But after coming here we demonstrated that the soil of these valleys, by being watered artificially, would produce crops; and the result of our experiment, for experiment it may be called, is that all this interior basin, formerly looked upon as an irreclaimable desert, is a choice land. The world once convinced of this, and population came to us, and the railroad came across the continent, and we find ourselves right in the center of the great transcontinental highway. If we were to go into any other land it would be the same—we should attract population and wealth, and the eyes of mankind would be directed towards us. (January 8, 1871, JD 14:28-30)

CONTACT WITH WORLD DESIRABLE. Those who are most familiar with the people know full well that whatever our peculiarities may be, we are not opposed to progress. . . .

When we came here, we sought isolation. We were utterly sick of everything we had been brought in contact with. We had suffered and were glad of an isolated retreat such as these mountains afforded, where we could dwell in peace and quietness for a season. We occupy a different position to that which we have ever occupied before. We desire to be more known. We have no desire to secrete ourselves, or to hide ourselves, or to hide ourselves from public gaze and scrutiny, and from contact with outside influences.

There was a time when, in our weak condition, we might have feared the results, but that day is past, and I trust forever. We court contact today, if it be of the right kind. We do not court nor invite aggression; healthy contact, legitimate acquaintance we desire. We want to be better known, and when we are better known, these absurd prejudices and misapprehensions which prevail now through the public mind respecting the "Mormons" and the people of Utah will be dissipated.

We may differ from them on many points; we may have our peculiarities of religion; but there is a standpoint, or platform on which they can meet with us, a common platform on which we can stand with the rest of our fellow-citizens. . . . (June 11, 1868, MS 30:500-501)

I would not give much for a religion which would not stand contact with the world. . . . If there is anything superior to that which we believe outside of our religion, let it come; we will welcome it. We are wedded to our religion only so far as it is true. So far as it is true we are wedded to it, and as such we have espoused it, as such we maintain it, and as such we hope to die believing in its tenets and practising them; but if any one else has something better let him come along. We have sacrificed enough for truth to show that we love it. . . .

A CITY SET ON A HILL. Jesus said to his ancient disciples, "Ye are the light of the world. A city that is set on a hill cannot be hid." [Matthew 5:14.] The eyes of the world were upon them. And in our day we behold the same effect. The

Latter-day Saints and their work have been like a city set on a hill. They have attracted the gaze of the nations, and that, too, without any especial effort on their part to make themselves conspicuous.

The clamor of our enemies has greatly contributed to this. What do their attacks accomplish for us? They advertise us and give us an importance to which we could not attain otherwise. Every effort that is made to destroy this work or to embarrass its onward progress or to deprive its leaders of their lives or of their liberties only enhances its importance in the midst of the earth, gives it publicity, preaches the Gospel, attracts attention, causes men and women to think, to reason and to investigate what it is about this people that creates so much excitement. (October 11, 1874, JD 17:261)

Every Latter-day Saint who is in the path of his duty, whether abroad among the people preaching the principles of "Mormonism" orally, or at home in the Valleys of Utah building cities and temples, or leaving the land of his or her nativity emigrating to the mountains, or engaged in any of the fields of labor assigned to us to fill, is disseminating a knowledge of "Mormonism" and is bearing so loud and powerful a testimony to its truth that the world will be left without excuse for rejecting it. (August 3, 1856, WS 189-90)

"IN" BUT NOT "OF" THE WORLD. It is true that we are in the world and must have association to some extent with its people. But it is not necessary that we should break down every barrier and wall of separation which the Lord has raised between us and them and become one with them. It is not necessary we should intermarry with them—give our daughters unto their sons nor take their daughters unto our sons. It is not necessary that we should foster and support them and give the power they seek for. It is not necessary that we should bow down to their gods or worship at their shrines. They who do these things are not friends of Zion; they are its enemies. (January 1, 1887, JI 22:12)

TESTING THE WORLD. The mission of the Gospel, or what is commonly called "Mormonism," appears to be to test men and nations and institutions, as nothing else will. It has the effect to draw to the surface, from the hidden resources of the human heart, manifestations that would, under other circumstances, remain entirely concealed. Every Latter-day Saint who has had any experience in the world has seen this illustrated. People whom they thought very honest, very truth-loving and very sincere have proved, when the Gospel has been brought in contact with them, to be the very opposite. People who have borne a high character for loving God, for believing the Bible and for a willingness to obey the truth have often been proved to be rank hypocrites when the Gospel has been brought to them. Men who have stood high in society, and who have had a fine reputation, have shown themselves to be utterly unworthy of confidence and to be enemies of truth. The Gospel has brought to the surface the true features of every character and has shown how many professions are false and hypocritical.

This has been the case in thousands of instances in the world where the Elders have gone carrying the Gospel. Men and women who received the truth gladly when it was preached to them and who joined the Church hastened with delight to their relatives and acquaintances to carry to them the glad message and were astonished at the reception they have had from many of these. Instead of being received with favor for carrying the truth, they have often been treated with scorn and contempt, and their relatives and friends have turned their backs upon them and shown hatred towards them. In this way many thousands of the Latter-day Saints have been disappointed. But this has not been without some profit for, by the means of the Gospel, they have been able to get a knowledge of human nature and an insight into the true characters of people whom they had previously known for years or, perhaps, all their lives and whom they had supposed they knew perfectly well. (March 15, 1890, JI 25:162-63)

DESTINED TO FILL WHOLE EARTH. This great work which God our Eternal Father has founded is destined—hear it all ye Latter-day Saints; hear it all ye ends of the earth—this great work is destined to fill the whole earth. It is the work that the Prophets spoke about. It is the work that they described in glorious language. The predictions of the holy Prophets upon this subject are the most glorious to be found in the volume of Scripture—we refer to the work of the last days—small as it is in the beginning, insignificant, destitute of influence, destitute of worldly advantages, it is a power, nevertheless, that will continue to grow; it will continue to increase; it will continue to spread, until from pole to pole, from the center to the circumference of our globe, in every land, the power and influence of this great work which our Father in heaven has laid the foundation of, will be felt. (February 24, 1889, MS 51:194)

OUR STRENGTH MUST BE PROVEN. We are bound to be lifted up. You cannot conceal us; it is impossible. We have got to stand contact with the world, and if our religion will not stand such contact, then it must succumb. But it will not. It will stand the test; it will pass through the ordeal purer and better, and men will recognize its beauty. Our destiny is to be brought in contact with the world. God has predicted it. We may hide ourselves in a corner, but God will bring us out to the light; we have to come in contact with the world to prove our strength, to prove what is in us and to learn many things, the knowledge of which we need. (June 12, 1881, JD 22:179-83)

SHALL WE BE OVERTHROWN? There is nothing plainer to my mind than this, that if the Latter-day Saints become luxurious and extravagant, if they love the world and forsake their former purity, if they forsake their frugality and temperance, and the principles which God has revealed unto them, and by the practice of which they are today the people that they are, we shall be overthrown as others have been overthrown. But I do not look for any such result, for I believe firmly in the prediction of Daniel that this work, when established, shall not be given into the hands of another people; it shall stand forever, and there will be means and agencies used and brought to bear on the minds of the people to prevent such a catastrophe as that to which I have alluded—to prevent the downfall of the system and the overthrow of those connected with it and to prevent the victory of that which is evil over that which is good, holy and pure. (October 8, 1872, JD 15:206)

THE LEAVENING EFFECT OF THE GOSPEL. The ideas that have been propagated by the Latter-day Saints, though they have not converted as many to our faith as they should have done, have had a most wonderful influence upon the religious, the philosophic and the scientific world. Ideas that men now believe in and receive readily, Joseph Smith was persecuted and denounced for proclaiming. And while there are millions who do not believe that he was a Prophet of God, or that the principles he taught were revealed from God, there is no mistaking the fact that his teachings, that the truths he advanced, and the ideas which he disseminated, have had a wonderful effect upon the human mind throughout Christendom. . . .

Although men and women have not become Latter-day Saints, nor have the mass of mankind received the religious truths in their entirety, as they were taught by Joseph, and as they have been taught by those who succeeded him, yet there has been a very visible and a marked advancement by men and women all over the world wherever the Elders of this Church have traveled.

So, it is not in the baptism of people; it is not in the gathering of the people together alone that we are accomplishing great results; but it is in teaching the world the principles that God has revealed to us and gradually indoctrinating the mind of mankind, to some extent at least, uplifting them from the prejudices and the darkness and the ignorance in which they have been enshrouded to a higher plane, to breathe a purer and a freer spirit of inquiry in religious and scientific thought. (April 7, 1878, JD 20:2)

GOSPEL TRUTHS BEING ACCEPTED. Simple, unadorned truth will win its way. Its onward march, as long as its believers and advocates live, is irresistible. Misrepresentation, falsehood and error flee from before its majestic presence and hide themselves in the recesses where it has not penetrated. . . .

By the revelations of the Lord through His Prophets a flood of light has poured forth. As men reason upon these things and become familiar with them, prejudice melts and the truth prevails. Men accept the new and truthful ideas but will not acknowledge the source whence it comes. . . .

Elders of the Church will yet be told that the bestowal of the gifts upon those who repent and are baptized as Latter-day Saints is no evidence that this is the Church of Christ, for miracles are wrought by people of other churches. By this the hearts of the people will be hardened against the truth. The Prophet Joseph said that the devil, in order to deceive the people and to cause them to reject the work of God, would work many miracles, and his followers would even cause fire to apparently come down from heaven.

It is very remarkable that the people of Christendom are gradually adopting the truths which the Prophet Joseph was inspired of the Lord to teach. Yet they will not acknowledge that he was a Prophet. . . . There were very many truths taught by the Prophet Joseph that the world kicked against and persecuted him and the Church for believing. But, wonderful to tell, there is scarcely one of these that is not believed in now in some form by thousands of people outside of this Church. They still reject the means by which they were obtained, and will not acknowledge the Priesthood, but they believe, in a certain way, the principles. And those which they do not believe are gradually working their way into notice and favor. The world is following the track of this Church. Slowly, perhaps, but surely it is adopting our thoughts and views. They are not conscious of this themselves, and the Latter-day Saints only perceive it when they compare the present with the past and see the progress that has been made. (February 15, 1883, JI 18:56-57)

TO REVOLUTIONIZE THE WORLD. "Mormonism" is destined to revolutionize the world. But how many are there who realize the truth of this saying? Some, no doubt, but not nearly all who have heard it, and yet that very revolution is going on, and they are helping to promote it; it commenced many years ago—the very moment the first revelation was given to the Prophet Joseph Smith.

But to revolutionize a world, with religions, political and social systems, the outgrowth of nearly six thousand years' experience is a slow process, and though "Mormonism" possesses a power belonging to nothing else on earth, and that nothing of merely human origin ever can possess, still its Almighty Author acts on natural and rational principles and does not seek by means alone of thunder, lightning, famine, earthquake, or other dread manifestations of superhuman power, to force or arouse His creatures to accept His institutions or to obey His laws.

For this reason the Kingdom of God upon the earth will not be characterized by a wonderfully rapid growth, like a mushroom; but, grappling ever with, and never ceasing the strife until it is victor over, error and evil of every kind, its foundations will be securely laid in the hearts and affections of those who love and live by truth and righteousness only. (October 26, 1872, JI 7:172)

A MARVELOUS WORK AND WONDER. It has been said very truthfully that God and one man are a great majority. God is doing a marvelous work and a wonder. He interposes and confounds the schemes of the wicked and controls by His invisible and irresistible agencies in such a manner as to accomplish His purposes. . . . There are powers unseen by mortal eye engaged in this contest. Behind this handful of people there stands, like a wall of living fire, the power of God. His command has gone forth. He has made promises. All heaven with its glorious array of mighty angels and just men made perfect are engaged in carrying out His purposes.

On the other side are the powers of darkness. They cannot withstand the almighty power of God. They are the weaker side, though according to mortal vision they are infinitely the stronger. Step by step, they must retreat until finally they will be overwhelmed and destroyed. Latter-day Saints, therefore, can take courage and press forward. They are the winning side and must eventually triumph. (August 15, 1883, JI 18:246)

Chapter 5

The Church of God—The Kingdom of God

ONLY TWO CHURCHES. After The Church of Jesus Christ of Latter-day Saints was organized, there were only two churches upon the earth. They were known respectively as the Church of the Lamb of God and Babylon. The various organizations which are called churches throughout Christendom, though differing in their creeds and organizations, have one common origin. They all belong to Babylon. God is not the founder of them, yet there are many sincere people who belong to them. These the Elders of the Church are commanded to warn, and they are commanded to gather out. The Spirit of the Lord moves upon the people who will listen to His servants to leave Babylon and join the Church of the Lamb. (April 1, 1882, JI 17:104)

THE KINGDOM OF GOD—A DISTINCTION. We are asked, "Is the Church of God and the Kingdom of God the same organization?" . . . The Kingdom of God is a separate organization from the Church of God. There may be men acting as officers in the Kingdom of God who will not be members of the Church of Jesus Christ of Latter-day Saints. . . .

The Kingdom of God when established will not be for the protection of the Church of Jesus Christ of Latter-day Saints alone but for the protection of all men, whatever their religious views or opinions may be. Under its rule no one will be permitted to overstep the proper bounds or to interfere with the rights of others. (March 1, 1896, JI 31:140)

We have been taught from the beginning this important principle that the Church of God is distinct from the Kingdom of God. Joseph gave us the pattern before he died. He gave his brethren an example that has not been forgotten up to this day. He impressed it upon them that men, not members of the Church, could be members of the Kingdom that the Lord will set up when He reigns. He picked out the youngest among them and told them to be sure and remember this. In the minds of all of us who understand this matter there is a clear distinction between the Church in its ecclesiastical capacity and that which may be termed the government of God in its political capacity. (April 5, 1897, DW 54:675)

You well-informed Latter-day Saints know that there are two powers which God has restored in these the last days. One is the Church of God; the other is the Kingdom of God. A man may belong to the Kingdom of God and yet not be a member of the Church of God. In the Kingdom of God, using it in a political sense, there may be heathens and Pagans and Mohammedans and Latter-day Saints and Presbyterians and Episcopalians and Catholics and men of every creed. Will they legislate for The Church of Jesus Christ of Latter-day Saints alone? Will the laws that they enact protect us alone and not protect others? No! Why? Because God is the Father of the Latter-day Saints as well as of every human being. . . .

TO PROTECT ALL WITH EQUAL RIGHTS. When He establishes His Kingdom, it will protect all in their equal rights; I as a Latter-day Saint will not have power to trample on my fellow-man who may not be orthodox in my opinion because I am a Latter-day Saint; nor will my fellow-man to whom I am heterodox have the power to trample upon me. Does not that look right? That is the kind of kingdom we have to contend for; that is the kind of kingdom we have to establish, and it is already provided for in the Constitution given unto us by God. (April 6, 1879, JD 20:204)

A CARDINAL DOCTRINE OF THE CHURCH. We have always looked upon civil government as entirely distinct from church government; and our views upon this subject ought to be so well known as not to leave room for accusation even. It has been proclaimed by Joseph Smith; it has been proclaimed by Brigham Young; it has been proclaimed by John Taylor; it has been proclaimed by Wilford Woodruff, and all the leading Elders associated with them, that God intended to organize a Kingdom on the earth that should not be composed of Latter-day Saints alone, but that members of that Kingdom should belong to other religious denominations, as well as to The Church of Jesus Christ of Latter-day Saints. This has been a cardinal doctrine of this Church—that is, with the Elders who have had experience and knowledge concerning that which is to come and that which the Prophet Joseph believed in and taught. . . . (October 6, 1889, DW 39:592-93)

SEPARATION OF CHURCH AND STATE. There is no necessity that there should be a blending of church and state. There is no necessity for this; it is not wise to blend church and state. I do not believe that as members of the Church we should pass decrees or laws that would bind other people. I have no such belief, never did have. I do not think I ever shall have. But, because a man is a member of a church and because a man is a servant of God and because a man bears the Priesthood of the Son of God, he should not be prevented because of that from acting in any civil capacity, from taking part in civil matters and executing the laws that are enacted by civil authority.

KINGDOM OF GOD A CIVIL POWER. The province of the Kingdom of God that Daniel saw, the Kingdom that would be established in the last days, is to be as a shield to the Latter-day Saints, to be as a bulwark around about that Church. . . . The Kingdom of God when it shall prevail in the earth—as it will do—will be the civil power which will shield and protect the Church of Christ against every attack, against every unlawful aggression, against every attempt to deprive it of its legitimate rights. (November 20, 1884, JD 26:12)

AMBASSADORS TO NATIONS. The Elders of Israel are now ambassadors to the nations from the court of heaven bearing the Gospel of salvation to the children of men; but the time will come when they will be called to act in a different ambassadorial capacity. The nations are not going to be all destroyed at once, as many have imagined, but they are going to stand and continue to some extent with their governments; the Kingdom of God is not all the time to continue its present theological character alone, but it is to become a political power, known and recognized by the powers of the earth; and you, my brethren, may have to be sent forth to represent that power as its accredited agents . . . and it is necessary that you should understand how to deport yourselves in every circle you might be called to move in. (January 3, 1862, MS 24:103)

KINGDOM OF GOD TO ASSUME LEADERSHIP. The Kingdom of God will not always occupy the humble position which it now does; neither will it continue to be confined to its present circumscribed limits. Many years will not pass away before it will take its place among the nations of the earth and assume a leading position in and exert a predominating influence upon the social, religious and political affairs of the world and when its disciples and ministers and representatives will not be treated with that contumely and contempt with which they are at present received.

In order that they may be prepared for this state of things and keep pace with the gradual but steady progress of the Kingdom, the Lord has said to his servants, ". . . seek ye diligently and teach one another words of wisdom; yea, seek ye out of the best books of wisdom; seek learning, even by study and also by faith." [D&C 88:118.] And again, "study and learn, and become acquainted with all good books, and with languages, tongues, and people." [D&C 90:15.]

We can readily perceive from these brief quotations, as well as from many other instructions which we have received upon this subject, that although the Lord has called "upon the weak things of the world, those who are unlearned and despised, to thrash the nations by the power of [His] Spirit" [D&C 35:13], yet, he does not design them to continue weak and unlearned and despised; but, on the contrary, He has commanded them to seek wisdom and knowledge and to study to make themselves acquainted with the manners, customs, languages and laws of the inhabitants of the different countries of the earth.

ELDERS TO REPRESENT KINGDOM OF GOD. The wisdom of pursuing such a course as this is already apparent to those Elders who have been sent abroad to proclaim the Gospel to the various nations of the earth; and it will be made still more evident, in a few years, when the Elders of Israel are called to go forth as the accredited representatives of the Kingdom of God and will necessarily have to move in what are called "the higher circles" of society. That time will certainly come; and it is easy to perceive how necessary it will be, for all who may be called upon to fill those responsible positions, to be possessed of general intelligence and cultivated minds, combined with a familiar acquaintance with the laws and customs of the people among whom they may be sojourning, in order that they may fill their appointed missions with honor to the government they represent and with pleasure and credit to themselves.

Besides, the time will also come when the servants of God, in possession of the Holy Priesthood, will be called upon to go forth and preside over the various communities, tribes and nations of the earth, and to administer the laws of Zion in their midst, in righteousness, justice and mercy. This they could not do if destitute of a knowledge of the past history, laws, customs, habits, etc., of the people; all these things must necessarily be taken into account in judging and governing a people righteously and wisely. (September 26, 1863, MS 25:616-17)

BUILDING THE KINGDOM OF GOD. We have not come out of our present location for purely spiritual performances but to lay the foundation of a system that should stand forever, that should be connected with man's existence here upon the earth, both his spiritual and his temporal existence, a work that should affect everything connected with man and his relationship to his fellow-man. . . .

The Lord is gathering out from every nation, kindred, tongue and people a community out of which He intends to form for Himself a Kingdom, not an earthly kingdom but a Kingdom over which He will preside in the heavens, a Kingdom that should be based upon purely republican principles upon the earth and, therefore, not a kingdom in the strict sense of the word, so far as its earthly location is concerned, but a republic. And for this purpose, as the Latter-day Saints have believed from the beginning, the Lord raised up the founders of our nation and inspired them—George Washington and others—to do the work that they accomplished in laying the foundation of a form of government upon this land under which that Kingdom that He should establish should grow and flourish and extend itself without interfering in the least degree with the genius of the government. (April 6, 1878, JD 20:81)

WORKING TO FURTHER THE KINGDOM. It does not matter what we are doing or where we are labouring—in the adobe yard, in the canyons, preaching the Gospel or doing anything else that God through his servants directs us to perform—if we labour faithfully, we are contributing to the accomplishment of a great and good work and are really doing much more than we think and labouring to bring to pass all those predictions that have been delivered respecting the generation in which we live. . . .

If we labour in the way and in the position in which the authorities have put us and directed us, we may rest assured that we are labouring for the accomplishment of all that which is required to be done by our Heavenly Father, and we are laying up treasures in heaven; and although we may not do as much here as we suppose we ought, there is an eternity before us in which we can labour . . . and we are to press forward until we attain the fulness of our desire.

It is so with the wicked in one sense—with the enemies of truth. All that they do contributes to the rolling forth of this great and mighty work. (September 9, 1860, JD 8:303)

WRONG-DOING BUILDS SATAN'S KINGDOM. Many do not think, even after they have obtained a knowledge in regard to the work of God, that every time they give way to the suggestions of Satan, and hearken not to the still small voice of the Spirit of the Lord, they virtually array themselves on the side of Satan, the arch-enemy of God. They do not think, when they disobey the counsel of the officers whom God has placed in His Kingdom, that they encourage, build up and give comfort to the rebel against God, the prince and power of darkness, and become his aiders and abettors in endeavoring to pull down the Kingdom of God. Yet this is the case.

Every man who giveth place to the adversary or his suggestions in his heart, or who giveth heed to him in any way, helps the usurper to perpetuate his power and prevents, in proportion to his disobedience, the consummation which God, angels and all holy and just men, both in heaven and on earth, are laboring to bring about. He is Satan's subject, because he is governed by him; and if he should not expel him with his influences from his heart, he will have power over him, not only here but hereafter. (June 5, 1857, WS 425-26)

ALL GOOD ACTIONS TO BEAR FRUIT. There never was a man who did a good action from the time of Adam down to the present time but that good action and its effects have lived, and they have contributed to the great work of human redemption. There is nothing, my brethren, that you have done or said, if directed aright, and in the discharge of your duties in the Priesthood, but has tended to the accomplishment of God's purpose. Whether you speak, write, or do anything else for the building up of the Kingdom, all will result, at some time, in the accomplishment of that which you desire. The seed you have sown will grow and blossom.

There is no Elder in this Church—no matter where he is, nor how small or limited his sphere of labor may be—but what all he does, if properly directed, will tend to consummate the the purposes of God. How many of you have preached over and over again and, comparatively speaking, have done but little in the way of bringing souls to the knowledge of the Truth. But the time will come, my brethren, when every word of truth, every testimony for the Truth you have uttered will be vividly remembered by those to whom you have spoken. You sow the seed, and, being eternal truth, it is imperishable and as undying as the men themselves are. People may reject the offer of salvation you make to them and may disregard your warnings, but every word you have uttered will be distinctly remembered at some future day by them. . . . In the depths of sorrow, misery, and, it may be, despair in which they may be involved hereafter, their minds will range over everything they have ever heard, and the words and testimonies of the truth you have declared, and probably thought fruitlessly because they fell unheeded, may be the means of bringing them forth to life, liberty and light.

We poor mortals are entirely too narrow in our conceptions of the nature of the Gospel. You have never given utterance to an expression but what will have an influence upon your lives; and the testimonies you bear concerning Joseph and the Work of God will be recorded in heaven and live eternally—coeval with ourselves—and those who hear your words will, themselves, be judged by them. . . .

ALL CARRY A SPIRIT AND INFLUENCE. As every good

thing we do tends to promote the cause of God, so everything that we perform that is unworthy of our positions and callings will go in the opposite direction. If you could see yourselves, you would find that there is not one of you but what carry a spirit and influence with you—a spirit and influence, whether good or evil, which can be sensibly felt by all who come in contact with you, especially if they have the gift of discernment. Did you ever feel, when you were in the presence of people who possessed a bad spirit, uncomfortable and an unwillingness to associate with such? And have you not felt how much more in accordance with your feelings and your own influence was the society of those who possessed a good spirit? The spirits are just as palpable to the understanding as men's words. (December 31, 1863, MS 26: 114-16)

GOSPEL WORTHY OF OUR UNDIVIDED ATTENTION. It is literally impossible for any man to remain a member of the Church of Christ who does not continually regard his religion and its requirements as matters of paramount importance. They may cling to it for a while; but sooner or later, unless they repent, they will be shaken off and left behind. If the Saints, therefore, wish to continue to be identified with the people of God and to progress as they progress, they must live in strict obedience to all the commandments of the Lord. . . .

The Gospel of the Son of God is either worthy of our sole and undivided devotion, or it is not worthy of a thought. If the Saints have the knowledge they ought to have relative to it, there will be no half-hearted feelings about it; they will feel like engaging in it with every faculty of their mind. (November 22, 1856, WS 253-54)

MEMBERSHIP IN CHURCH SHOULD BE VALUED. A standing in the Church is not viewed as of very great moment by many people. They think too lightly of it, and the line of distinction between those who are members of the Church and those who have lost their fellowship is not drawn with sufficient plainness to impress the people concerning it. This is especially the case with many young people. They cannot perceive as they should do the great difference between a membership in the

Church and being outside of the Church. Where this state of feeling exists and men and women, or boys and girls, are indifferent concerning their standing, they are liable to take steps that may endanger their fellowship and be a means of losing their connection with the Church. It is this indifference that frequently causes young people to lose their standing, and they take no particular pains to avoid the evil consequences which follow a course of life that is improper.

APOSTASY A DREADFUL CRIME. Ought not the lesson to be impressed upon every heart, so that all will shun the commission of acts that will endanger their standing in the Church of Christ? Apostasy is a dreadful crime. No matter who it is that apostatizes from the truth, breaks the commandments of God, violates the covenants that he or she has made with the Almighty and denies the faith, it is a dreadful crime. It cannot be glossed over; it cannot be made light of; it is a serious offense, upon which God has set the seal of His condemnation. Children should be taught this in their early life. The mother, when she gathers her children around her knee and teaches them to pray, should teach them to pray that they may be preserved in the truth, that they may be kept from sin, that they may be enabled to maintain the faith; and she should impress upon them the greatness of the blessing they enjoy in being permitted to be members of the Church and to be in covenant with their Father in Heaven.

If proper pains were taken in teaching the rising generation these truths, our children would dread apostasy; they would shun the commission of sin and would view with horror anything that would be likely to endanger their standing in the Church of Christ. They would avoid quarrels; they would suffer wrong rather than to do wrong, because in so doing they would be more likely to preserve the fellowship of their brethren and sisters. This feeling would grow with their growth and strengthen with their strength; and if it ever should become necessary for them to face death for their religion, they would do so, if not gladly, at least with resolute determination rather than deny the faith.

OUR GREATEST HONOR. Every member of the Church —young and old—should be taught to appreciate the fact that to be admitted to covenant with God, to have communion of the Holy Ghost, to have the fellowship of the Saints, is the greatest honor and blessing that can be bestowed upon mortal man; and their daily prayers should contain thanksgiving to God that they have been permitted to enjoy this exalted privilege. (January 15, 1895, JI 30:55-56)

TRANSGRESSORS TO BE CUT OFF. Men who are doing wrong, by being dealt with, may sometimes see their folly and repent of it; but if they are left to themselves, they may go from bad to worse until they have gone too far for repentance. Besides, the example of such characters may lead others astray. . . .

We know that many are tender-hearted about their relatives, their friends and their acquaintances. They dislike to deal with them and to expose them; but this is mistaken kindness and always results badly. If the man who drinks liquor and gets drunk be taken in hand in time, he may be induced to repent and lead a new life; but if permitted to go on, he may go until he indulges in acts of violence and perhaps becomes a murderer. Then which of the shepherds will be responsible for permitting him to remain with the flock and be called by the holy name of our Master? What a reflection for a Teacher! What a reflection for a Bishop, if a man, through his neglect of duty, goes step by step on the downward road until he stains his hands in innocent blood and stands a murderer before God! Every Teacher and every Bishop and every President of Stake and every Apostle should take warning. . . .

The officer who permits these things to exist in the Church, God will not hold guiltless. (July 1, 1886, JI 21:200)

EXCOMMUNICATED MEMBERS LOSE BLESSINGS. Those who are severed from the Church lose all the rights and privileges which they enjoyed as members of the Church. . . .

He has forfeited, by his misconduct and suffering himself to be severed from the body of Christ, all the blessings pronounced upon him in holy places and can lay no claim to any promises of that character. . . . Every blessing, every promise, every power that is made unto the faithful is withdrawn from and forfeited by the transgressor who loses his standing in the Church. . . .

Any man whose case has been acted upon in that way by the legal authority of the Church can only obtain restoration of those promises and blessings by doing his first works over again —by repenting truly and sincerely, confessing his sins, being baptized and confirmed a member of the Church; and to have the blessings of the temple and the promises which he may have received through its ordinances in full force upon him, he should have them confirmed again upon him by one having the authority. (October 15, 1891, JI 26:622-23)

Chapter 6

True and False Religion

MORALITY AND RELIGION. Occasionally we find people who disclaim having anything to do with religion; at the same time they profess to believe in the practice of what are known as good moral principles. Such people do not seem to understand that morality is religion—that the Gospel is but a system for the development of moral principles. Without morality religion is but a useless form, and without the aid of the ordinances of the Gospel morality cannot be brought to perfection. There is no dividing line between the laws of morality and the laws of the Gospel. The Gospel includes them all, and any system of morality which does not embrace all the principles of true religion is imperfect or incomplete.

It may be supposed that obedience to the Gospel requires the observance of practices that have no connection with morality. It is true that the Gospel inculcates ordinances and duties that seemingly are not necessary to the practice of moral principles. They appear to be arbitrary requirements. But when the philosophy of these Gospel ordinances is understood, it will be discovered that they are but necessary aids to the practice of moral principles.

Prayer for example may be regarded by some to be strictly a religious duty, having no connection with moral obligations. If prayer were only a form, this might be true. But prayer is for the purpose of obtaining Divine aid in order to more fully perform moral duties. Without the assistance of the Lord a person cannot live a strictly moral life; hence, prayer is as much a part of morality as of religion. One who lives a moral life cannot be otherwise than a religious person, at least to the extent of his obedience to what he regards as moral laws. As long as he rejects the Gospel ordinances that to him may appear to be unnecessary for moral development he will never reach that moral perfection which may be attained by those who render obedience to all the Gospel requirements. (October 15, 1898, JI 33:699-700)

RELIGION AND AUTHORITY. Morality in and of itself, however skillfully and beautifully taught, is not sufficient to save mankind. . . . It is apparent that something more than a knowledge of moral precepts is necessary to save the world and to unite the people to make them one. . . . The Lord has revealed that the presence of the Holy Priesthood is necessary to accomplish this; without authority the words and ordinances of life and salvation cannot be rightfully administered, neither can mankind attain to the fullness of His Glory.

The Christian ministers of today have no more authority in this respect than the heathen teachers. . . . Belief in God and in the Savior lies at the foundation of true religion, and in that respect those who have this belief are nearer to God and to the truth than those who do not have it. But belief in God and in the Lord Jesus Christ does not alone give men the authority to officiate in the ordinances of the Gospel. That authority must come from God. It cannot be self-assumed.

Now, this is the great deficiency among these teachers of morality of which we have spoken. Many of their views are grand and, when carried out practically, ennoble men and women and help them to live comparatively pure lives. This is admirable and attended with excellent effects as far as it goes. To progress, however, in true righteousness, to be united, to have the soul filled with the light of heaven and to grow to the stature of men and women in Christ Jesus, there must be ordinances administered by those having the authority from God to administer them. (March 1, 1890, JI 25:146-47)

TRUE AND FALSE RELIGION. The religion of Jesus is one of mercy, love and kindness. Where it prevails, the people are meek, lowly and gentle. They suffer wrong rather than do wrong. They never oppress. They never bind heavy yokes upon their fellows. Hence, in the history of our world that religion has never stood a fair chance. Its followers have always been driven to the wall. It would be so in this age also had not God promised that His Kingdom should be established and prevail over the whole earth.

In the case of false religions the very opposite of this picture is the true one. Where false religion prevails, men persecute and oppress those who are not of their own faith; they are frequently fierce, cruel, pitiless and do not feel content unless they are waging war against those who possess pure religion or who are striving to obtain a knowledge of it. The history of false religion is the history of crime and the most dreadful and shocking persecutions of men by their fellows.

Man has tried to do what God never did; God gives every man the right to worship according to the dictates of his own conscience; he is free to worship the Lord or not. But men, when filled with false religion, have not been content with this; they have sought to prescribe rules and frame religion for their fellow men, and in many instances have killed them because they would not accept them. (April 1, 1871, JI 6:52)

FREEDOM OF WORSHIP. If our belief and practice are erroneous, will they not fall before light, intelligence and truth? Truth has the Creator for its support. It is eternal as He is eternal. Give it a fair field and it will prevail. It is only error which needs the support of the Government, which requires to be bolstered up by the strong arm of power. . . .

If our doctrines are false and our practices are not what we think they are—according to the will of heaven—we shall be the sufferers and not those who do not believe or indulge in them. So long as we do not intrude upon our fellow-men or interfere with their rights and happiness, it is not their right to punish us. The punishment of false doctrines is the prerogative of the Great Creator. He has reserved that to Himself, for such deeds are an offence against His majesty, and for them He has reserved the proper punishment. . . .

The Latter-day Saints have positive views respecting the Gospel of the Son of God. They are satisfied that many doctrines taught by popular sects are false, that many practices flowing from those doctrines are contrary to the will of heaven; but what of that? Have they the right to interfere to prevent such acts of worship upon the part of their fellow-men? Certainly not. If they were vastly in the majority, and full of strong convictions upon those subjects, as they are, they would not have any such right. They might reason and teach, use moral suasion and Biblical argument, but beyond that they could not go without an offence to the great Creator, neither can others be justified in going beyond this with them.

If, as all who receive the Bible as the word of God believe, the Lord will hereafter reward and punish men and women for the deeds done in the body, is it not plain that man trenches upon His domain, when, for entertaining religious opinions and the practice of acts of worship which do not interfere with his enjoyment or his rights, he attempts to anticipate the Almighty and rewards and punishes these things at his pleasure here?

One would think that those who believe that sinners against heaven will be plunged into the lake of fire and brimstone, never by any possibility to be extricated therefrom, would be satisfied to wait until the offender died and not attempt to give him a foretaste of that torment here. But many, while loudly avowing their belief in the horrible sufferings which they describe as awaiting those who do not worship as they do, are not content to let the few short years allotted to man on the earth pass away without making those who, in their eyes, are sinners, feel their vengeance. They act as though they were afraid that, without excessive watchfulness on their part, those wicked wretches might escape the knowledge of the Lord. (1879, *Review*, 43-46)

EXTREMES—THE ERROR OF MANKIND. There is, perhaps, no error which the Saints, in common with the rest of mankind, are more liable to fall into than that of running from one extreme to the other. From the hypocritical sanctimoniousness or ignorant bigotry and fanaticism which characterize the various sects of the religious world too many are inclined to fly to the opposite extreme of irreverence and profanity of feeling if not of expression and of treating with lightness and levity the most sacred subjects connected with man's present and future happiness and exaltation—from that man-worshipping spirit, which has been the fruitful cause of so much evil in this and other countries, to one no less fraught with direful consequences, that of undervaluing, if not despising, the authority, power and dignity of the Priesthood—and from a profuse and unwise liberality to its opposite, a mean and contracted penuriousness. (October 25, 1862, MS 24:680)

NECESSITY OF SPIRITUAL NOURISHMENT. I often remark that our spiritual wants need to be supplied just as much as our physical wants. There are many even among the Latter-day Saints who undergo a species of starvation through neglect in attending meetings and availing themselves of the opportunities which God has given unto us. They do not get that spiritual nourishment which is as necessary to make the man or the woman in Christ Jesus perfect as it is that we should partake of earthly food to sustain our bodies. (April 27, 1890, DW 40:833)

SPIRITUAL DECLINE OF WORLD. It is one of the duties of our mission to establish faith in the earth and also to set examples to the children of men. Through the lack of faith on the part of our fathers and the traditions which have come down to us from them, we today occupy a very low plane, so far as God and Godliness is concerned. The world has made great progress in many directions, but the spiritual decline of the world is perhaps more apparent than its growth in other matters. There has been a complete decadence spiritually. Faith has declined, spiritual growth has ceased and God's power is not recognized among men. Men have grown into the belief that there is no necessity for His power. The spiritual part of man in this age is dwarfed, stunted, stifled, and the growth of mankind is altogether one-sided.

Now, this is not right, and God will correct it. He will be acknowledged in the earth. The day will come when every knee shall bow and every tongue confess Him. The cause of this decay in spiritual matters is due to false doctrines, to false teachers, to men professing to be ministers of Jesus Christ and yet denying the power of God. Instead of stirring the people up to seek for the gifts and graces that adorned the Church in ancient days and for the power that the members of the Church possessed, the effort has been apparently to stifle every aspiration of the human soul after higher things and after greater faith. (July 5, 1896, DW 53:162)

THE UNBELIEF OF THE AGE. We attribute a great deal of the skepticism of the age to the unauthorized utterances of self-constituted representatives of Deity. Their conflicting opinions as to divine truth, their contradictory explanations of sacred scripture, and their clashing, contending organizations, each claiming to be the Church of Christ, and each denying many of the doctrines and ordinances incorporated in the Church established by the Savior and his Apostles, have the effect of creating more doubt than faith, and of driving people to the conclusion that, as there is no evidence of God's power or presence in those religious institutions, there is no Church of God at all and that religion altogether is a humbug and delusion. . . .

Between the fanatics who insist upon the verbal inspiration of every word of the Bible, and the clerical infidels, in the disguise of "Reverends," who turn its history and facts into metaphor, its doctrines into sentiment and its ordinances into non-essential customs, the anxious inquirer falls to the ground of total unbelief, and becomes a scoffer of all that pretends to be divine.

Between true science and true religion there can be no conflict. All truth emanates from the same source. The light that reveals a fact in science is from the same Spirit of intelligence which unfolds the principles of religion. Its communications must necessarily be in harmony. But the speculations and theories of scientists ought not to be taken for science, neither should the opinions and fancies or rhapsodies of religious ministers be mistaken for religion. The truths of religion and the rules which govern spiritual things are just as positive as the facts of science and the laws which control the physical universe. True theology is as exact a science as chemistry, and cause and effect are as sure in one as the other. But the necessary conditions must be complied with in the practice of either, or the desired result will not follow.

Faith, repentance and baptism, properly administered and received, are as sure to bring remission of sins as the combination of certain substances, in fixed proportions, to produce certain chemical changes; and the Holy Ghost is as sure to be imparted by the laying on of the hands of authorized servants of God, if the foregoing requirements precede it, as the production of electricity is to follow the manipulation of the correct process. So much in illustration of doctrine. And it will be found that when God reveals anything in relation to the method or order of creation, or in regard to the earth, the starry worlds or any principle that pertains to their organizations, progress or destiny, it will be in perfect harmony with everything which is developed through patient investigation, or flashed upon the mind by the natural inspiration that is open to all mankind according to their organic powers of conception and their efforts to receive it.

But "religious" men add their notions to God's revelations and cover up the divine truth by their human imaginings; and "scientific" men weave in their own deductions and conclusions with the weft of actual demonstrations, and thus, in both instances, the eyes of the general multitude become blinded and confused, skepticism is the consequence, and God himself is doubted and denied, while the evidences of His Being and the marks of His wisdom, power, love and Fatherhood, are spread all around the pathway of humanity, glittering in the firmament on high and pressing close to the soul of every breathing mortal.

The unbelief of the age is great and deplorable. But so are its sins. Faith and licentiousness do not run together. Dishonesty and divine inspiration are not companions. Lying and prayer do not harmonize. An age of fraud is sure to be an age of infidelity. And an evil and adulterous generation may seek for signs, but they do not appear, because eyes filled with lust cannot discern spiritual things. (December 3, 1877, MS 39:804-805)

PERSECUTIONS LED BY RELIGIOUS LEADERS. Among the first persecutors of this Church, when its members were few, were those who were themselves religious teachers. The earliest persecutors of Joseph Smith were religious teachers, and the mobs in Missouri and the mobs in Illinois were led by religious teachers. Even the mob that murdered our beloved Prophet and Patriarch and wounded our revered President [John Taylor] was led by a local Baptist preacher, and our people were driven from Nauvoo . . . by a mob headed by a preacher.

And to-day, those who are inciting mobs against this people, those who go to Congress and incite persecutions against us, those who fulminate threats and frame petitions, those who meet together in conventions, those who gather together in conferences, are those who belong to this "mother of abominations," this "whore of all the earth" [1 Nephi 14:10], and it is through the influence of that accursed whore that they gather together and marshal their forces in every land and against the Latter-day Saints, the Church of the living God. . . .

Here in this city, who has done as much or more than any

one else? The religious teachers, men who came here to preach what they call the Gospel. They are stirring up strife continually, instead of making peace, going back to other religious associations in the east and telling the most abominable falsehoods about us, exciting the public mind, in order that they may get money with which to come here and accomplish their wicked designs. They tell lies without number about us.

FALSEHOODS EXPOSED. Our newspapers have exposed such people time and time again, and yet they shamelessly go forth and repeat those lies about the wickedness of this people, about the intolerance of this people, about the dangers they run when here in this country, when they know, as we all know, . . . that they have never been molested and that we have never injured them, nor interfered with them in any form but that we have always treated them with that respect and kindness with which we desire to be treated ourselves. (April 6, 1884, JD 25: 127-28)

Chapter 7

Preaching the Gospel to the World

A DUTY TO PREACH THE GOSPEL. The duty which devolves upon us as a people is to patiently labor in disseminating the Gospel of Jesus Christ throughout the nations of the earth. . . . This is our duty; and this Gospel of the Kingdom, as we have been told, must be preached as a witness unto all nations before the end comes. It is a labor devolving upon us as a people; and though it may cost many precious lives to do this, the obligation rests upon us nevertheless, and we cannot be freed from it only by the discharge of the duty. (August 31, 1884, JD 25:270)

WORLD INFLUENCED BY MISSIONARIES. The world is being benefited by the preaching of these young men who are going out continually to the various missions throughout the earth. They may think themselves that they are not doing much good; but no man can teach these divine principles that the Lord has revealed without their having their effect upon the human family. I am a great believer in the idea that no seed of truth is ever sown unsuccessfully. It will find a lodgment in some heart, and it will remain there. It may not germinate immediately, but the time will come, either in this life or in the life to come, when it will sprout and bring forth fruit.

I believe, therefore, that the Elders, in going forth and bearing testimony that this is a divine work and that Joseph Smith is a Prophet of God, though they may think they do not accomplish very much, they do, in my opinion, do a great work, and some time in the great future it will be seen that their labors have not been fruitless. Although men and women may not have been converted or baptized, nevertheless the labors of the Elders will contribute to their salvation and their redemption. (January 22, 1898, MS 61:115)

NATIONS LEFT WITHOUT EXCUSE. We have been told that all the nations of the earth will have to be warned. This Gospel will be preached as a witness, Jesus said, unto all nations; then the end shall come. I have felt that some of our folks sometimes have been considerably exercised at the thought that every creature would have to hear the sound of the Gospel. But God has ways of warning the inhabitants of the earth as well as by the voice of His servants. The nations of the earth have received very great and powerful testimonies that will leave them without excuse, although they may never have had an Elder visit them.

It has been thought that a great many thousands of people that ought to hear the Gospel were left in ignorance and that we have not done our full duty in warning the rich and the learned and those who were outside of the circle which our Elders generally reach. Now the facts are these, when we look at it properly: It seems to me that the inhabitants of the earth are left without excuse because of the knowledge of this work that has gone forth among this nation and among all the nations of the earth. It is true, there have been a great many falsehoods told about it, and a great many honest people have been deceived by these falsehoods. But, nevertheless, the sound of this Gospel has gone to the remotest ends of the earth, and the character of this work is such that the inhabitants of the earth are left without an excuse—at least, in many of the nations. They are held without excuse, if not for rejecting us, at least for not investigating the principles of the Gospel. . . .

GATHERING VIEWED BY WORLD. I remember myself, on one occasion, chartering a ship in Liverpool that carried some nine hundred Latter-day Saints, and in that ship's company there [were] no less than eleven nationalities represented. But if you had asked those persons, in their own language, where they were going, they would have told you they were going to Zion; they were going to the House of God that was being reared in the tops of the mountains. If you had asked them what they were going there for, they would have replied, each in his own language: "I am going to be taught in the ways of God and walk in his paths" [see Isaiah 2:2-3]—just as the Prophet declared thousands of years ago. And this has been going on in sight of all Christendom.

Here is this great people in the tops of these mountains—different from any other people that are now on the face of the earth. And who has not heard, among the various nations, concerning our persecutions and the strangeness of our union? Is there any educated man in Christendom that has not read about this? And if he has had the Spirit of God at all—and all men do have a portion of it—and has been honest, he must have felt in his heart that there was something more about this than usual.

The persecutions that we have endured . . . have been published throughout the entire civilized world. There is scarcely an ear that has not heard something concerning us and the attacks that have been made upon us. We have been advertised as no other people have been, and every reading man in the country has known something about us. In this way I believe the civilized nations of the earth have been warned, and they will be judged according to the knowledge that they have had concerning these events which have been of so striking a character. (August 3, 1890, DW 41:485-86)

A message such as the Latter-day Saints profess to be the bearers of is of such extreme importance to the whole family of man that they cannot be justified in passing it by unnoticed. Even if the people should have no cause to think it true, it becomes a duty, situated as they are, the moment they hear the message to investigate and give heed to it. (February 21, 1857, WS 346-47)

OUR MISSIONARIES. One of the remarkable features of the work of God in the last days has been that uneducated and sometimes illiterate men have gone out as ministers of Christ. They have had to meet and discuss with the learned men of the world, whose lives have been devoted to the study of religious questions, and who have been supposed to be thoroughly familiar with theology. Looking at the Elders of this Church from the standpoint of the world, it would seem to be impossible for them to meet with any success while opposed by such ability and odds. The only advantage that they possessed—and it has been a most stupendous advantage—has been that they have been called of God and ordained as His servants. Like the humble fishermen of Galilee, this has been their only strength.

But what extraordinary results have attended their labors! Wherever they have gone, those who have listened to them have been pierced to the heart by the truths which they taught. In simple and unadorned language they have told the message of which they were bearers, and no music that ever saluted mortal ears has been sweeter to the ears of honest lovers of truth than have been their words and testimonies. Gladness and joy have attended their footsteps. They have carried peace and light and knowledge to the abodes of men, where uncertainty and doubt and darkness reigned before. (June 25, 1892, JI 27:373)

DON'T APOLOGIZE FOR WEAKNESSES. I do hope that, as soon as you get into your fields of labor, you will not apologize to the people for your weaknesses, and tell them how incapable and unfitted you are for such positions as you may hold. . . . Go into your fields of labor as men of God, appointed by Him to minister unto them the things pertaining to their salvation, and they will find that you have power which no other men, devoid of the authority you have, possess.

The people will realize, my young brethren, if you will pursue a course that becomes the servants of God, that, although young in years, you have a power superior to that possessed by the generality of men—a power which comes, alone, from our Father and God. There is a power and an influence with Elders from Zion which are very much felt. . . . Do not, therefore, go and tell the people how inadequate you are for the responsibilities which rest upon you. Do not say, when you arise to address a congregation upon the principles of the Gospel, "unaccustomed as I am to public speaking," etc., or anything bearing the same idea. There is no necessity for you to mourn over your weakness and want of that ability which is possessed by men of the world. Go to work and do the best you can. (January 5, 1864, MS 26:196)

HOW TO PREACH. It is right that the Elders should "treasure up in [their] minds continually the words of life. . . ." [D & C 84:85.] It is proper that they should ponder upon the things of the Kingdom and the principles of life and salvation. They should store their minds with all knowledge, for the Lord has, in several revelations, given commands to this effect. It is evident that it is His wish that His servants should be fully informed concerning principle, doctrine, the laws of the Gospel and all things that pertain unto the Kingdom of God, and also that they should "obtain a knowledge of history, and of countries, and of kingdoms, of laws of God and man." [D&C 93:53.]

In bestowing time and thought in studying the principles of

intelligence and truth the Elders obey the command of God. It is evident, however, the Lord designs that His servants should trust in Him to give them His Spirit to bring forth the principles and instructions best adapted to the condition of the people whom they address. No man, by his own wisdom and knowledge, can judge correctly concerning the spiritual wants of his fellow-man. It is the Lord alone who knows the hearts of His children, and when His Elders stand up before a congregation and put their trust in Him, He will, through His Holy Spirit, suggest to them and lead their minds to speak upon those points of doctrine and to give that counsel that shall be best adapted to the condition of the listeners. . . . It is the Spirit of God that reaches the hearts of the honest. A few words accompanied by that Spirit, though they may be awkwardly expressed, will have more effect upon the people than the most eloquent discourses which are not sealed upon the hearts of the listeners by the Holy Spirit. . . .

Undoubtedly the Lord knows that which is best for His Elders and people. It is for Him to dictate how His Gospel shall be preached, and His Elders have no right to depart from His instructions upon this point. . . .

The experience of all men who have had any knowledge of or practice in public speaking is that the man who is trained to speak extemporaneously is a far more ready and effective speaker than one who has been accustomed to rely upon notes or to write out his discourses or lectures in full. The man most ready in off hand speaking, or in answering a sudden call, is one who has never depended upon notes, but who has stored his mind with truth and knowledge in the manner that the Lord has suggested to His Elders. . . . That which they do say, though it may not be so elegantly framed as it might be if time were taken to write it, reaches the hearts of the hearers and has a much better effect upon them than a speech would be that had been carefully prepared and written. (April 1, 1890, JI 25:210-11)

GOOD SPEAKERS IN DANGER OF FALLING. The danger of the young brethren being overcome was not now when they feel their weakness but after they came to rely more on their own individual ability and ceased to trust in the arm of God. There is little fear of Elders falling so long as they call upon

God and depend entirely on him. But when Elders become accustomed to speaking in public and they begin to imagine that it is their own ability that accomplishes the labors in which they are engaged, and they rely upon their own strength, they have commenced to transgress the laws of God, and they are in danger of falling. If you will peruse the history of the Church, you will find that the greatest speakers have in this manner fallen. You will find they have been unable to stand in the Church while they have indulged in these feelings.

The man who is endowed with natural ability to speak in public must be exceedingly careful. The devil is ever ready to whisper in his ear that he has talent. This reminds me of an instance which occurred in the experience of one of our leading Elders. He was on a mission to the Eastern States and was considered to be a very gifted speaker. He had been speaking on one occasion to a very attentive congregation, and at the conclusion of the meeting one of the brethren stepped up to him, apparently well satisfied with the remarks that he had made; and he said, "Brother, you have preached an excellent discourse." "Brother," replied he, "the devil told me that before you did."

The rebuke was truthful and well-timed, for the devil is ever ready to tell an Elder when he has preached an "excellent discourse" and that he is a very wonderful and effective speaker, without having the aid of his brethren and sisters to tell him such things. If you allow such insinuations to have weight with you and allow men and women to tell you how able you are and what excellent speakers, etc., you are, the result will be, my brethren, that you will be overcome. When you preach under such circumstances, your words will not give that degree of instruction and satisfaction that the broken remarks of a more humble brother will. If your words do not savor of the Spirit of God, they will not profit those to whom you speak.

GET THE SPIRIT BEFORE SPEAKING. I speak to the young men, and what I say to them on these points will suit the old men as well. Seek for the Spirit of God, and when you rise to proclaim the words of life and salvation, let them be accompanied by that Spirit. If you rise devoid of that Spirit, it will be far better for you to sit down, although in doing so you may be mortified and your vanity wounded; but, brethren, sit down rather than attempt to address a congregation without this Spirit. Have it with you constantly that its influence may, in all your preaching, accompany the words you utter that they may prove beneficial and saving. I know that the man who cultivates the Spirit of God is the most calculated to do good and to move forward this work. (December 31, 1863, MS 26:113-14)

CONTROVERSY TO BE AVOIDED. Controversy is a thing which, in a general way, had better be refrained from by the Elders. Their special duty is to preach the Gospel and administer its ordinances; and although they may at times have to face unsought opposition in various forms, it is not for them to stoop from their high and holy calling as ministers of the Gospel of peace to . . . take the challenge of any petty antagonist who may audaciously confront them to dispute their testimony and teachings. They have something better to do—a higher and holier work to perform—than engaging in . . . encounters with those who seek, by polemic warfare, to waste the time of the Elders and gain at their expense the inglorious fame of "Anti-Mormon" champions. (April 19, 1862, MS 24:249)

DON'T RIDICULE OTHER CHURCHES. In proclaiming the principles of the Gospel the Elders should remember that it is not necessary to indulge in the denunciation of any sect or belief. Errors of doctrine and practice may be exposed and the truth be plainly taught without calling to your aid sarcasm or ridicule. We know that it is a gratification to some of the Elders to denounce the fallacies of sectarianism and demolish the feeble defences of its advocates, and whenever an opportunity of this kind offers, the temptation is almost too strong to be resisted. But a practice of this kind is rarely, if ever, attended by good results. Men are not won, generally, by such a style of reasoning.

There are very few who cannot—after hearing the truth preached in simplicity and tasting of the Spirit of Truth—draw their own contrasts between truth and error, the Gospel of Jesus and the systems of men, and arrive at correct conclusions upon the subject. The great duty which devolves upon the Elders is to teach the truth and render the children of men all the assistance in their power in comprehending it, and this certainly can be done without our descending to abuse opposite systems of their advocates. (July 11, 1863, MS 25:440-41)

Assailing a man's belief or exposing the weakness of his religion is not the best plan to adopt to convince him of his errors or to convert him to the truth. Arouse a man's combativeness and make him angry, and he will fight; he will regard neither reason nor argument under such circumstances but will cling to and defend his opinions, right or wrong, to the extent of his ability and power against every assailant.

If men are to be convinced, it must be done by showing them the truth and setting before them its beauties in a simple, mild, kind manner. . . .

As a people, we should be most kind in all our intercourse with those who do not believe as we do. The knowledge which we now possess of the truth, contrasted with our former ignorance of its saving principles, should fill us with charity for those who are in the position we were in when the Gospel found us. (February 1, 1862, MS 27:74)

HONEST IN HEART WILL ACCEPT GOSPEL. Those who sincerely, humbly and honestly desire to know God will know that the Elders of Israel are His servants the moment they hear the testimony of the Elders, for the Spirit of God will bear witness to them of its truth; and I am not afraid to say that all the honest in heart among the nations will, sooner or later, obey the Gospel and receive a testimony of the truth. There is no man or woman who is honest and sincerely and truly humble before God but will, sooner or later, receive the testimony of the truth.

There is a power in testimony—one that is irresistible to the honest soul; and where there is a man or woman who desires to know the foundation on which their faith is based, they seek unto God for it, and when they hear the truth and the testimony of men who have the principles of salvation to proclaim unto the people, they are ready to receive them, because they take the right course to obtain a knowledge of the truth for themselves. (April 12, 1863, MS 25:307)

PREACH ONLY FIRST PRINCIPLES. It is advisable that the Elders, when preaching to the world, should confine themselves as much as practicable to the first principles and leading doctrines of the Church. Such subjects as . . . the second advent of Christ, the resurrection, the millennial reign, the nature of the Godhead, etc., although interesting and important matters in their place to those concerned, are sadly out of place when unnecessarily dragged before the attention of a mixed audience, who more particularly need establishing in those principles and doctrines which pertain to their immediate salvation and present requirements.

There are many subjects that can be advantageously discussed privately which it would be unwise to dilate upon publicly, except when circumstances render it specially advisable. When an enquirer after truth clearly understands and embraces the first principles of the Gospel, he is then prepared for a consideration of those which are more advanced. But to crowd upon him matters for which he is unprepared is like attempting to erect the walls and compartments of a building which has no sure foundation upon which to rest them. (April 12, 1862, MS 24:234)

A TENDENCY TO STRAY. It requires constant watching on the part of those whom God chooses to be His servants to keep out of the Church of Christ false doctrines, false practices and false conceptions concerning duty. Well did the Apostle say that the Lord had placed certain officers in His Church "for the perfecting of the saints, for the work of the ministry, for the edifying of the body of Christ" [Ephesians 4:12], because a very little experience with mankind will show how necessary it is that there should be men inspired of God in charge of His Church —shepherds who are under the guidance of the Great Shepherd in caring for the flock. Errors are liable at all times to creep in—errors in doctrine, errors in practice, errors which lead the people astray and would result, if not checked, in great injury to the Church, if not its overthrow.

It was in this way, doubtless, that the primitive Church fell into darkness and became apostate. The Apostles were slain; others who bore the Priesthood and enjoyed revelation from God were also destroyed. But the Church did not immediately fall into utter darkness. It was by degrees, yielding a little in one direction and yielding a little in another, until there was a complete departure from many of the pure principles of the Gospel of the Son of God.

In our own day we can see the tendency there is to stray from the exact path. . . . (November 1, 1893, JI 28:668.)

MANY GREAT NATIONS YET TO WARN. We have a large portion of the world yet to warn. Instead of crowding into English-speaking countries, it seems to me that our Elders must begin to crowd into lands where the English language is not spoken and to exercise faith for the gift of tongues and for the gift of interpretation. These gifts have been given for this purpose. Elders will have to exercise faith before God in acquiring foreign languages so that they can go and warn the people of the earth and carry the glad tidings of salvation to them, because God has said that from every land under heaven there shall be people gathered to swell the hosts of Zion. Every nationality must be visited; and when we cannot go, as the Lord has told us, we must send His word. . . .

God has commanded us that we must preach the Gospel to every land, to every people; and where we have men join the Church belonging to a foreign nation, as soon as they are able and qualified they should be sent to their land to bear testimony of what God has revealed to them. . . . The preaching of the Gospel now is like the gleaning of grapes after the vintage is over. That is the comparison used by the Prophet, and a most striking one it is. . . .

We do not expect to convert all the inhabitants of the earth—but we expect to warn them. We expect to gather out every honest soul, and the Lord will deal with the rest. We have to do our duty so that no people will be able to say that they never heard of the work God is doing in the earth. (DEN, August 18, 1900)

Chapter 8

God's Covenant Peoples

THE ELECT AND THE CHOSEN. We find in the writings of the Apostles mention frequently made of the "elect" and of the "chosen." Well, we could do the same thing, writing in our day. How strange it is, and how it gives rise to this view, the experience that we have in the world in preaching the Gospel! We go into a neighborhood, and we gather in a few. The great masses of the people pay no attention to the message of salvation that we declare. Now, who are those that listen? Why, we might call them very truthfully the "elect," the "chosen," according to the grace of God as the Apostles so frequently did.

Yes, we are chosen, but it is not because the others are not chosen. It is because we, in the providence and mercy of God, have had our hearts softened so that we have believed the truth when we heard it; we have received it and rejoiced in it. Therefore, we can be rightfully called the elect. But it is not because others are debarred from these privileges, but because we have chosen to accept the message of salvation.

In this way the Lord inspired His servants in ancient days to speak and write as they did. They spoke about foreordination, about the blest and the chosen. But Paul . . . tells us who they are plainly, that "they are not all Israel, which are of Israel." [Romans 9:6.] There are a great many that inherit the blessings of the covenant, who are of the seed of Abraham, who do not prove themselves worthy of it, and therefore they are not all Israel. If they had obeyed the commandments of God, they would have been; they would have received all the promises made to the fathers. For be it known unto you that God make covenants with men, and He blesses men, and He will bless their posterity.

This ought to be an incentive to every man to live as he should do, not only for his own sake but for the sake of his posterity. But are there not good men that have wicked children? Certainly. Nevertheless, God makes promises to His faithful children. He did to Abraham, yet Abraham had descendants who were wicked and who did not live to inherit the blessings that God had promised to their great ancestor. But others received these promises; and all the families of the earth are blessed through faithful Abraham, so we are told, and they are adopted into his family. (April 27, 1890, DW 40:837)

CHILDREN OF THE COVENANT. In restoring the Priesthood to the earth the Lord made a new and everlasting covenant with the people who would listen to and obey His voice. A people with whom the Lord makes a covenant are greatly favored, and they ought to be the most humble and grateful of any people on the face of the earth, for it is a great honor and distinction and means of glory to men to be in covenant with the Almighty. The men with whom the Lord made covenant in ancient days are the men whose names come down to us in sacred history. We honor and revere their memories. The people who are descended from them are peculiar objects of God's care, for this is according to the promises which He has made, and when God makes a covenant or gives a promise, He never forgets to fulfill it to the very letter. . . .

The Lord has again made covenant with man, and those with whom the covenant is made are greatly favored, and they and their children will feel the blessed effects which accompany such a covenant. We have now thousands upon thousands of children who have been born in the covenant. Those who have not been thus born can have the privilege, if faithful, to become sealed or adopted and thus receive the benefits of the covenant, the same as if they had been born in it. In this way the entire Church of Christ, where the members have not been born in the covenant, can enter into the covenant by adoption.

In this way all will receive the benefits and blessings which flow therefrom and will receive, not only in their own persons but in their posterity, the fulfillment of the promises. The children of the Latter-day Saints through this covenant enjoy many advantages. Many blessings are promised unto them, and they become a favored race. This will be more and more apparent as time rolls on. The distinction between them and the people who are not of the covenant will be more and more marked, for God will not forget His promises to His servants. A faithful man and woman, by means of their diligence and faith, can secure blessings for their children. They will find favor in the sight of the Lord, and He will exercise His wonderful Providence in their behalf.

A NOBLER CLASS OF SPIRITS. Without doubt a nobler class of spirits are permitted to come forth as children in the covenant because of the advantages which they have when born in this way. There are differences in spirits, as there are differences in men and women. Some spirits are more capable than others because of past faithfulness in times of trial. When Lucifer, who was once a mighty angel before the Lord and held great power, became rebellious and sought to lead away the children of God, he was followed by one-third of the hosts of heaven. Of the remaining two-thirds some were, doubtless, more valiant than others. In the exercise of their agency there would be a great difference in the conduct of the spirits thus left to choose for themselves. Take any number of human beings and place them in a position where there is a division between two leaders and great decision is required, and it will be found that some are more decided and positive and determined than others. There will be some who will scarcely know which side to take, and they will be greatly influenced by the opinions and actions of others.

Doubtless this was the case with the spirits in heaven. There were some who were valiant, decided and full of integrity, who did not waver nor doubt, while there were others who, while they did not take sides with Lucifer, were fearful and uncertain and probably stood aloof, watching which side would win. This being the case, is it any wonder that there should be differences in the spirits who come here?

Some are chosen to occupy prominent positions and seem to be favored, and many wonder why this is so. They do not understand that there may be causes for these differences which reach back into eternity before our spirits had taken tabernacles. Hence, as it is a great advantage to be born in the covenant, it is but reasonable to suppose that noble spirits will seek the opportunity to come into families where they will have all the blessings and promises which pertain to the covenant. The Latter-day Saints will undoubtedly become a great people, for God has made promises to them, and this will be one of the means by which their greatness will be developed. (November 1, 1890, JI 25:690-91)

BLESSINGS FROM PROMISES TO FATHERS. It is through the promise that God made to our fathers that we are here today and that we have received the Gospel. The fathers and mothers of many who are here received it; their hearts were touched; God poured His Spirit upon them, and they came "one of a city, and two of a family" [Jeremiah 3:14] to Zion, while the rest of the kindred rejected the Gospel. It is because of the promises that God made to our fathers that we have received the truth; and if we are faithful, we can obtain the same blessings for our posterity.

When my boys go out on a mission, I say to them, "Boys, God is your father's friend; He has always been his friend; you can trust Him and can call upon Him with confidence; for I tell you that while I live and keep His commandments, God will watch over my children and will preserve and bless them." And He has done it. So it will be with every faithful man and woman; God will remember them and their seed after them; and He will see that they will have representatives in His Church at the very last when Jesus shall come. (February 16, 1896, DW 52:387)

IMPORTANCE OF A FAITHFUL POSTERITY. Our future as a Church and as families depends upon our children being trained in righteousness. . . . All the records that have come to us from righteous men convey with plainness the great importance of having a faithful posterity. . . . Men of God have always endeavored to exercise faith in behalf of their posterity. The Lord made covenants with Abraham, Isaac and Jacob, and with the sons of Jacob, concerning their posterity, and these covenants the Lord holds in great esteem and has promised that in the last days they shall be fulfilled. It is the same in our day; the posterity of faithful men may stray from the Church, but the Lord will feel after some branch of their family and bring it back in days to come to the covenant people.

At times it has been a matter of surprise to some individuals that they have been enabled to join the Church and receive the truth while so many around them have turned deaf ears to it. But, if we understood the past as we do the present, we would doubtless see that there are reasons for this which have existed long before we were born. There is no doubt in my mind that the gathering together of this people from the various nations of the earth and the manner in which they have received the Gospel is due to the promises made to their fathers. (April 5, 1897, DW 54:673)

BORN THROUGH A NOBLE LINEAGE. Our lineage is not known to all of us. We may not know our origin; but this we may be assured of, that we who have received the truth are choice spirits. . . .

Where do you think this nobility of character has come from? It has come from ancestors who obtained promises from God, through their faithfulness, in regard to their posterity. Our ancestors may have come through poverty and obscure channels, and some of them may not have possessed any noted characteristics; but when our ancestry is known, it will be found that the noblest men and women of God have been the progenitors of this people. (April 8, 1894, DW 48:701)

OUR LINEAGE PREARRANGED. It was arranged before we came here how we should come and through what lineage we should come. . . . As the Lord has taught us, . . . our Priesthood has been hid with God. He says:

> Therefore, thus saith the Lord unto you, with whom the priesthood hath continued through the lineage of your fathers—
>
> For ye are lawful heirs, according to the flesh, and have been hid from the world with Christ in God—
>
> Therefore your life and the priesthood have remained, and must needs remain through you and your lineage until the restoration of all things spoken by the mouths of all the holy prophets since the world began. [D&C 86:8-10.]

I am as convinced that it was predestined before I was born that I should come through my father as I am that I stand here. (April 8, 1894, DW 48:545)

A WORK OF GLEANING. We have gathered the people, through the blessing of God, from the various nations of the earth; but we have gathered them by small handfuls, as it were. There has been no great influx into the Church from these nations; but . . . it has been exactly like a gleaning of grapes after the vintage is over. And it is a remarkable fact that the great bulk of the people who form this Church—that is, those who were adults when they became members of this Church—were anxiously waiting arrival of some such message as the Elders brought. . . .

ISRAEL EASILY CONVERTED. It is a remarkable fact . . . that, wherever we have gone among those people whom the Book of Mormon tells us are the descendants of the house of Israel, we have had no trouble in converting them by hundreds, and it may be said by thousands, to the truth. They were ready to receive it without any difficulty whatever. It seemed as though their hearts had been prepared by the God of heaven; all that has been necessary has been to tell them the truth, and they were natural Latter-day Saints, natural believers in the Gospel of the Son of God.

GENTILES NATURALLY UNBELIEVERS. I myself went as a missionary . . . to the Sandwich Islands, the natives of which I believe to be either a branch of the Indians of this continent or of some other portion of the House of Israel. There was no trouble in baptizing them, and there is no trouble in baptizing any of the Polynesian races. They are ready to receive the Gospel, ready to be baptized, very different in this respect from us Gentiles. There is a spirit of unbelief among the Gentile race; there is a hardness of heart; there is a want of faith that prevents the blessings of God from descending as they did in ancient days upon His covenant people. Gentiles are naturally unbelievers. It is difficult to convert them, difficult to control them, difficult for them to receive the truth in plainness and simplicity. (May 25, 1884, JD 25:171-72)

THE GENTILES AND APOSTASY. We are a nation of Gentiles. We who have come here, what are we? We are called from the Gentile nations. The promises are not made to us that are made to people who are the unmixed descendants of Israel. In many respects, when they come into the covenant and are baptized, and the power of God rests upon them, you will see a different work than you see at the present time. It is just as much as we, with our Gentile traditions—an inheritance we have received from our fathers, which have come down through generations—it is as much as many of us can do, with all the power we can exercise, to remain in the Church. . . .

During my experience among that people, a red skinned race, I never knew a man, because of transgression or anything else, after he received the truth—I never knew one of them to turn around and fight this cause in the manner that we witness men doing among our race. How is it with the Gentiles, the race of which we are a part? When a man gets a testimony from God and falls into transgression, he is almost immediately seized with the spirit of murder. He wants to shed the blood of innocence. He wants to kill the servants of God, is full of bitterness and hatred and seeks to find vent for his wicked passions. (November 2, 1897, JD 21:271)

BLOOD OF ISRAEL ACCEPTS GOSPEL. No doubt many of you have been led to wonder in your experience how it was that you should receive the Gospel and that others who had equal opportunities with you, probably belonging to the same household and numbered among your friends and acquaintances . . . could see nothing desirable or attractive about it, while your hearts were kindled into a glow and felt like fire within you when you heard the testimony of the servants of God concerning the Gospel that He has revealed.

Nothing that I know of more plainly demonstrates the fact that this is the blood of Israel that has been gathered out, that we are of the chosen seed, though we have been mixed, or our fathers have been mixed, among the Gentiles. God has saved to Himself a seed among all nations; and when the Gospel came to the lands where this seed dwelt, there was, on their part, a natural affinity, a natural attraction to the principles of righteousness, and they received them gladly and were gathered out by the wonderful power of God to this land and are numbered now among His Saints. . . . (November 16, 1884, JD 25:361)

PECULIARITY OF POLYNESIANS. There is this peculiarity about them—every one of them is a natural Latter-day Saint. I never yet knew a native with whom I could converse for any length of time but what would admit that the doctrines we believed in and taught were of God; and in every instance nearly where access could be obtained to them they were ready for baptism. However, there are other influences at work among them as there are among the Gentile races.

But they are a people ready to believe the Gospel and render obedience to it; there is this peculiarity about them that is not about our race, when they become convinced of the truth, if they commit sin and have to be excommunicated from the Church, I never knew them to become an enemy to the work and to be bitter in their feelings against it.

With our race it is different. When Gentiles turn away from the truth, when they commit sin after receiving the truth and the light, it seems as though the adversary has great power over them, and they become bitter enemies to the work of God and to the servants of God. . . .

HOUSE OF ISRAEL NATURALLY RECEPTIVE. It is a remarkable peculiarity that wherever the Elders of this Church go carrying the Gospel among the descendants of the house of Israel, they find friends; they find those who are ready to do everything for them they can, to receive them just as the seed of Israel scattered among the nations has done. When the Elders first went to Great Britain, there was a certain class of the English people who were ready to open their doors to entertain them and do all they could for them to prosecute their ministerial labors. All such were natural Latter-day Saints. It seemed to them when they heard the Gospel first as though it was something they had almost known but which had faded from their memory. It was as natural for them to believe the Gospel as it was for them to believe anything they knew absolutely.

This was the case throughout Great Britain and Ireland, and it has been the case throughout the Scandinavian nations; it has been the case among the Germanic races that have heard the preaching of the Gospel by our Elders. It has been the case in every land and among every people wherever the Elders of this Church have gone carrying this message of life and salvation, this Gospel of the Son of God; they have been recognized as Gentiles, but their readiness to receive the Gospel when it saluted their ears bears witness of the fact that they are of Israel. (January 12, 1890, DW 40:159)

JERUSALEM FOR JUDAH. These are the "times of restitution of all things, which God hath spoken by the mouth of all his holy prophets since the world began." [Acts 3:4.] The purposes of Jehovah cannot be frustrated. The descendants of His ancient covenant people will reap the fruits of the promises planted in the hearts of the fathers. The signs of the times point to the speedy redemption of Jerusalem, and the spirit of the great gathering is beginning to take hold of the Jewish heart. The war now waging will be one of the instruments in the hand of the Omnipotent to prepare the way before the feet of the sons of Jacob, and the Hebrew, not the Latin, will come in upon the land like a flood.

There are no people who watch the events transpiring in the old world with greater interest than do the Latter-day Saints. The gathering of the Jews to Palestine is one of the important incidents of the work to which their lives are devoted. Their destiny is associated with the ultimate triumph of Judah. And the fulfillment of the predictions of ancient Prophet and modern Seer is taking place so rapidly and significantly, that they are almost ready to proclaim, "Speak ye comfortably to Jerusalem, and cry unto her, that her warfare is accomplished, that her iniquity is pardoned: for she hath received of the Lord's hand double for all her sins." [Isaiah 40:3.] . . . The soil is reserved for Judah, and the "Mighty God of Jacob" [D&C 109:68] will turn and overturn until the dominion is established. The dispersion of the House of Israel was clearly predicted by their Prophets, and they literally became "a hiss and a by-word . . . among all nations." [1 Nephi 19:14.] "He that scattered Israel will gather him." [Jeremiah 31:10.]

The prophecies concerning the restoration are just as clear and definite as those in relation to the dispersion. If the latter have been fulfilled, have we not good reason for expecting the accomplishment of the former? The great theme of the inspired Jewish bards and seers was the latter-day glory of their nation. The events which they associated with the restoration and the re-building of their ancient capital are now transpiring, and we therefore look for the complete fulfillment of their sayings concerning the triumph of Judah.

This re-establishment of an old and once powerful nation

upon the site of its former splendor and dominion is one of the important scenes in the great drama of the last days, and a precursor of the "restitution of all things." [Acts 3:21.] It will surely be accomplished, and will aid in the vast revolution that is about to be inaugurated by the powers on high, which will result in the "end of the world" [D&C 45:22], or, in other words, the destruction of man's misrule, and the setting up of His Kingdom whose right it is to reign, whose dominion shall be everlasting, and whose sway shall be "from the rivers even unto the ends of the earth." He is the "Lion of the tribe of Judah" [Revelation 5:5]; He will sit upon the throne of his father David, and all nations and kingdoms will serve and obey Him. (October 29, 1877, MS 39:707-708)

THE GATHERING OF THE JEWS. After the Church was driven out of Missouri, two of the Twelve Apostles, Orson Hyde and John E. Page, were appointed by the Prophet Joseph to take a mission to Jerusalem. John E. Page did not fulfill his mission. Brother Orson Hyde did go there and dedicate the land, as he had been instructed to do, to the gathering of the House of Israel.

Subsequently, two other Apostles, George A. Smith and Lorenzo Snow, also visited the land of Jerusalem, and they too prayed to the Lord and invoked His blessing upon the land that it might be so blessed that fertility should be restored to it and that the curses that had rested upon it might be removed by the power of God.

It is very remarkable that since that time the work of gathering the Jews has gone on with considerable rapidity and in such a manner as to attract attention and fill the hearts of believers with great delight at seeing such a plain fulfillment of the word of the Lord.

The Jews are undoubtedly turning their attention to the land of their fathers. Circumstances are being so shaped by the Almighty as to favor the colonization of the Jews on their ancient heritage. It is an easy thing for the Lord to cause His word to be fulfilled respecting that land and its people; and He will use the nations of the earth as His instruments. They will think, doubtless, that they are accomplishing their own ends in making combinations that will favor the settlement of the Jews and give them the liberty which has heretofore, to a great extent, been denied them. . . .

The Lord Jesus when He was upon the earth said that Jerusalem should "be trodden down of the Gentiles, until the times of the Gentiles be fulfilled" [Luke 21:24]—that is, the Jews should remain in their scattered condition until then. The Lord further says that in that generation shall "the times of the Gentiles be fulfilled." [Luke 21:24.] The gathering of the Jews, then, was to be a sign that the times of the Gentiles were fulfilled. To the Latter-day Saints this event is full of great importance. We are looking forward to the coming of the Lord Jesus, according to the promise that He should again descend from heaven, this time in power and in great glory. But before that awful day a remnant of the Jews will be gathered to Jerusalem, and the ancient city will be rebuilt; the land of Palestine will be re-peopled by the descendants of the covenant people of the Lord.

Many of the Jews will gather in unbelief; but the Prophets in the Book of Mormon convey the idea that they will gather in belief. "The Jews . . . shall begin to believe in Christ . . . and to gather." [2 Nephi 30:7.] Then shall they know their Redeemer and be gathered from the four quarters of the earth. It seems from their words that belief in the Savior will precede the gathering of the Jews together again. Heretofore the Jews have been apparently impenetrable to the Gospel, and many will doubtless still remain in this condition of unbelief; but on the other hand, we are told, when "they shall be restored to the true church," they "shall be established in all their lands of promise." [2 Nephi 9:2.] And again it is said, "When they shall come to the knowledge of their Redeemer, they shall be gathered together again to the lands of their inheritance." [2 Nephi 6:11.]

There will doubtless be a mighty work performed in the gathering of this race, whose fathers the Lord entered into covenant with. His word cannot fail; and although it may seem an almost impossible thing to be accomplished, yet the Jews will be gathered to their own land, and they will build up the waste places, and they will be prepared for the events that are to come. (September 15, 1896, JI 31:558-59)

A SIGN OF APPROACHING END. We have always been led to expect that Russia would figure very prominently in the events of the last days connected with the Jews and the holy land . . . .

Every power that has been unfavorable to the gathering of the Jews and their re-establishment in the land of their fathers will sooner or later be removed so that no serious and certainly no insurmountable obstacle will be in the way of the fulfillment of the words of the Lord. . . .

The fulfillment of prophecy is dependent upon these movements of the nations. We can see how one nation finds it necessary for the furtherance of its policy to checkmate another nation. In doing this the nations appear to know nothing about what the Lord has promised, but they are prompted entirely by self-interest. They make moves for the preservation of their power and for the bringing to pass of that which they desire; and the Lord overrules these for the fulfillment of His purposes. They are really blind instruments of doing that which He has foretold many centuries ago. But to us these movements are full of meaning. The gathering of the Jews is one of the signs that the end is approaching. The Jews will be gathered to Jerusalem, when the Lord will appear in power and great glory. (November 1, 1896, JI 31:642-44)

STAKES OF ZION IN PALESTINE. It appears that the time must soon come when a gathering place for those who obey the Gospel in those regions must be appointed so that they can be taught the principles of righteousness in a body and not be left in their scattered condition. . . .

It is probable . . . that when the converts in the Orient become sufficiently numerous to make it necessary for them to gather together, a place will have to be selected, probably in Palestine itself, that will be suitable for this grand purpose, and a Stake or Stakes of Zion be organized there. It may be necessary, in the progress of events, for experienced Elders with their families to go from Zion to the land of Jerusalem to help lay the foundation of the work there in teaching these people the arts of true civilization from which they have fallen through the transgressions of their fathers. (August 15, 1889, JI 24:391)

FUTURE FATE OF THE RED MAN. Improbable as it may seem, it is nevertheless true that the Indians . . . are not destined to be crowded off the face of the land by the whites; neither will the whites ever witness their utter extermination. In ancient days the Lord made covenants with various individuals in relation to their descendants—that he would bless them, etc., and would not suffer them to perish from the face of the earth, but would remember them in the last days, and would reveal unto them the abundance of peace and truth. . . . The Book of Mormon, the record containing the ancient history of America, plainly states that the Lord did also make such a covenant with the ancestors of the present American Indians, and with other holy men who formerly inhabited this continent. . . .

Instead, therefore, of there being any likelihood of the Indians being exterminated, or meeting the fate many imagine to be inevitable, there is much more danger that the whites themselves will be the people who will experience this fate, or something approximating thereto. The only way they can avoid it is by receiving and obeying the fullness of the Gospel. Yet, this they as a nation have rejected. (December 13, 1856, WS 270-71)

INDIANS RECEPTIVE TO GOSPEL. Strange to say—if anything can be said to be strange connected with the work of God—the descendants of those ancient covenant people of the Lord have gladly received the testimony of the servants of God. Wherever we have gone and mingled with those people, with those Red Men, and been able to communicate to them the truths of which we are in possession, which God has revealed to us, they have received the same gladly, not only upon this continent but upon the islands of the sea; . . . everywhere where those men with red skins dwell, they have gladly received the testimony of God's servants concerning the Gospel, and they rejoice in its fullness and in the knowledge that their fathers once possessed and of the redemption that Jesus Christ has wrought out for them. Most wonderful has this prediction been fulfilled in this respect. (April 6, 1884, JD 25:123-24)

THE INDIANS TO BUILD NEW JERUSALEM. The Latter-day Saints should remember who these red men are and the predictions which have been made concerning them. They are our brethren, being of the house of Israel and containing a purer strain of Israelitish blood than many members of the Church. It has been predicted, and the word of the Lord will no more fail in this respect than in any other, that they will yet become a white and delightsome people, possessed of a very high degree of cultivation.

They are to build the New Jerusalem, and we, who are of the Gentile nations, are to assist them in the work. The prospect of such a condition of things may humble our pride, but we may as well look squarely at the destiny which is before [them] . . . in the due time of the Lord they will be redeemed. . . . (February 1, 1895, JI 30:75-76)

TEN TRIBES TO RECEIVE BLESSINGS FROM EPHRAIM. It is written that the ten tribes will come forth from the north country, and they will come here to those who hold the keys in this dispensation, to receive the blessings they do not have themselves. Here is Ephraim, and Ephraim holds the keys. The ten tribes are there, but the authority to hold the keys is here.

God is doing a mighty work among the nations of the earth, unknown to us to a great extent. Powerful agencies are operating under His direction in all the nations to bring to pass the fulfillment of His designs. While this is all going on, and we may seem only like a little handful in the midst of the millions of the earth, here in the midst of this people the authority is held which God recognizes, and here are the keys by which the purposes of God will be fulfilled.

All that has been spoken by the mouths of the holy Prophets will be accomplished. There will be a highway cast up; the ten tribes will return, and they will come to the children of Ephraim to receive their blessings. (October 6, 1897, CR 56)

Chapter 9

Salvation for the Dead

PLAN OF SALVATION FOR ALL. We must remember that God's work is not confined to this life; that God's plan of salvation extends throughout eternity; that according to our belief it began to operate in eternity, if it ever began at all. It never really in truth began; it always operated, operated from eternity and will operate to eternity, for all the children of men, for every human soul.

The plan of salvation devised by our Father and God is intended to save every human being that will be saved, to reach them all unless, during this probation, they commit what is termed the unpardonable sin, the sin against the Holy Ghost, and become sons of perdition, in which event salvation ceases (so far as they are concerned) to operate; they put themselves outside of the pale of salvation. (November 9, 1884, JD 26:79-80)

ALL TO HEAR VOICE OF SALVATION. Those heathen nations, like our ancestors who died in ignorance of the Gospel of Christ, will yet hear the voice of salvation. Jesus and those associated with Him will minister to them, for we are all the sons and daughters of God. . . .

The little space of time we live here upon the earth, important as it is to us, compared with the eternities of our God, is only like one grain of sand out of the immensities of grains that are upon the sea shore. Our God is endless and eternal. His Gospel is endless and eternal, and as long as there is a soul to be saved, He, and Jesus, Who died for all, and all associated with Them who have the same Priesthood, will labor anxiously until every soul will be brought back who can be brought back, who has not committed the unpardonable sin by sinning against light and knowledge. . . . Every soul other than these will be felt after throughout the eternities of our God.

Hell itself will be sought; every crevice of it, every part of it will be penetrated by Jesus, and by the Saints of God, in search of the souls of the children of men, until from every crevice and from every recess in the regions of the damned they will be brought forth to light and glory, if they will obey the glorious Gospel of the Son of God, if they will bow in submission to the sceptre of King Immanuel. That is all they have to do, repent of their sins, repent of them whether in this life or in the life to come, and put them away far from them. (May 25, 1884, JD 25:174-75)

JUDGMENT IN ACCORDANCE WITH LAW. We as a people . . . do not believe that God our Heavenly Father will condemn any human being unless he has been made acquainted with the law which He has revealed; in other words, to use the expression of one of the Apostles, "Where no law is, there is no transgression." [Romans 4:15.] Unless a law is proclaimed unto men, that they may understand it, there can be no transgression of that law, and consequently no condemnation following its transgression; and if condemnation follow, there must be a knowledge of law. There must be a comprehension of a law and wilful violation of it before condemnation can come.

There is no room for the exercise of pity to a person who, knowing a law, violates it. We do not have any feelings of pity to men who violate our laws when they understand them. We may regret their course, but when we know that they understood the law and had power to live above it, and that through yielding to their weaknesses and to their propensities they have violated the law, we feel to say, "Let justice take its course, the punishment is a just one, and they must abide by it."

So it is in the Gospel, you will not be condemned for that which you do not understand, neither will any other people that ever lived, that now live or ever will live in the future. They will be condemned according to their knowledge; every man will be judged according to the deeds done in the body. (January 12, 1873, JD 15:293-94)

GOSPEL TO THE DEAD. The Apostle Peter sets forth in great plainness this doctrine when he said:

> By which also he [Jesus] went and preached to the spirits in prison; which sometimes were disobedient, when once the long suffering of God waited in the days of Noah. [1 Peter 3:19-20.]

Noah had declared to them how they could be saved, but they had rejected his words, and they were destroyed. Their spirits were committed to a prison which the Lord had prepared for them, and there they remained in torment, being punished for their great wickedness, until the crucifixion of the Savior. After His Spirit left His body, He went and opened the prison doors to them and declared to them the Gospel of salvation. They then had the opportunity of repenting.

And thus it is, as we are taught in this dispensation, the Elders of this Church are engaged, while in the spirit world awaiting their resurrection, in preaching to the millions of human beings who once lived upon this earth, but who died in ignorance of the Gospel of Jesus Christ. They preach to them as living Elders now preach to living people upon the earth, declaring to them that they must believe in Jesus Christ, the Son of God, the Redeemer of mankind. They must also repent of all their sins and all their wicked thoughts and deeds, and bring forth an acceptable offering of a broken heart and a contrite spirit.

No doubt thousands, yea millions, of men and women who have lived upon the earth listen to these tidings with joy, these words of hope, this heavenly message which comes to them freighted with so many glorious promises, and feeling humble and contrite they receive the truths which they are taught and live as best they can according to the light given to them. (May 15, 1893, JI 28:318)

ALL IN SPIRIT WORLD HEAR GOSPEL. The Gospel shall be preached to them that are dead; the Savior shall carry the glad tidings of salvation to them, and not only to those who were disobedient in the days of Noah, but to all the spirit world, to every soul of Adam's race that had up to that time died who had not received the Gospel in the flesh. He commenced the work there just as He did here.

He commenced by preaching the Gospel, by revealing it to His disciples, by giving them the authority to preach it, and then He descended into Hades or hell, and He there, doubtless, chose His ministers, the men who had the authority of the Holy Priesthood, and set them to the same labor that was commenced on the earth, the labor of preaching His everlasting Gospel to all the spirit world, to the millions of spirits who had died either in disobedience to the Gospel of Christ or in ignorance of that Gospel, never having heard the sound of it. The Gospel was sent to the entire spirit world, except to those sons of perdition who had committed the unpardonable sin, or the sin against the Holy Ghost, and the labor has doubtless continued from that day until the present time in the spirit world. . . .

VARIOUS GRADES OF SPIRITS. In the spirit world there are grades of punishment just as there are grades of spirits. Some are ignorant. Some men who never heard the name of Jesus have lived according to the light that God gave them; for God has given to every man that is born into the world, according to the revelations we have received, His Spirit. He has given unto every man and woman His Spirit, not the gift of the Holy Ghost, but His Spirit by which they are led and guided. (November 9, 1884, JD 26:82-85)

REDEMPTION FOR THOSE WITHOUT LAW. The words of Mormon recorded in the 22nd verse of the 8th chapter of Moroni . . . read as follows:

> For behold that all little children are alive in Christ, and also they that are without the law. For the power of redemption cometh on all them that have no law; wherefore, he that is not condemned, or he that is under no condemnation, cannot repent; and unto such baptism availeth nothing.

. . . There are two classes referred to in this verse, namely, little children and they that are without the law. Upon both of these classes redemption cometh, so far as the consequences of the fall are concerned. Upon little children because they are not accountable and upon those that are without the law because they are ignorant. . . . The Prophet Mormon says, "Little children cannot repent." [Moroni 8:19.] This being the case, baptism would be of no avail to them.

But the question remains, how about those "that are without the law"? Why cannot they repent? And why is baptism of no avail to them? They cannot repent because they are not under condemnation, and the reason they are not under condemnation is, they are ignorant. And being ignorant of the law, and therefore not under condemnation, the law of baptism does not apply unto them any more than it does to little children. It requires knowledge of the law to bring men under condemnation. When they possess that knowledge, they become accountable and are in a condition to repent; and when they repent, or are capable of repentance, they can then be baptized.

This is the meaning of the Prophet Mormon's teaching in the verse referred to. He does not mean that this class will never be under condemnation, that there never will be a time when they cannot repent and never be a time when baptism will be of any avail to them. But while they remain ignorant of the law or, to use his own language, while "they are without the law," they are under no condemnation and, therefore, cannot repent and be baptized.

This is in precise agreement with all the teachings of the Prophets recorded in the Book of Mormon. King Benjamin . . . says:

> And moreover, I say unto you, that the time shall come when the knowledge of a Savior shall spread throughout every nation, kindred, tongue, and people.
>
> And behold, when that time cometh, none shall be found blameless before God, except it be little children, only through repentance and faith on the name of the Lord God Omnipotent. [Mosiah 3:20-21.]

This is the law as this Prophet and king clearly sets it forth. Men are no longer blameless before God when this knowledge, of which the angel speaks to King Benajmin, comes to them. . . . The angel in the next verse told King Benjamin that even his own people would be found no more blameless in the sight of God, after he had declared these things unto them, only on the conditions which the angel had declared—"repentance and faith on the name of the Lord God Omnipotent."

Now, it is pertinent to ask at this point, if this is the case with men in the flesh, will not the declaration of this law, or the imparting of this knowledge, to men in the spirit world be followed by the same consequences? It is the making known of the law of the Gospel—the conditions of salvation—that brings mankind under condemnation, that requires from them faith and repentance and that brings to them remission of sins through the ordinance of baptism.

Before the knowledge of a Savior had spread, men were blameless for not obeying His law. They were not under condemnation. They did not know the will of God concerning them, and if they broke any of His laws, they did so ignorantly.

Alma .,. . asks very pertinently:

> Now, how could a man repent except he should sin? How could he sin if there was no law? How could there be a law save there was a punishment? . . .
>
> Now, if there was no law given—if a man murdered he should die—would he be afraid he would die if he should murder?
>
> And also, if there was no law given against sin men would not be afraid to sin.
>
> And if there was no law given, if men sinned what could justice do, or mercy either, for they would have no claim upon the creature? [Alma 42:17, 19-21.]

This agrees with what the Apostle Paul says: "Where no law is, there is no transgression." And, of course, where there is no transgression there is no condemnation. Again he says: "Nay, I had not known sin, but by the law." [Romans 7:7.]

According to the words of Jacob. . . :

> Wherefore, he has given a law; and where there is no law given there is no punishment; and where there is no punishment there is no condemnation; and where there is no condemnation the mercies of the Holy One of Israel have claim upon them, because of the atonement; for they are delivered by the power of him.
>
> For the atonement satisfieth the demands of his justice upon all those who have not the law given to them, that they are delivered from that awful monster, death and hell, and the devil, and the lake of fire and brimstone, which is endless torment; and they are restored to that God who gave them breath, which is the Holy One of Israel. [2 Nephi 9:25-26.]

In the next he says, "But woe unto him that has the law given, yea, that has all the commandments of God."

The atonement of Jesus brings to pass the deliverance of all those who have died without the law, both those who died before the coming of Jesus and after His coming. It is declared by Abinadi that these, "not having salvation declared unto them . . . have a part in the first resurrection, or have eternal life, being redeemed by the Lord." [Mosiah 15:24.] He puts little children also in the same class. . . .

After examining these passages, let us return to the words of Mormon, as recorded by Moroni, and let us read those words in the light of the sayings of the Prophets which we have quoted. He says, "For the power of redemption cometh on all them that have no law."

Why is that? Because they are not under condemnation, not having violated any law knowingly, and, therefore, they cannot repent. How can a man repent of that which is not sin? For, as Alma says, "how could he sin if there was no law?" Therefore, until the law is declared, such people are not sinners; and if they cannot repent, of what avail would baptism be? We would not baptize a man that had not repented. He must be convicted of sin. He must see that he must obey the laws of God. He must know that it is his duty to believe in Jesus, to repent of his sins, and to be baptized in His name.

This is the salvation which Abinadi speaks of. It was not declared unto those who died in ignorance of the plan of salvation. But when it was declared unto them, then sin began. They then needed to repent and to be baptized.

There is this distinction between children and adults: children are not accountable and are not sinners until they reach the age of accountability, which the Lord has said is eight years; and, therefore, they cannot repent, neither is baptism necessary for them. But it is different with adults who died in ignorance of the law of God. The time will come when every creature, both those who are living now and those who have lived and those who will live, will hear the law of salvation declared unto them, and when they hear that law, they come under condemnation, if they do not obey it. Those who are in the spirit world will hear it, and when they do hear it, they will become amenable to the law of God; and though they themselves cannot be baptized, they can believe in Jesus and repent of their sins, and others in the flesh can be baptized for them, so that the whole law will be maintained. Unto such baptism will be of avail, because they are in a condition to repent, and the law has force upon them. (February 15, 1892, JI 27:122-24)

THE WORK OF THE MILLENNIUM. There will be a thousand years' rest, during which period Satan will be bound, and when the seed of the righteous will increase and cover the land. In that glorious period everything on the face of the earth will be beautiful; disease and crime and all the evils that attend our present state of existence will be banished; and during that period, as God has revealed, the occupation of his people will be to lay a foundation for the redemption of the dead, the unnumbered millions who lived and died on the earth without hearing and obeying the plan of salvation. (December 3, 1871, JD 14:321-22)

A NEVER-ENDING MISSIONARY LABOR. When this life is ended, when this mortal is laid aside, we shall go into the spirit world, endowed with the same Priesthood and authority of the Son of God; clothed with that authority, enveloped with it, even the fullness of it, we shall go into the sipirit world and continue this glorious labor of warning our brethren and sisters who once were in the flesh, until throughout the spirit world the Gospel of salvation shall be heard from one end of it to the other.

It is a never-ending work that we have taken upon ourselves. It will never terminate until this earth shall be redeemed, until the power of Satan shall be subdued, until wickedness shall be banished from the earth, until He reigns whose right it is to reign, and every knee shall bow and every tongue confess that Jesus is the Christ, the Son of God. Then will this labor cease so far as the family of man is concerned; but it will never cease until all who belong to this earth, who ever were born upon it—no matter in what age, no matter what time, no matter what nationality—shall be redeemed who can be redeemed. (November 9, 1884, JD 26:86)

REPRESENTATIVES OF ALL NATIONS. God has chosen us from the various nations for this purpose. There are men in this Church from almost every race of men, and if representatives from all the races are not now, they will be in. God scattered the seed of Israel through all of the nations of the earth so that in the great gathering of the last days He might be able to get representatives of all the families of men. And we are chosen for this purpose.

The seed has been scattered among the nations; and when the descendants of Israel here heard the sound of the Gospel, it was indeed the glad tidings of salvation to them. They knew the voice of the Shepherd; it was like telling them something they had been waiting for; the sound thereof was most delightful to the soul.

The reason that the sound of the Gospel had such an effect upon us was because we were chosen from before the foundation of the world for the express purpose of coming forth in this day to receive it, and well may it be said that your lives have been hid with Christ. You have come forth in these last days to be instruments in His hands of bringing souls to a knowledge of the truth as it is in Christ Jesus. . . .

A DUTY TO TRACE GENEALOGIES. It is your duty now to rise up, all of you, and trace your genealogies and begin to exercise the powers which belong to saviors of men, and when you do this in earnest, you will begin to comprehend how widespread, how numerous your ancestors are, for whom temple work has to be performed, in order that they may be brought into the fold; and when you get stopped, the Lord will reveal further information to you; and in this way the work of salvation and redemption will be accomplished. . . .

It is true we have been scattered among Gentile nations and are called Gentiles, but, nevertheless, we are of the pure seed, having come through Gentile lineage that we may be the means of saving them, and through our faithfulness we shall stand at their head. This is the blessing which rests upon us as descendants of Abraham. . .

PRAYERS FROM WORLD OF SPIRITS. When you think that you are chosen to be saviors to the children of men, to stand as a medium through whom salvation shall flow unto unnumbered thousands, what manner of people ought we to be? They pray for you today in the spirit world, as they have been no doubt from the beginning praying for their descendants that they may be faithful to the truth. You cannot tell the interest felt in eternity for you by those of our dead who have gone before us. Their hearts yearn after us, their constant desire being that we may be faithful and maintain our integrity and be prepared to bring salvation to them and redeem them by going forth and obeying every ordinance which God has established in the Church for the salvation of the living and the dead. (October 31, 1880, JD 22:129-31)

REPRESENTATIVES OF THOUSANDS OF SOULS. A people like this, gathered from all nations of the earth, will comprehend in our labors entire nations. There are but few of us, but we represent a vast number of the families of the earth. Hence the anxiety there is on the other side of the veil in regard to us. Streams of blood from a thousand different sources may concentrate in one man or one women, and that man or woman be the representative of thousands of souls. . . . There is no sweeter joy ever received by a human soul than that experienced in the labor for the redemption of the dead. . . .

God has taught us that there is hope for every soul that has not committed the unpardonable sin. . . . There is not as much difficulty in getting the inhabitants of the spirit world to accept the Gospel as we have here on earth. . . . We will administer punishment to the men who mock and deride us, and what will be our revenge? We will be baptized for them and redeem them. We will heap coals of fire upon their heads. (April 1893, quoted in *Era* 34:479 [1931])

ORDINANCE OF ADOPTION OR SEALING. Marriages of the children of men are only binding as between themselves while the covenant lasts. Our fathers made their covenants with our mothers for time, and when time ended, of course, the covenant and the union ended also. Now, the Holy Spirit revealed that this being the case, every man and woman and every child born as the offspring of these unions would stand separately, unless a new bond were formed. Without this should be done, there would be no binding link to unite woman to man and children to parents, for all the obligations and all the covenants had terminated; therefore, members of families would each stand separately, without any connection of a binding character between themselves.

Of course, there was what we call the bond of blood existing (there is no blood, however, in resurrected beings) or, in other words, there was the bond that arose through kindred. That would remain. The Lord has taught us, however, that this is not all that is required; there must be an authority exercised by which parents should be bound together, and then their children bound to them.

We have been taught also that through the revelation of the Priesthood and its bestowal upon men, and the exercise of that Priesthood in sealing wives to husbands, the children begotten in these marriages are born, as we phrase it, in the covenant; that is, they are recognized by the Lord as legitimate children of the covenant, He having recognized the marriage of their parents, having given the authority to man on the earth to bind on earth, and that bond should be sealed in heaven. In this way the Latter-day Saints are being bound together in the new and everlasting covenant, wives being sealed to their husbands, and children, the offspring of these marriages, being born in the covenant under the blessing and the recognition by the Almighty of the bond that exists between their parents.

Thus, you see that there is a new order of things growing up among us. It is not necessary, where parents are thus sealed together by the authority of the Holy Priesthood for time and for eternity, that their children should be adopted or be sealed to them. They are legitimate heirs of the Priesthood and of the blessings of the new and everlasting covenant. But not so with those who have been born outside of this covenant. There has to be some ordinance performed in order to make them legitimate; and that ordinance, the Prophet Joseph revealed, was the ordinance of adoption; that is, that word covers the ordinance or law, although we do not use the word adoption when we seal children to parents; we call that sealing. But to illustrate the principle and explain the law the word "adoption" is used. (April 8, 1894, DW 48:544)

THE EFFECT OF GENEALOGICAL WORK. The effect of temple labors upon the Latter-day Saints will become very marked. The researches which they will make to obtain knowledge of their ancestors will broaden their minds and enlarge their sympathies and make them more cosmopolitan than other people. They will feel a bond of sympathy as well as of blood for mankind in general. There has been such an intermingling of the races in times that are past, and the blood of Ephraim has been so widely scattered throughout the nations of the earth, that the tracing of genealogy will establish a kinship between the Latter-day Saints and a great many races and nations. This will have the effect to remove narrowness and those sectional feelings that are too apt to grow up in the minds of individuals and communities. And as these causes continue to operate, every generation will exhibit more distinctively the traits that the belief and practices of the Latter-day Saints develop.

One effect will be that young men and young women who come of honorable ancestry will feel that it depends upon them to maintain its reputation and do nothing unworthy of their lineage. While our Church is too democratic in its teachings and organization and all its views to permit pride of birth to grow up to any extent, yet there will be what may be . . . termed pride of character and a disposition to maintain the honorable reputation which the family may have; and it is to be hoped that this will have an elevating effect upon the people. Marriages will be contracted with more care. Young men and women of good families, whose attention will be directed to their lineage, will naturally be more careful respecting alliances that they may form, and they will not be nearly so likely to form hasty and ill-considered connections. (June 1, 1895, JI 30:354)

THE LORD TO REVEAL GENEALOGIES. We need not be in such a hurry as to create confusion. The Lord will give us time enough to do it all; and when we have gone as far as appears possible, He will give to us opportunities that, at the present time, we are ignorant of; we will find that everything will be made plain, and each man will trace his genealogy clear back; we will know our connection and what to do in relation to these matters, for the Lord will reveal it to us. (April 8, 1894, DW 48:545)

A TEMPLE-BUILDING PEOPLE. God did not permit David, a man after His own heart, to build the temple at Jerusalem, because he was a man of war, but He gave unto His peaceful son Solomon, who was a peaceful ruler and had no occasion to fight, the privilege of building His holy temple. We are a temple-building people. God has given unto us a mission of this kind, to build temples in which we shall perform the ordinances of life and salvation, and it seems to be meet in His providence that we should refrain from everything that would unfit us for the discharge of this high and holy calling. (August 31, 1884, JD 25:272)

Temple building is one of the most prominent and important features of this latter-day dispensation. The Saints are aware of the stupendous issues that hang upon the earnestness of the teeming millions of the dead, as well as of those of the living who will give ear to the voice of invitation and warning that is now resounding. They are consequently interested in every thing pertaining to the progress and prospects of the rearing of structures that are to be used for the sacred purposes of salvation. (December 24, 1877, MS 39:836)

TEMPLE BUILDING BRINGS INCREASED POWER. Every foundation stone that is laid for a Temple, and every Temple completed according to the order the Lord has revealed for His Holy Priesthood, lessens the power of Satan on the earth and increases the power of God and Godliness, moves the heavens in mighty power in our behalf, invokes and calls down upon us the blessings of the Eternal Gods and those who reside in Their presence. There is no doubt whatever of this in my mind. (September 17, 1877, MS 39:743)

I fully believe that when that temple is once finished there will be a power and manifestations of the goodness of God unto this people such as they have never before experienced. Every work of this kind that we have accomplished has been attended with increased and wonderful results unto us as a people—an increase of power and of God's blessings upon us. It was so in Kirtland and at Nauvoo; at both places the Elders had an increase of power, and the Saints, since the completion of and the administration of ordinances in those buildings, have had a power they never possessed previously. . . .

I fully believe . . . that when this and other temples are completed there will be an increase of power bestowed upon the people of God and that they will thereby be better fitted to go forth and cope with the powers of darkness and with the evils that exist in the world and to establish the Zion of God never more to be thrown down. (April 18, 1871, JD 14:125-26)

SATAN ENRAGED BY TEMPLE BUILDING. Every temple that we build excites additional hatred, increases the volume of opposition, the volume of hostility and the threatenings of the wicked. Every temple that we have thus far completed—and every temple of which we lay the foundation—has been another testimony in favor of God and has brought strength to the people of God in enlisting the hosts in the eternal world upon our side; but at the same time there has been stirred up, from the very depths of hell, all the damned.

Satan and his legions unite with their agents upon the earth in an endeavor to destroy this work and to do everything in their power to obliterate it from the face of the earth; hell is enraged at the work we are doing; hell is stirred up at that which we are accomplishing. Satan sees that which he dreads, . . . and seeing this he is determined to exert every power, every influence that he can muster for the purpose of preventing the spread and growth of this work. (October 5, 1884, JD 25:326)

What is there connected with baptism for the dead that should cause feelings of opposition? All the Christian world believe that Jesus died for us and that through His vicarious atonement and sufferings we are redeemed. This principle of vicarious action lies at the very foundation of the whole Christian religion. (January 28, 1900, MS 62:162)

Satan rages as he views his domain trenched upon, his captives delivered, and the souls of men wrenched from his grasp by the labors of the living for the dead in and through those sacred ordinances that belong alone to the Gospel of the Son of God, administered in holy places by His chosen servants and handmaidens. And it must not surprise us if the rage of the arch-enemy of mankind increases and his emissaries grow more relentless and cruel, more brutal and inhuman in their efforts to stay this work, as the number of temples increases and the thousands of Israel go in thereto to minister the ordinances of salvation for their ancestors and departed friends. (October 6, 1886, MS 48:715)

He [Satan] understands very well that if the children of men will enter into such holy buildings and receive the ordinances there administered and be faithful thereto, his power over them is lost forever, and his kingdom must go down. The struggle with him is a desperate one. He wishes to retain his supremacy on the earth—the territory which he has usurped and over which he held dominion, by all the trickery and violence of which he is capable, for so many generations. God designs to overthrow him, to break his power and to have His children live for one thousand years free from his domination. Great issues are involved in this struggle; but God's Kingdom will triumph, and His people will be freed from the thraldom which Satan seeks to impose.

HOUSES OF LEARNING. There is another use to which temples are put that will prove of great benefit to the rising generation of the Latter-day Saints. The Lord has commanded His people to "seek ye out of the best books words of wisdom; seek learning, even by study and also by faith." [D&C 88:118.] He has commanded us to make our temples houses of learning in which His people may receive instruction in every useful science. In the temple in Kirtland much valuable instruction was given to the Elders. The Prophet Joseph himself, through instruction received there, made considerable progress, especially in a knowledge of languages. Others of the Elders also studied diligently there and acquired much useful knowledge. (August 15, 1884, JI 19:248)

SECTION 2

LIVING THE GOSPEL

Every Latter-day Saint who is in the path of his duty, whether abroad among the people preaching the principles of "Mormonism" orally, or at home building cities and temples, or leaving the land of his or her nativity emigrating to the mountains, or engaged in any of the fields of labor assigned to us to fill, is disseminating a knowledge of "Mormonism," and is bearing so loud and powerful a testimony to its truth that the world will be left without excuse for rejecting it.

—George Q. Cannon
Western Standard
August 23, 1856

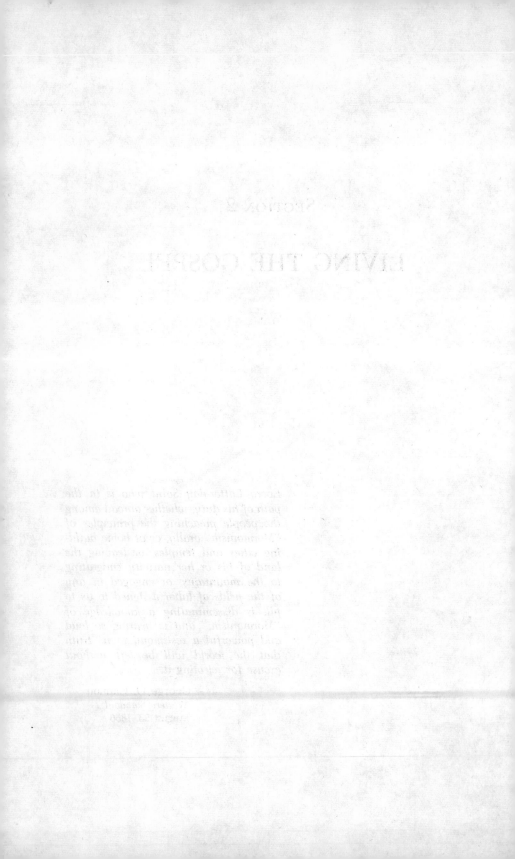

Chapter 10

Courtship and Marriage— Home and Family

MARRIAGE NOT TO BE POSTPONED. Young men make a great mistake to postpone marriage when they reach the proper age. It is a groundless fear for any young man of industrious habits to think that he cannot support a wife. A healthy, industrious young fellow has no reason to fear about making a living in this country. If he is intelligent and energetic, he will find plenty of opportunities to make a living for himself and for a wife.

There is a blessing attends marriage when rightly entered upon. The experience of the world, in all societies, is that married people do better, even in a worldly sense, than the unmarried. A young man finds that he can support himself and wife as easily as he supported himself. When a child is born, the married couple find it no harder to live than they did before. And as the family increases, their ability increases in proportion. There is a providence over every human being, and our Father, Who provides for the wants of the sparrows, does not forget His children.

Shall I be pardoned if I quote my own case? When I went on my first mission, I was engaged to a young lady. After a lengthy absence, I came back as poor as missionaries generally do. But I got married twelve days after my return. I tried to get employment; but up to the day of my marriage had not obtained it. The next day after marriage I secured employment. I had only been home five months when I went on another mission; and though it was in the winter time I made means so fast that when I started on this mission, having been called to take my wife with me, I left Salt Lake City with a very excellent outfit—mules and wagon, provisions, etc.

My own experience, therefore, warrants me in saying to young men: Do not be afraid of marriage, even though you may be poor. Select for yourself a good partner—a faithful, honest, industrious girl—and get married. If you are energetic yourself, and not afraid of work, you will have no trouble in making a living, and you will increase your happiness very much by doing so. The fact of your having a wife and the prospect of children will arouse your energies and make you think and exercise your brains. This of itself will have a beneficial effect. . . .

A generation who marry reasonably early is a happier, a stronger and a purer generation than one in which marriage is deferred till later in life. Frequently a remark which I once publicly made concerning marriage is quoted to me. I said that any large element of unmarried young men in a community after they are twenty-four years of age is a dangerous element. Some, in speaking of it, have supposed that I referred to individual young men. Of course, this was not so. I did not refer to individuals; for there are many young men of twenty-four who, through being on missions or for other causes, are not married; but I referred to the danger to society of any considerable element of unmarried men over that age in a community. Does not the experience of mankind prove that this is correct? I certainly think so. I should deplore the increase of unmarried young men beyond twenty-three or twenty-four years of age in any of our communities, as I am satisfied that the effect on society would not be good. (January 15, 1898, JI 33:66-67)

LAWS OF NATURE REQUIRE YOUNG MARRIAGES. To marry and to marry rightly is part of the religion of the true servant and handmaiden of the Lord. In our eyes it is far more than a mere civil contract; it is a command of God, just as binding as though it were one of the ten written by the finger of Jehovah on the two tables of stone amidst the thunderings and lightnings of Sinai. Many, however, are inclined to treat this relationship far too lightly, as though it were something with which religion had no concern. . . .

The laws of nature and the word of God require that mankind should marry in their youth. The longer this union is put off the more opportunity for evil and, as a rule, with increasing years the less inclination to enter into it. The postponement of marriage has, all through the world's history from the very beginning, been a sign of the decline of any nation where it prevailed. It generally follows the increase of riches and consequent growth of luxury and is itself followed by corruption and decay. Such was the history of Greece and Rome and other rulers of antiquity, and such is the growing story of some of the nations of modern Christendom. It is not a good sign among the Latter-day Saints. (January 15, 1901, JI 36:49-50)

MARRIAGE IS A DUTY. Every young man of proper age should be taught that it is his duty to take to himself one of the other sex as a wife. It should be enforced upon men as a duty which they owe to themselves, to their parents and to society at large. It should not be left as a matter of personal convenience or inconvenience alone but should be made to appear in their minds as something of far greater and higher importance. . . .

In view of these things, parents cannot be too careful in training their daughters, so that they will have correct feelings upon this subject. They should be made to understand that happiness does not consist in fine clothing nor in fine furnishings nor in elegant surroundings but that where true love exists between husband and wife a humble cottage may be made the abode of a purer happiness than can be found many times in the richest habitations in the land.

Our girls should be taught that if they obtain a suitable companion, however poor he may be, if he be a man of good habits, full of faith in the Lord, he can by industry, with his wife's help, lay the foundation for future reasonable comfort, and perhaps wealth. (May 15, 1892, JI 27:304-305)

But, girls, remain maids until you are a hundred years old if you cannot get men who are men of God. Better to remain unmarried all your lives than to connect yourselves with unworthy men and afterwards have to be divorced. (May 19, 1889, DW 39:18)

CULTIVATION OF MUTUAL RESPECT. Young people of the right character who enter into the married condition do not get bored by being together; they arrange their lives so that the society of one will always be agreeable to the other. Marriages are sure to be unhappy where the parties become tired of each other, and prefer the society of others to that of their companions. Mutual respect must be cultivated, for without this, love cannot exist. The polite attentions which lovers show to each other should be kept up through life, and not be confined to the honeymoon. Where married people maintain this conduct in their treatment of each other, they are very likely to lead happy lives.

It is a beautiful sight to see a family where these amenities are maintained. The children partake of the spirit of their parents, and they live in love and harmony. The parents respect each other, and the children respect the parents. The influence of the example of the parents is plainly visible in the demeanor of the children. Even in poor circumstances, families who live in this manner are happy. Poverty may sometimes be painful, but the pain and irritation are wonderfully eased where the domestic virtues are cultivated.

HUSBANDS TO BE GOOD PROVIDERS. I have already given my views on the advantages of early marriages. As a rule, people assimilate in their dispositions and manners much better when they are young than when they are beyond middle age. They can adapt themselves easier to each other's ways and are more likely to become congenial. The absence of money may prevent the procuring of some comforts and conveniences in the outset, but the common exertion and toil to obtain these have an enduring effect on both husband and wife.

Every young man should seek to qualify himself to become a good provider for a wife and children. Skill should be cultivated. Industry should be a fixed habit of life. Time should be valued as more than gold. The young man who values his minutes and his hours, and permits none to pass in idleness, is sure—all other things being equal—to become a useful citizen and to make a good provider for a family. There ought to be no trouble in this country for any industrious young man to make a reasonably good living for himself and family.

WIVES TO BE GOOD HOUSEKEEPERS. On the other hand, the girls should qualify themselves to be good housewives. Every girl, when she marries, should seek to make her home attractive. The contrast in the mind of her husband between her abode and that of others of her class should always be in her favor. The husband should always have reason to praise his wife's qualities as a housekeeper. Especially should the art of cooking food be cultivated, for though some may think that a matter of but little importance, experience will prove that it enters largely into domestic happiness. One of the poets says:

> We may live without poetry, music, and art;
> We may live without conscience, and live without heart;
> We may live without friends; we may live without books,
> But civilized man cannot live without cooks. . . .

A tactful wife will not fail to perceive the effect of a good, well-cooked meal upon her husband. If she have any troubles, she will not obtrude them upon him before he has had his meal. She will watch her opportunity to present a disagreeable subject at a time when she knows her husband is in the best mood to hear it. The husband also, on his part, if he be a man of good sense, will not come into his house, when his wife is perhaps tired and fretful through overwork or the annoyances which the children may give her, and throw in sight the cares and perplexities under which he labors. He should let all these slip off his shoulders when he crosses his threshold.

Domestic peace and tranquillity in the family are most desirable. People who live such lives are likely to live to advanced age. Care and worry attendant upon earthly existence ought to be softened and overcome by the sweet rest and entire absence from friction in the family circle. (March 1, 1898, JI 33:195-96)

BUILD A HOME BY UNITED LABOR. A properly constituted young woman, if she finds a partner of her choice, will be content to struggle with him in obtaining the comforts of life. Every addition to the furnishings of their home or of their surroundings obtained by their joint exertions forms another link in their happiness and binds them closer together. . . .

Young people marrying in this manner and building themselves a home by their united labor, enjoy that home as they could not possibly a home that might be furnished for them beforehand. Everything in it brings to remembrance the pleasures of the past. It represents hopes and exertions, recalls incidents that are pleasant to reflect upon, and they learn to appreciate the value of that which they possess because of the exertions they have made to obtain it.

HAVE CONGENIAL MARRIAGES. Parents, and others who have influence with the young, should be careful to have marriages congenial. No true happiness can result from an ill-assorted marriage. . . .

The marriage of an ignorant person with an intelligent one is not always attended with happy results. There should be some similarity of taste, of disposition, of training, and certainly of belief, to make a couple congenial. A young man, therefore, in seeking for a partner—and the same may be said of young women—should bear in mind that to live happily through life in the wedded condition they should have partners of congenial tastes and of similar training. An intelligent, educated girl who marries an ignorant man must either lift him to her level, if she would lead a pleasant life and maintain her self-respect, or she must descend to his level. It is seldom that a woman can lift her husband in this way; she is more likely either to become discouraged and alienated from him, and separated from him, or descend to his level. If she does the latter, she cannot escape the feeling that she is lowering herself and descending from the station she might have occupied. The young man who marries a girl who is not his equal in education or in intelligence is more likely to lift her up to his level, and to inspire her with noble thoughts, and to develop her higher attributes, than in the other case. (May 15, 1891, JI 26:316-17.)

A STRICT MARRIAGE COMMAND. When Latter-day Saints marry those who are not of their faith, I look upon it as a great misfortune to those who do so. If those barriers were to be broken down which ought to exist between us and the world, I should view it as a great calamity. One of the strictest commands that the Lord gave to Israel in olden times was that they should not marry with the nations surrounding them; this law is equally binding on us, and we should do everything in our power to maintain it inviolate. (October 31, 1881, JD 22:284)

Many of the evils that fell upon Israel were due to intermarriage on their part with women who were not of their faith, and who were from nations who did not have the same worship that Israel had. Marriages of this nature are contrary to the command of God.

We are commanded not to marry with those who are not of our faith, and no woman ever did it, no girl ever did it that has not sooner or later had sorrow because of this. God is not pleased with such marriages, and it is not in the nature of things to expect blessings to follow such inter-marriages. (August 26, 1883, JD 26:319)

MARRY THOSE STRONG IN THE FAITH. Many girls have supposed that the husband's love for them would be the means of bringing them into the Church; but the experience of our many years . . . has proved the fallacy of that hope. There have been exceptions, it is true, but they are very rare. The most frequent result has been that the girls have lost their faith and succumbed to the influence of the husband, and they and their children are aliens to the covenant. . . .

For a marriage to be a truly happy one among us, a young man or young woman in seeking a partner should make it a matter of the first consideration to find one who is strong in the faith which he or she possesses. This forms the principal foundation for future concord and happiness. Following this care should be taken upon the point of good habits, good temper, industry and agreeable tastes.

A man that is not of the right character before marriage ought not to be trusted to reform after marriage. It is seldom that such changes occur. The girl deceives herself who trusts to have such a result follow her marriage with a man of this kind. Her love for him should not blind her to his defects; in fact, if she would take the right course, she would never allow herself to become entangled in such a way as to place her affections upon an unworthy person. The society of such should be shunned; and if care be taken in this direction, there is but little danger of improper attachments springing up.

Marriage is the most important step in a young woman's life. It should be entered upon with the greatest care. Both sexes should earnestly seek the guidance of heaven in a matter so momentous as the forming of a contract as husband and wife. It ought not to be formed for a day, or for a few years, but with a view to being continued as long as life shall last, and then throughout eternity. (November 1, 1891, JI 26:664-65)

It should be the aim of every father in Israel to have his daughters married to those who are of the right lineage, who have a claim upon the blessings of God, through their descent, added to their own faithfulness in keeping the commandments of God. I deem it of great importance to us as a people that we should look to this. . . .

MARRIAGE TO GENTILES CAUSES UNBELIEVING OFFSPRING. There are some men who have so much Gentile blood in them that their offspring partake of it and of the unbelief of the father, and in such cases it is impossible for a mother who has such a husband and children, with all her faith, with all her zeal, with all the pains that she takes, to instil into the minds of her children faith in the God of Israel and faith in the covenant that He has restored. They seem to belong to another flock. It seems as though they have no susceptibility for the truth. There is no good soil in their hearts to receive the seeds of truth, the Gospel of the Son of God. . . .

A girl of our faith may marry a Gentile, and he may be a pretty good man as far as his conduct is concerned; he may be a good citizen, a truthful man, but there will be a lack of susceptibility to the truth about his offspring. There will be a lack of faith there. Some of the children may have a little faith in the truth, but many of them, probably, will have no faith whatever and will give the mother uneasiness and trouble and sorrow, and she will have no satisfaction whatever in her children. . . . When women make alliances of this kind, they are not sure, in the least degree, as to the character of their posterity. They may have faithful children, but as likely as not . . . they will go back to their old element and to their old associations, and it seems impossible to prevent them from doing so.

JOSEPH SMITH YET TO HAVE A FAITHFUL POSTERITY. There may be faithful men who will have unfaithful sons, who may not be as faithful as they might be; but faithful posterity will come, just as I believe it will be the case with the Prophet Joseph's seed. Today he has not a soul descended from him personally in this Church. There is not a man bearing the Holy Priesthood to stand before our God in the Church that Joseph was the means in the hands of God of founding—not a man to-day of his own blood, that is, by descent—to stand before the Lord and represent him among these Latter-day Saints. But will this always be the case? No.

Just as sure as God lives, just as sure as God has made promises, so sure will some one of Joseph Smith's posterity rise up and be numbered with this Church and bear the everlasting Priesthood that Joseph himself had. It may be delayed in the wise providence of our God. There are many things that we cannot understand, cannot see the reason why they should be so, but these promises are unalterable; God made them to Joseph during his lifetime, and they will be fulfilled just as sure as God made them. He [Joseph] will have among this people some one descended from his own loins who will bear the everlasting Priesthood and who will honor and magnify that Priesthood among the Latter-day Saints.

Therefore, it is a blessing from God for a woman to bear children to such a man, or to any man who bears or holds the everlasting Priesthood of the Son of God, and who magnifies his calling, and through magnifying it, receives promises from God to himself and his posterity after him. . . .

REVELATION NEEDED FOR PROPER MARRIAGES. Out of all the sons of God there are comparatively few, I say, who are capable through their faith and faithfulness, and through their keeping the commandments of God, of leading the daughters of Zion in the path of exaltation and leading them into the Celestial Kingdom of our God; therefore, it is of the utmost importance in these matters we should be exceedingly careful.

We should seek by revelation to obtain a knowledge for ourselves respecting these matters. Our daughters should be taught to control their feelings and affections and not let them go out without any regard to these circumstances to which I have alluded. A woman should be exceedingly careful, a girl should be exceedingly careful, and parents should be exceedingly careful in instilling into her mind the principles that must be observed by her and by her husband to obtain exaltation in the Celestial Kingdom of God. . . .

MARRY INTO FAITHFUL FAMILIES. According to our faith no woman should be connected with a man who cannot save her in the Celestial Kingdom of God. What I mean by this is that if a man apostatizes and breaks covenants and loses his standing in the Church of Christ, he is not in a fit condition to save himself, much less to lead his wife aright. He cannot lead her in the path of exaltation, because he has turned aside from that path; he has gone into another path. If she follows him, she will follow him to destruction; she will take the downward road. She will never find, while following him, and he in that condition, the path of salvation. Therefore, how carefully men should be that in marrying they should marry into good families and not marry into apostate families. . . .

MARRIAGE BY AUTHORITY OF PRIESTHOOD. Our people are commanded to marry in their own Church. We are commanded to marry those of our own faith and not to go outside of our Church for partners. Instead of being married by Justices of the Peace, or by other civil authorities, God has placed in His Church a Priesthood, and one of the offices and functions of that Priesthood is to marry the sons and daughters of God—to marry them one to another in the new and everlasting covenant and to seal upon them and their posterity the blessings that pertain to that new and everlasting covenant; and any man who desires to be a happy husband and to have a happy home, and any woman who desires to be a happy wife and a happy mother, and to have joy in their associations, will never permit themselves to be drawn aside to be married by any authority except that which God has instituted, namely, the authority of the Holy Priesthood. (November 16, 1884, JD 25: 365-69)

SACREDNESS OF FAMILY RELATIONS. The life of a Saint is not simply a personal perfecting, it is also a factor in the entire scheme of earth's redemption. No one can be saved alone, by himself, or herself, unassisted by . . . others. The weight of our influence must be either for good or harm, be an aid or an injury to the work of human regeneration, and as we assume responsibilities, form ties, enter into covenants, beget children, accumulate families, so does the weight of our influence increase, so does its extent broaden and deepen.

The Scriptures inform us that God created this earth as a habitation for man, and He placed man on it that he might have joy, a joy that is to be eternal. To accomplish these purposes, the preparatory one of peopling the earth, and the ultimate one of man's eternal happiness, He, the Creator, established marriage, and commanded those He first placed here on earth to be fruitful and multiply. This institution He regulated by strict laws given through His servants to His people in their various dispensations; and His Son, our Savior, emphasized these commandments by most unequivocal teachings with regard to the sacredness of the marriage covenant, and of the sinfulness of divorce for other than the most grave departures from the spirit and intent of that covenant.

In this is wisdom, for the experience of the world, in all its ages, proves that where lax ideas exist with regard to marriages and divorce, more especially where those ideas find expression in lax legislation, there we discover peoples and nations whose code of morals is inferior, and where sexual irregularities and sins increase, until that righteousness, which has been so truthfully said "exalteth a nation" [Proverbs 14:34], ceases to have an existence in their midst.

To a people who believe as we do, that true marriage was divinely instituted for the multiplication of mankind, and is not a union for time alone, but reaches into the eternities, the disruption of families by divorce is an evil of no ordinary character, not only bearing a harvest of sorrow and suffering in this life, but also having a far reaching influence into the world beyond the grave, and possibly involving others in the ruin who had no voice in the separation or power to avert its occurrence. For this reason the Latter-day Saints of all people should be most loath to sunder sacred ties once formed, and most determinedly opposed to the severance of unions made in holy places in God's appointed way, for light and trivial causes. (October 6, 1886, MS 48:716)

BIRTH CONTROL—A GREAT SIN. From what we have heard we are led to believe that the spirit is abroad in the earth, and is making some headway among the Latter-day Saints, to look with reproach upon women with large families, and the desire seems to be growing among some of the younger population, to desire only one or two, and not to exceed three, children. We have heard that many of the diabolical practices of the world have been introduced . . . among some who profess to be Latter-day Saints, to prevent the bearing of children. No sin, unless it be that of murder, will meet with a greater condemnation from God than this evil of tampering with the fountains of life. Such sins will destroy the strength of any people that practices them, and the nation whose people yield to such vices is in great danger of destruction. No Saint can practice or encourage such corruption without incurring the displeasure of an offended God. (July 15, 1895, JI 30:451)

I refer to the practice of preventing the birth of children. I want to lift my voice in solemn warning against this, and I say to you that the woman who practices such devilish arts, or the man who consents to them, will be cursed of God. Such persons will be cursed in their bodies, cursed in their minds, cursed in their property, cursed in their offspring. God will wipe them out from the midst of this people and nation. *Remember it.*

Mothers, teach this to your daughters, for I tell you it is true. I need not pronounce any curse, whatever my authority may be, but I say to you that women who take this course, and men who consent to it, will be cursed of God Almighty, and it will rest upon them until their generation shall be blotted out, and their name shall be lost from the midst of the Saints of God unless, as I have said, there is deep, thorough and heartfelt repentance. (October 7, 1894, DW 49:739)

ABORTION—AN UNFORGIVEABLE SIN. I say to you, my sisters, you teach your daughters against this accursed practice, or they will go to hell; they will be damned, they will be murderers, and the blood of innocence will be found upon them. A man that would sanction such a thing in his family, or that would live with a woman guilty of such acts, shares in the crime of murder. I would no more perform the ordinance of laying on of hands on a woman who is guilty of that crime, if I knew it, than I would put my hands on the head of a rattlesnake.

We must set our faces like flint against such acts. These dreadful practices are coming up like a tidal wave and washing against our walls. . . . Now just as sure as it is done, and people yield to it, so sure will they be damned, they will be damned with the deepest damnation; because it will be the damnation of shedding innocent blood, for which there is no forgiveness; and I would no more, as I say, administer to such women, baptize them, or perform any ordinance of the Gospel for them, than I would for a reptile. They are outside the pale of salvation. They are in a position that nothing can be done for them. They cut themselves off by such acts from all hopes of salvation. (November 20, 1884, JD 26:14-15)

GREAT POWER BESTOWED ON WOMAN. A great glory is bestowed on woman, for she is permitted to bring forth the souls of men. You have the opportunity of training children who shall bear the Holy Priesthood and go forth and magnify it in the midst of the earth. It is a glorious mission which God has assigned to His daughters, and they should be correspondingly proud of it, and should realize its importance and seek to be missionaries in their own families, training up their children in the fear of God.

It is an established fact . . . that scarcely any great men ever had a poor weak-minded mother. If you read of the great men of antiquity, or of modern times, you will find that in almost every instance they have had great mothers, who have moulded and fashioned the plastic minds of their sons according to their own notions of greatness and sent them forth to battle with the circumstances of life, like gods almost.

Great interests are in the hands of mothers. God has reposed in them great power; if they wield that power for good, it will be productive of peace and happiness and exaltation to them. They will be blessed in seeing the greatness of their posterity. Their hearts will be gratified in having a posterity who will rise up and call them blessed. (March 3, 1867, JD 11:338-39)

GOD PLEASED WITH WOMEN OF CHURCH. The women in this Church are worthy of all praise. They are more attentive to their meetings, more faithful in the observance of the duties that devolve upon them and have proved stauncher advocates of the truth and shown less treachery . . . than the men have. I know that God is exceedingly pleased with the women of this Church, for they have shown characteristics that are worthy of the angels in heaven. I know that God will bless the mothers and the daughters of Zion for their fidelity to the Gospel and for the devotion that they manifest. And the men of this Church might take lessons from the sisters in the way they attend to meetings and perform the other duties that devolve upon them. (June 20, 1882, DW 45:257)

THE INFLUENCE OF MOTHERS. I have noticed in my experience that where girls are indifferent about whom they marry, and with whom they associate, it is very frequently traceable to the influence of the mother. A mother may have a careless husband; she may have a man that is indifferent to the duties of his religion; but if she be a faithful woman herself and exercise proper control, and does have control over her children, she can bring up her children to be faithful men and women in the Church.

Go where you will and examine the households of the people, and you will find that the mother's influence is a very wonderful influence, not only upon the children but upon her husband, but particularly so with her children. She can teach her children to pray in early life, and she can instil into them feelings and desires that remain with them throughout their life. (January 1, 1897, DW 54:289-90)

Women can wield a most potent influence, and it would be folly to ignore the fact. With women to aid in the great cause of reform, what wonderful changes can be effected! Without her aid how slow the progress! Give her responsibility, and she will prove that she is capable of great things; but deprive her of opportunities, make a doll of her, leave her nothing to occupy her mind but the reading of novels, gossip, the fashions and all the frivolity of this frivolous age, and her influence is lost, and instead of being a helpmeet to man, as originally intended, she becomes a drag and an encumbrance. Such women may answer in other places and among other people, but they would be out of place here. . . .

NECESSITY OF GOOD COOKING. He who said that "cleanliness was next to godliness" might with truth have said that it was a part of godliness. Cleanliness among the Latter-day Saints should be universal, for no man or woman who are uncleanly in their persons and their houses can be Saints in the true sense of the word. And we firmly believe that a man who is habitually compelled to eat badly-cooked food, served up in slovenly style, cannot be so faithful a man, so pleasant a companion, so good tempered a husband as he would be if his victuals were properly cooked and served up tastefully. He is apt to become dyspeptic. Every woman in our community, whatever her station, should possess the art of making food wholesome, palatable and nutritious. She should be able to compete with the physician in cures, and surpass him in the prevention of disease. A good, well-cooked meal—not a glutonous feast—is a mighty civilizer; it brightens the faculties, helps the health and produces good temper. . . .

If women knew how much of human health and happiness depend on good digestion, they would never rest until they had acquired the art of rendering food tender, wholesome and easy of digestion. Young ladies who are in possession of this art are far more likely to secure and retain the respect and love of husbands, when they get them, than if they were fully conversant with the round of fashionable accomplishments, and yet incapable of serving up a good meal. Before marriage love answers very well as food, in some cases; but, after that happy event, something more substantial has to be provided—the heart has had its turn, and the stomach steps forward and asserts its claims, and it will not be disregarded. (June 19, 1869, MS 31:400)

THE FOUNDATION OF SOCIETY. The family organization is the foundation of all society, and the character of a community or nation will correspond with the general character of the families that compose it. It is amongst the latter that we must look for the germs of those virtues or vices that distinguish the former, and either exalt them in the scale of mental and moral worth, or sink them into degradation and contempt. It is from the home circle that must radiate those benign and purifying influences which are destined yet to effect a mighty revolution in the world, to reform, moralize and re-organize its inhabitants, and to banish from their midst every cause of crime and misery, when of course their effects will disappear also. . . .

TEACH CHILDREN THE GOSPEL. In the Gospel we have a scheme of education which is applicable to all classes of society and all grades of intellect, and is calculated, as we progress in the knowledge of its principles, to ensure a better and more perfect development of the faculties of our minds and the energies of our bodies and through which there is, or should be, even now, a universal and uniform course of instruction going on in the family of every Latter-day Saint, in whatever quarter of the world they may reside. The Lord has wisely made it obligatory upon every head of a family to instruct his children in the principles of the Gospel of Jesus so soon as they are capable of understanding them, and when the Government of God is established upon the earth, those who neglect so plain and natural a duty will, according to one of the established laws of that kingdom, "be had in remembrance before the judge of my people." [D&C 68:33.] . . .

We are not merely required to teach our families the truth, but to teach it in such a way as shall render it attractive instead of repulsive to them. . . . Now, the truth may be presented in such a way as to repel instead of attracting and to leave disagreeable instead of pleasing impressions; and as children are very susceptible to these feelings, and very quick to observe, they will of course prefer to associate with those who, though they have less truth, or even a great deal of error, are more agreeable; and as a natural consequence they imbibe the views and feelings, the prejudices and errors of those they associate with, and thus the influence and power we might have gained over their minds and used for their present and future good are lost forever. . . .

It is the bounden duty of every parent, and the pleasure of every one who is fit to be a parent, to present the truth in as attractive a garb as possible to his children. We should clothe it in the habiliments of beauty and cheerfulness, and as we shall of course be regarded by our children as the embodiment and exemplification of the effects of the principles we teach, we should be careful to let our own life be a practical illustration of the cheerful and happifying results of obedience to the truth. . . .

LOVE SHOULD PREVAIL IN HOMES. Home should be the center of attraction to young people. It is there that all the beautiful effects of the truth should be practically exemplified in the lives and actions of its possessors, and those sweet and cheering influences should be felt which radiate like a halo of glory and happiness around the family altar and the domestic hearth and make home the dearest and most cherished spot on earth. It is the duty of parents to make home attractive and the fireside cheerful; every cause of discord, contention and bitterness should, so far as possible, be banished from the hallowed precincts of the family circle, and love and kindness alone should predominate in their midst. Neither is this so difficult to accomplish as it may at first appear, for if the head of the household is governed by the principle of love and a desire to make others happy, the same spirit will be sooner or later diffused through every member of his family. No parent should ever play the part of a tyrant in his family and rule with harshness or correct in anger. If we cannot control ourselves, we cannot control our children and are consequently not fit to have any. Love is the only correct governing principle. (November 1, 1862, MS 24:696-98)

EXAMPLE OF PARENTS. Where parents set proper examples to their children, and with those examples join good precepts, the influence is felt throughout the lives of their children. There may be some who will forget or disregard that which is shown and taught them, but they will be the exceptions. As the children grow in years, they will think about the examples and precepts of their parents. Increasing years will add weight to all that they have said and done. (January 1, 1892, JI 27:28)

CHILDREN SHOULD RESPECT PARENTS. The Apostle Paul, in writing to Timothy, foretold many things concerning the last days. He said "perilous times shall come," and he predicted that men should be very selfish or, to use his own language, "lovers of their own selves" [2 Timothy 3:1-2]; they should be covetous, boasters, proud, blasphemers. He also said they should be disobedient to parents and without natural affection.

Certainly, his words have been and are being fulfilled. Disobedience to parents is one of the sins of the age. The want of natural affection is also a prominent feature of our times. Is it possible that the children of the Latter-day Saints partake of this spirit which the Apostle Paul, through the gift of prophecy, said should be seen in the last days?

Whatever other people may do, certainly Latter-day Saints should not be guilty of this wickedness. Their children should be taught to avoid disobedience and to cultivate natural affection. Parents should respect and love their children. Children should respect and love their parents.

How gratifying it is to affectionate parents to have their children manifest interest in their health and welfare! It is a beautiful feature in family life, when children and parents separate for the night, to have them shake hands and exchange the kiss of affection, and express one to the other their good wishes for their safety through the night; also, in the morning when they meet, to exchange salutations in like manner, and loving enquiries concerning the condition of their health. (December 1, 1891, JI 26:729-30)

OBEDIENCE TO PARENTS. To a person who understands the value of obedience it is painful to be where it is neglected, to hear a mother request a child to do or not to do a certain thing and see the child pay no regard to it, to hear a father request that certain things should be done and find that his request is entirely unheeded. Such carelessness is ruinous to the character of the child, and produces a most injurious effect upon it that will be felt throughout its future life.

Too much stress cannot be laid upon the importance of teaching children to obey. The parent should be exceedingly careful not to make an improper request of the child; but when the request is made it should be enforced, and the child should be taught that its will should be subject to the will of the parent, and that the parent's wish should not be contradicted nor departed from but be carried out exactly as stated. In this way the habit of obeying without question is formed; and it adds greatly to the happiness of both parents and children when this kind of obedience is established.

Children should be taught to take pleasure in submitting to and carrying out the wishes of their parents, and not to murmur when they are told to do anything, or to ask why someone else could not do it better than they. (January 15, 1893, JI 28:58-59.)

A loving, well-trained child takes delight in complying with the wishes of its parents. It is its highest pleasure to do that which they require. Such children obey their parents with alacrity. If they know their parents' wishes, they do not wait to have them told to them. Where such children dwell, there are no frowns; there are no expressions of a wish not to do as they are told. Such children are not heard making the reply to their mothers or to their fathers, "Why cannot someone else do this?" Neither are they heard saying, "I don't want to," in reply to a request that is made of them to do something. Such remarks are evidence of bad training, and every sensible boy and girl should be too ashamed to ever give utterance to such replies.

If children only knew the pains that their parents have taken with them, how they have cared for them in infancy and watched over them night and day, frequently exhausting themselves to render them assistance, their hearts would overflow with gratitude to their parents, and they would feel that they could not do them sufficient kindness to repay them for all that they had done for them in their childhood and youth. (August 15, 1888, JI 23:248)

CORRECT FAMILY GOVERNMENT. There is such a thing as governing too much. This is attended with as grave evils as laxity in governing. Too many exactions and too great severity of treatment lead to rebellion, and if they be continued, children, when they grow older, are apt to break away from proper restraints and pursue their own course, regardless of the wishes of their parents.

The best family government is that in which the judgment of the children is appealed to and they are shown, by kind words, that the requests made of them are for their benefit and happiness. Parental authority can be built up in this way in the minds of children to such an extent that disobedience would be one of the last things children would think of. There is this advantage which attends correct family government, the children grow up to be good members of society. They honor all lawful authority. As members of the Church they are obedient in their sphere, and there is no difficulty in controlling them. Young men who are properly brought up, when they are sent into the missionary field, become faithful, industrious, counsel-obeying Elders. They reverence the authority which God has given to His servants, and they have no difficuty in submitting to all proper requirements. As husbands they make the best of companions.

Girls brought up in this manner gladden the household of which they form a part. They make their husbands' lives happy ones, for they have been taught to restrain themselves and not carry out every whim or caprice that may suggest itself to their minds. They have been taught self-control, and this of itself is an important lesson. (July 15, 1891, JI 26:442)

OBEDIENCE TO PARENTAL AUTHORITY. While few individuals who have carefully noted the spirit of the press . . . can doubt that its teachings have had much to do in promoting the lawless and revolutionary tendencies of the people, the real source of such tendencies must be sought in a very different direction—namely, in the family circle, where every bias is given to the human mind, and where the germ of every evil as of every good principle is planted and developed. Disregard of law and authority under the parental roof leads inevitably to utter disregard and contempt for all law, authority and restraint; and when was there an age in the whole history of the world more notorious for this one thing, than the present? It is one of the crying sins of the age! Why, the fifth commandment is almost entirely disregarded.

It is decidedly unfashionable for children now-a-days, except of very tender years, to submit to parental restraint; and instead of being a blessing and an honor to parents, children too often are almost a life-long source of trouble and anxiety; and home, instead of being, as it ought to be, the very commencement and foundation of an eternal heaven, is, alas! in innumerable instances a scene of discord and turmoil, and an embryotic hell. This spirit and disposition influencing the home circle, affects communities in a corresponding ratio, and here is the real and only source and foundation of that spirit of lawlessness and defiance now so general.

Among the Latter-day Saints, whose aim and whose mission

is to restore true principle, and re-establish the order of heaven through all the ramifications of human affairs, respect for and obedience to all legitimate authority is the invariable rule. In their midst, and forming a part of their religious faith, the father is the Lord and head of his family, and implicit, unquestioning obedience to parental authority, when judiciously exercised, is strenuously insisted upon. We do not wish to be understood that this desirable consummation has been fully or nearly reached; but the foundation is laid. This is the end kept in view, and it will never be relinquished until obedience to parental authority even unto death, if necessary, as manifested of old by Abraham's son and Jephthah's daughter, will be willingly rendered.

This line of policy commenced in the family circle, as it most assuredly has been, its happifying influences will gradually unfold and develop themselves, until the whole community will eventually reap the inestimable blessings and benefits arising from its full consummation. Thus will the principles of true government be established, legitimate authority be unmurmuringly and implicitly obeyed, until peace and concord become the rule, and finally the dreams of Prophets and poets will be realized in universal peace on earth and good will to men. (April 25, 1868, MS 30:257-58)

A SAINT OF GOD. Is it a man's duty, or right, or privilege, to carry his cares into his family and disturb the peace and serenity existing there by relating his troubles? Certainly not. When his foot rests upon the threshold of his door, no matter what his difficulties or perplexities may be, he should enter with the spirit of peace in his heart and with the love of God burning within him. If there is irritability existing, his presence should be soothing to every member of his household, and particularly in talking with his children they should feel the influence of his presence; if there should be any improper feelings existing, they should be calmed. . . .

A Latter-day Saint! Think of the nature of the name. A Saint of God! Why, he should be next to an angel the most perfect of the human family. He should be perfect in his sphere, as God is perfect in His sphere. He should be free from fault. If he has a fault, he should seek daily and hourly to correct it and not rest satisfied as long as he is aware of the existence of a fault until he conquers it, pleading with the Father in the name of Jesus for strength to overcome his weakness, for power to put it away, carrying with him the spirit of love, the spirit of serenity, the spirit of peace, that when he appears in society, no matter where he may be, all who come in contact with him may feel his influence and feel purified and strengthened by his example and by his words and by his very presence. And this is what God designs we should be as Latter-day Saints. (July 27, 1879, JD 20: 290)

FEMALE CULTURE AND TRAINING. Too great care cannot be taken in educating our young ladies. Great responsibilities will devolve upon them. To their hands will be mainly committed the formation of the moral and intellectual character of the young. Let the women of our country be made intelligent, and their children will certainly be the same. The proper education of a man decides his welfare; but the interests of a whole family are secured by the correct education of a woman. It is a noticeable fact in the history of mankind that men who have attained to distinction among their fellow-men have been the sons of wise, judicious mothers. Their mothers' influence has, in the most instances, had more to do with the formation of their characters than their fathers'.

But to have a race of capable women, they must be healthy. . . . If the choice must be made between the mind and the body, and only one of these can receive the proper training, we would say, much as we would deplore the absence of mental cultivation, let it be the body. It would be better for posterity and the future of the world for the physical portion of woman's nature to receive the proper care than for the mind to be developed at the expense of everything else. . . .

Many of our families who now complain of a want of health and vigor could bring about a wonderful change in themselves and their feelings by changing their habits. Instead of remaining immured in their houses from one week's end to another, they should spend more time in the open air. They should exercise their bodies in outdoor exercises and employments—walking, riding, and gardening. The excuse now frequently made for not taking this course is the want of time. But if a certain amount of outdoor employment and exercise were to be viewed as of primary importance, and were to be strictly attended to, the in-door labors would suffer but little, if any, for the physical energy to perform them would be so much greater that they would be accomplished with pleasure. Regular exercise in the open air should be required by mothers of their daughters as a part of their daily duty.

Another point of great importance in the education of young ladies in our community is to impart to them a thorough, practical knowledge of all kinds of domestic employments. Mothers who have an idea that labor is degrading and unbecoming, and do not give their daughters a thorough training in household employments, are not true friends to their children. If they could see all the anxieties, vexations, and perplexities which their daughters would have to endure, after they become wives and mothers, in consequence for their lack of training, they would see their mistake. It may cost mothers more care to teach their daughters to be excellent cooks and thorough housewives; but the time and pains will be spent, and in days to come their daughters will bless them for such training. Every woman, however wealthy, should understand everything connected with the care of a house and family to be able to teach her help whenever necessary. By such a training poverty itself is deprived of many of its inconveniences. (June 13, 1868, MS 30:369-70)

TEACH CHILDREN HOW TO DO THINGS. It is a great deal easier, as many of us know by experience, to do a large proportion of household and other tasks than to teach children how to do them. Through ignorance, lack of judgment, want of skill, they waste time and material and tax our patience sadly. They always want to do the very best things they cannot do, and such tasks as are suited to their capacity they complain of as drudgery. Far too many parents, rather than assume the labor of teaching their boys and girls how to do the more difficult tasks of daily life, prefer to do the work themselves and keep the child at the same routine of petty choring. This is altogether bad policy for both parties. It discourages the child and effectually prevents the parent from reaping the full benefit of the child's capacity.

If the mother cannot have patience to teach her daughter how to make bread and cake, how to sew and how to manage the niceties of housekeeping, who will teach her? And what unkindness it is to let her grow up in practical ignorance of these things, and then suffer the bitter consequences of such ignorance when she goes to housekeeping on her own account. As a reward for drudgery faithfully done the growing girl should be allowed to attempt tasks even a little beyond her ability. . . .

The same is true of boys. Those boys who are taken into companionship and fellowship with their fathers and gradually initiated into ways of doing business, entrusted according to their capability with the management of important transactions and instructed how to achieve results, will almost certainly pass, with no unpleasant transition, from boyhood to manhood. (July 15, 1895, JI 30:433)

DON'T HIDE THINGS FROM PARENTS. Another thing, I wish to say to you, boys and girls, never do anything in secret that you would be ashamed of your parents knowing about. Never use language, say words or be guilty of actions you would be ashamed of your father or mother learning of. Always remember this. If any of you, boys or girls, ever feel inclined to do anything which you would not like your father to know of or your mother to see, avoid it, shun it, and never keep the company of those who would do such acts, for associating with such boys and girls would have an evil influence upon you; better quit their society than be guilty of things you would be ashamed to have known to your parents. There are a great many wrongs committed through boys and girls doing things in secret which they would be ashamed of their fathers or mothers knowing about. (August 2, 1873, JI 8:124)

THE COURTESIES OF HOME. The happiness of human life can be greatly increased by paying attention to those little courtesies which belong to our daily associations. It is an important lesson to teach children to observe these details so that the observance may become habitual to them. When the habit is once acquired, it is not easily forgotten. Children should be taught to be respectful and courteous to their parents, to pay them the honor that is due to them, to listen attentively to their instructions and requests and to always manifest a spirit of cheerful obedience. . . .

It is not only in the intercourse that children have with their parents that they should observe civility and courtesy, but it is in their association with their brothers and sisters and, in fact, with all with whom they are brought in contact. Boys should be taught to treat their sisters with as much kindness, respect and courtesy as they do girls who are not related to them; and girls should be taught to treat their brothers with as much affability and sweetness as they do boys who are not their kindred. . . .

There should be no shadow of displeasure or anger enter into the habitation of any family in Zion; if the parents dwell together in love and affection and exhibit that feeling in their daily association, the children will partake of that influence and will grow up under it, and it will always be in their minds the proper way to live. . . .

There can be no true happiness maintained in a household where these things are neglected. Men should be as much disposed to be attentive to and careful of their wives after marriage as they were when they were endeavoring to secure their love before marriage. Women should understand that to maintain the affection and devotion of their husbands after marriage they should take as much pains to please them and to make them have a good opinion of them as they did before they entered into covenant with each other. . . .

It should be made a constant rule in every household to enforce the observance of proper respect between parents and children, children and parents and brothers and sisters. Children thus brought up will find their pathway in life, all other things being equal, much smoother than if they should be left to neglect these things. They will be beloved wherever they go, and they will always have friends, because it is by such conduct that friendship is secured and preserved. (July 1, 1891, JI 26: 410-11)

QUALITIES THAT PROMOTE HAPPINESS. Men should never treat their wives with disrespect. They should manifest a feeling of love for them, and more especially when they become advanced in years. There is nothing that will excite love in a man's heart so much as to see a wife as willing, even in her advanced years, to sacrifice her own comfort to his sake as she was when they were first married; and I am sure it must have the same effect upon a woman—to have the husband, when her charms are fading and she is growing old, and perhaps not so attractive as she was—to have the husband tender and kind and loving, not forgetting her good qualities nor what she has done. When a woman sees a husband manifest that feeling towards her, she in return will manifest her kindness and love for his thoughtful attentions.

TREAT CHILDREN WITH RESPECT. These are little things, but how much they contribute to our happiness and to our peace. We should therefore cultivate these qualities ourselves and teach them to our children. Our children should be made to feel that we love them and that we are disposed to treat them with proper respect. When we ask a child to do a favor, we should ask it as though he were a gentleman, or if a girl, as though she were a lady. A man should never talk to his children as though he were a tyrant. He should address them in kindness and as though they were gentlemen and ladies, and they will grow up with that feeling and treat others with the same respect. . . .

Women should talk to their children in kindness, not harshly and not in a spirit of scolding. . . . A man or a woman who is always scolding loses influence with children and with everybody else. (June 20, 1883, JD 24:226)

Chapter 11

The Sabbath—The Lord's Day

THE LORD'S DAY. The reason why The Church of Jesus Christ of Latter-day Saints keeps Sunday as the day of rest and worship, instead of Saturday as observed by devout Jews and Seventh Day Adventists, is because the Saints have been commanded of God by revelation to keep "the Lord's Day" as the Sabbath. This law was given on Sunday, August 7, 1831, as follows:

> And that thou mayest more fully keep thyself unspotted from the world, thou shalt go to the house of prayer and offer up thy sacraments upon my holy day; for verily this is a day appointed unto you to rest from your labors, and to pay thy devotions to the Most High;
>
> Nevertheless thy vows shall be offered up in righteousness on all days and at all times; but remember that on this the Lord's Day, thou shalt offer thy oblations and thy sacraments unto the Most High, confessing thy sins unto thy brethren, and before the Lord. [D&C 59:9-12.]

"The Lord's Day" [Revelation 1:10] is the day on which He rose from the dead and on which His disciples at that period assembled to worship and break bread in His name. That was the "first day of the week" [John 20:1; Acts 20:7], as they counted time. This custom was observed in the primitive Christian Church, and the Seventh Day was also observed by the Jewish disciples for a time. But Paul and other leading Elders of the Church set themselves against the observance of the rites and rules of the Mosaic law and proclaimed the liberty of the Gospel, the law having been fulfilled in Christ. He chided those who were sticklers for special days as required by the law but himself observed the Lord's Day—the first day of the week.

It is the spirit of Sabbath observance that is acceptable to God rather than its letter. One day out of seven is to be a day of rest and worship. It would not matter which day of the week that was but for the sake of order and uniformity. So the Lord has designated for the Saints which day they should keep holy, and that is the "Lord's Day," commonly called "the first day of the week."

Respecting the seventh day and the first day of the week, it should be remembered that that which is the seventh day in one part of the earth may be the sixth day, or the first, in another part of the earth. (August 15, 1896, JI 31:481-82)

The children of Israel observed the seventh day as a day of rest—the day known to us as Saturday. But the Lord was crucified on Friday and arose from the dead on the first day of the week. It was therefore called "The Lord's Day." It seems that the day of Pentecost that year fell on the first day of the week, when the disciples "were all with one accord in one place." [Acts 2:1.]

In the Acts of the Apostles it is recorded that St. Paul and his companions arrived at Troas and "abode seven days. And upon the first day of the week, when the disciples came together to break bread, Paul preached unto them." [Acts 20:6-7.]

Paul himself also alludes to it:

> Now concerning the collection for the saints, as I have given order to the churches of Galatia, even so do ye. Upon the first day of the week let every one of you lay by him in store, as God hath prospered him, that there be no gatherings when I come. [1 Corinthians 16:1-2.]

The Apostle John describes himself as being in the spirit on the "Lord's Day." [Revelaton 1:10.]

It would seem from these allusions that the disciples, after the death of the Savior, made a practice of meeting together on the Lord's Day. This was not the Jewish Sabbath, neither was it recognized by law as a Sabbath until the time of Constantine. He prohibited judicial proceedings on the Lord's Day, and after that it was probably observed as a Sabbath in the place of Saturday, the old Jewish Sabbath, and grew into use as a day of rest and worship. We now observe it because it is sanctioned by law, and it seems to make but little, if any difference, whether we call it Saturday or Sunday. It happens that the day we observe is called Sunday. But the great point is to observe one day in seven and have it kept as a day of worship, a day of rest, a day when worldly thoughts and business shall be banished from our minds and from our habitations. It is in this spirit that Latter-day Saints should observe this day. (May 1, 1892, JI 27:286-87)

OBSERVANCE OF THE SABBATH. If there was in every breast a strong desire and determination to keep the Sabbath Day holy, other times could be found sufficiently ample to gratify the taste for amusements. . . . If the lives of those who keep the Sabbath Day holy be observed, it will be found that they have quite as much enjoyment, and certainly a greater feeling of satisfaction, than those do who break the Sabbath day to gratify their inclinations for amusement or other enjoyment, for those who keep the Sabbath day holy have an approval of conscience that gives them greater pleasure, because they are doing that which the Lord has commanded.

There should be a feeling of reverence for the Lord's Day taught to our children and cultivated in all their minds. The force of such teaching and cultivation has a strong effect upon all men and women. Boys and girls who have been taught in their childhood to keep holy the Sabbath Day grow up with that feeling so strong that it is painful to them to be compelled, as sometimes all of us are, to do anything that can be construed into a violation of that day.

There have been times in the history of our people when work had to be done on the Sabbath Day. We refer to times in crossing the plains and on other occasions when it seemed absolutely necessary to travel or move from one camp to another or from one place where grass and water were scarce or very poor to a better camping place. It is true, as we have been taught by the Lord, that man was not made for the Sabbath but the Sabbath for man. At the same time it is our duty to observe the Sabbath and refrain from all kinds of work and amusements that would be considered a desecration of the day. It should be made a day of worship and a day of rest.

Children who are brought up in this way, and in whom this feeling is instilled, will not willingly break the Sabbath; they will not go skating nor swimming nor fishing nor hunting nor pleasure seeking; but they will use the day in the manner in which the Lord has commanded.

It is a great mistake to suppose that the man who goes off riding on Sunday obtains more rest than the man who goes to meeting. There is a refreshing influence connected with the Spirit of the Lord that brings health and strength and ease to those who receive it, and time spent in meeting, listening to the word of God and partaking of the sacrament is well spent, and both body and spirit are refreshed. Men and women who thus observe the Sabbath day are prepared on Monday morning, with invigorated bodies, enlightened and comforted minds, to enter upon the serious labors of the week and to perform them with ease and pleasure. While in meeting and under the influence of the Spirit of the Lord troubles and perplexities are cast away, burdens are lifted, anxieties are removed and peace and joy fill the soul.

We know whereof we speak when we thus write, and we sincerely trust that all . . . will do everything in their power to impress upon the children . . . the great importance of observing the Sabbath day. This observance lies at the foundation of all true character. Children who observe the Sabbath day grow to be men and women who observe the Sabbath day. (February 1, 1891, JI 26:86-87)

SABBATH BREAKERS TO LOSE SPIRIT. Children should not be permitted to attend public gatherings without older persons accompanying to guard them from accident and from the contamination of the ungodly. The responsibility for the evils attending violations of these instructions will rest upon parents, guardians and the local Priesthood in the various wards and settlements.

Persons who habitually desecrate the Lord's day cannot be held in fellowship, and members of the Church who neglect public worship and the partaking of the Sacrament and do not remember the Sabbath day to keep it holy will become weak in the faith and spiritually sickly and will lose the Spirit and favor of God and ultimately forfeit their standing in the Church and their exaltation with the obedient and faithful. (April 8, 1887, MS 49:298)

RECREATION AND THE SABBATH. Among the sins into which some who are called Saints have been betrayed is Sabbath-breaking and over indulgence in useless pleasure. "The Sabbath was made for man, and not man for the Sabbath." [Mark 2:27.] But it is The Lord's Day and should be spent as He directs. We are not left to the doubts and queries which enter into the polemics of sectaries on this important matter. We have the word of the Lord upon it, direct. . . . [See D&C 68:29; 59:9-13.]

These commandments of the Lord do not admit of Sunday excursions to the lake or the canyons or other places any more than manual labor. That day will be held sacred to the service and worship of God by every true Latter-day Saint. Those who desecrate it reject the word of the Lord and will not be held guiltless. We admonish all members of the Church to obey this commandment and the officers of the Church to see that it is not broken with impunity.

The mania for recreations of various kinds which has seized upon many of the people is harmful in several ways. It unfits them for the regular duties of life. It renders them restless and impatient of proper restraint. It obstructs business. It tends to contract habits of dissipation. It throws our young folks into the company of persons whose society should be shunned. It cultivates worldliness. It conduces to many evils, and the spirit of purity, temperance, holiness and peace will not abide in resorts such as have been established for the purpose of enticing the Saints into folly. . . .

We have no disposition to deprive either young or old of proper amusement. It is necessary to perfect health and rational enjoyment. It should be provided by those who have the watchcare of the people, especially for the young, and conducted without sinfulness and without excess. (October 6, 1886, MS 48:714-15)

LIGHT-MINDEDNESS TO BE AVOIDED. The Sabbath is ordained as a day of rest and a day on which the Saints should specially devote their attention and turn their thoughts to spiritual matters. It is expected that the Saints will refrain from seeking amusement, as well as to avoid work at this time, and it is not right for young people to spend their time in games of any kind on the Lord's Day, though meeting together and engaging in elevating, interesting and instructive conversation is not at all improper.

The Saints should not put on a sanctimonious air and long face, which at one time were thought to be necessary to the proper worship of God, nor should they be more anxious on the Sabbath to serve God than they are upon any other day. But there is an appropriateness of conduct and of action which all Latter-day Saints should adopt on Sunday which will cause them to refrain from light-mindedness and folly and prompt them to make it indeed a day of worship and of rest. (February 1, 1894, JI 29:79)

SABBATH DAY LABOR UNPROFITABLE. A man deceives himself when he thinks that by working on Sunday he advances his labor or his interests. So also with those who take that day for excursions and pleasure hunting. A man who strictly confines his labors to six days, and will not work himself, nor suffer his animals to work on Sunday, will perform more labor during the year and be prospered to a far greater extent than the man who is careless upon this point.

So also with those who seek pleasure; they lose by using the Sabbath for that purpose. If they would select some other day, they would find themselves better off at the end of the year than they would be in using Sunday for this purpose. It should be an inflexible rule with every man, woman and child in the Church to hold Sunday sacred for the worship of the Lord and never to perform any labor on that day if it can possibly be avoided. (September 2, 1871, JI 6:140)

ATTENDANCE AT MEETINGS RESTFUL. I have always felt (as soon as I reached an age to reflect upon this subject) that our spiritual natures require as much care as our physical natures need nourishment. I believe that we can starve our spirits, impoverish them and dwarf ourselves by so doing.

I have found in my own experience—although I have labored a good deal mentally—that by attending meetings regularly on the Sabbath Day it has been a day of rest to me; yet many persons might be disposed to excuse themselves by saying that their brains were tired and going to meeting on Sunday only added to the weariness. I know by experience we can rest by attending meetings and partaking of the Spirit which generally prevails and which should always prevail in our meetings. (September 2, 1889, DW 39:461)

BENEFICIAL RESULTS OF CONFERENCES. It is very interesting to us to meet together as we do from time to time, according to the appointments which are made, to have brought to our attention our condition and circumstances as a people. Even if we hear the same truths told that we are familiar with, when they are told under the influence of the Spirit of God, there is a freshness, a sweetness and a novelty, I may say, about them that makes them interesting to us, and we feel refreshed and strengthened in our spirit by listening to them and contemplating them in the Spirit of God. That is one peculiarity which the Gospel possesses; when men and women live as they should do, it is always sweet and attractive to them and does not become worn and threadbare or wearisome.

When we come together in conferences like these, if we come in the right spirit and with the right feeling, we are sure to receive the instruction that is adapted to our circumstances, and when we leave the conference, we feel that we have been profited and that our hearts have been made to rejoice in the truths that have been dwelt upon by the brethren who have spoken. (January 18, 1885, DNW 34:50)

THE OBJECT OF SUNDAY SCHOOLS. Our Sunday Schools are for the purpose of teaching our children the principles of the Gospel. . . . We want to make Latter-day Saints of our children. If I send a child to Sunday School, I want the child taught the Gospel. He can read and learn history and a great many other things outside of the Sunday School that ought not to be taught in the Sunday School. In the Sunday Schools we should confine our labors to the object for which they have been established. . . .

We want to teach the children the simple principles of the Gospel. Care should be taken by the superintendency to see that this is done and that the time of the Sunday School is not occupied in teaching subjects, the knowledge of which can be obtained outside of the Sunday School. I wish this could be impressed upon the minds of our superintendents and teachers. The Sunday School is a school, as I have said, and as you all ought and do understand, for the purpose of giving our children instructions in the principles of the Gospel, to indoctrinate them in its principles, and, if we give them any history at all, it should be the history of our Church and the dealings of God with His people—that is, from a sacred standpoint, a religious standpoint.

Of course, information concerning the history of peoples can be given, or brought to bear occasionally, illustrating God's dealings with mankind to prepare the way for the carrying out of His work. This is proper, but it is not proper to go into extended lessons upon secular history. (October 6, 1897, JI 32:749)

TEACHERS TO SET EXAMPLE. Our brethren and sisters should always remember that the work of teaching in our Sunday Schools imposes upon them a moral obligation to make their daily walk and conversation accord with their teachings. Of all lessons, the living lesson is the best. Children are surprisingly shrewd in detecting inconsistencies between the instructions and habits of their instructors. Besides, the teacher who seeks to live up to his own advice not only benefits his scholars, but his teachings exert a salutary influence upon himself, and he profits by his own lessons. (April 8, 1887, MS 49:299)

Chapter 12

The Sacrament of the Lord's Supper

THE SACRAMENT—A SACRED ORDINANCE. We partake of the sacrament for one most important reason, that we may always remember that sacred body that was offered up for our salvation, by which the ransom was paid and we were brought into communion with the Father and made heirs of salvation and joint heirs with Him who made the sacrifice. To rob the ordinance of any of its significance by omitting any of its parts is not pleasing to the Lord, for to do so obviously weakens the intent for which it was established as an ordinance of the everlasting Gospel. So effectually and permanently does the Lord wish to impress the remembrance of that great sacrifice at Calvary on our memories that He permits us all to partake of the emblems—the bread and wine. . . . So that we may all remember Him, all who are members of the Church are permitted to partake as are also the unbaptized children who have not reached the years of full accountability. . . . (November 15, 1899, JI 34:704-705)

THE SOLEMN NATURE OF THE SACRAMENT. It is very important that our children should be made to understand the importance and solemn nature of the sacrament. It is administered with some regularity in our Sunday Schools; but the mere eating and drinking by the children would be of little or no benefit to them if they did not understand why they eat the bread and drink of the cup. Great care should, therefore, be taken to teach them the object of the sacrament.

The Lord has commanded His people to meet together oft and eat and drink in remembrance of Him, of His sufferings and death, and to witness unto the Father that they are willing to keep His commandments which He has given them, that they may always have His Spirit to be with them. This is the purpose of the sacrament, and that these things might be kept constantly in mind, the Lord's people are required to partake of the sacrament often.

EFFECT OF NEGLECTING SACRAMENT MEETINGS. Yet, there are members of the Church who seem to attach no particular importance to these meetings. They will allow weeks, yes and months, to pass without having the least anxiety or desire to avail themselves of the privilege of partaking of the Lord's Supper. Can there be any wonder at such people being barren, spiritless and indifferent about the work of the Lord? They neglect the means which the Lord has provided for the nourishing of their spiritual natures, and they are in a state of spiritual starvation—a starvation which is as fatal in its effects upon the spirit as the continued refusal to eat food has upon the natural body.

No Latter-day Saint who places proper value upon his standing before the Lord will be guilty of this neglect. Circumstances may, at times, prevent him from joining with his brethren and sisters in eating and drinking in the way appointed in remembrance of the Lord; but this will always be a cause of regret to him, and he will hasten at the first opportunity to the meeting where he can share with the Saints in the sacrament. (February 1, 1893, JI 28:89)

FORGIVENESS OF SINS AND THE SACRAMENT. The ordinance of baptism is instituted for the remission of sins. The sacrament of the Lord's Supper was not instituted for that purpose. Yet, when people partake of that sacrament worthily, they no doubt obtain the forgiveness of their sins on the same principle that we obtain the forgiveness of our sins whenever we confess them and repent of them. . . .

On the Sabbath Day we assemble together to partake of the Lord's Supper. We are commanded not to partake of that ordinance unworthily; that is, we should eat and drink with a spirit of penitence in our hearts in remembrance of the Lord and witness unto Him that we are willing to take upon us the name of the Son and keep His commandments. If we have sinned publicly, we should, before we partake of that ordinance, confess publicly and obtain the forgiveness of the Church, as well as the forgiveness of the Lord. If our wrong-doing be against the Lord alone, then we should humble ourselves before Him in secret and confess to Him, and all this before we partake of the sacrament. Can there be a doubt in anyone's mind that, under those circumstances, if the sacrament be partaken of in the right spirit, the Saints do obtain the forgiveness of their sins? Certainly they do. . . . [See James 5:14-15.]

There is a case recorded by Matthew where the Lord Jesus, seeing the faith of the people who brought to Him a man sick of the palsy, said to the man, who we have no reason to believe was a member of the Church of Christ: "Son, be of good cheer; thy sins be forgiven thee." [Matthew 9:2.]

But does it follow, because of . . . this act of our Savior's, that we should set forth that our sins will be forgiven by having hands laid upon us by the Elders when we are sick?

However true it may be that sins are forgiven under such circumstances, it is not for the forgiveness of sins that that ordinance was instituted. It was for the healing of the sick. So also with the Lord's Supper. Even if penitent Latter-day Saints are forgiven their faults when they partake worthily of the sacrament, they do not eat and drink for that purpose, but in remembrance of the Lord and of His blood that was shed for our salvation that they may have His Spirit to be with them.

The ordinance of baptism is for the purpose of obtaining a remission of sins. If a means of obtaining forgiveness of sin be held up to our children, the ordinance of baptism is the proper means, and to teach anything else is liable to mislead. (July 15, 1890, JI 25:442-43)

ONLY WORTHY ONES TO PARTAKE OF SACRAMENT. Before we come here to partake of this bread and to drink of this cup, we should know that there is nothing in our hearts or conduct that will prevent us from eating and drinking without condemnation and without sin attaching to the act. If we are not in this condition, then we are not as we should be.

It is the imperative duty of the officers of this Church, if they know that there is a man or a woman whose life is not what it should be, to forbid that person from eating of this bread or drinking of this cup, that they may not do it unworthily. If they do not take this course with their brethren and sisters who are in transgression, or who are not living as they should, the sins of such individuals are likely to attach to them. . . . [3 Nephi 18:28.]

Our lives should be such that when we go away from this place, after partaking of this holy ordinance, we may be filled with the Spirit, refreshed, feeling that our souls are filled with the bread of life and that our spiritual strength is renewed. (May 26, 1889, DW 38:710)

NON-TITHE PAYERS UNWORTHY TO PARTAKE OF SACRAMENT. Reflect upon this, ye Saints; if you are not willing to pay your tithing, to gather with the people of God, to receive and obey every principle and ordinance which He has instituted, you are not willing to keep His commandments, and, therefore, you can not partake of the sacrament; you are unworthy of it, as in partaking of that ordinance you witness unto God, the Eternal Father, that you are willing to always remember Jesus and keep His commandments which He has given you. No Elder would be justified in administering it unto you under such circumstances. And if you cannot partake of the sacrament, whose are ye? Ye cannot be Christ's, neither will you be His at His appearing upon the earth. (March 27, 1857, WS 377)

IMPORTANCE OF THE SACRAMENT. There are various causes for the loss of the Spirit and decrease of faith among the Saints—adultery, lust, murmuring against the Priesthood, neglect of prayer and other duties, etc.; but there is, perhaps, no single cause more frequently productive of these evil consequences than the partaking of the sacrament by the Saints while in possession of a wrong spirit and feeling. To commit adultery, every one who has had any experience or understanding of the work of God knows, will inevitably result, unless speedily and sincerely repented of, in the apostasy of the adulterer. So also in the commission of other sins, though the denial of the faith by the one thus sinning might not follow the sinful act so quickly as in the other instance.

But the partaking of the Lord's Supper appears almost to be so unimportant in the estimation of some (probably through partaking of it often) that they think it a matter of no consequence whatever, whether they are at that time filled with love to God and their brethren, or whether they are filled with enmity—whether they eat and drink in remembrance of the Lord Jesus, or whether His death and sufferings are never thought about by them. The eating of a piece of bread, or the drinking of a little wine, or its substitute, under ordinary circumstances, might not be expected to excite any particular emotions in those thus partaking; but it is nothing less than solemn mockery for men and women, professed followers of the Lord Jesus, to assemble together and unite in a prayer to have the bread and the contents of the cup blessed and sanctified to their souls, and then eat and drink with feelings of enmity in their bosoms to some one or more individuals of the same faith and hope with themselves and in total forgetfulness of their Lord and His precepts.

PARTAKING UNWORTHILY MAY CAUSE SICKNESS. No individual, whether officer or member, can pursue a course of this kind and escape condemnation. Such was also Paul's faith in ancient days; for he wrote to the Corinthian Branch of the Church that in consequences of their partaking of the Lord's Supper unworthily many were weak and sickly among them and many had slept. [1 Cortinthians 11:26-30.]

The Lord Jesus himself attaches so much importance to the sacrament that He has commanded His servants not to knowingly suffer any one to partake of His flesh and blood unworthily when they shall minister it. They are required to forbid such, because they who eat His flesh and blood unworthily eat and drink damnation to their souls. [3 Nephi 18:28-29; D&C 46:4.]

A SAFEGUARD AGAINST APOSTASY. This places the Elders under solemn obligations to see that iniquity does not exist among the Saints, for iniquity of any kind would render whoever practiced it unworthy of this ordinance. If there are feelings of enmity in the bosom of one against another—if there is evil speaking one of another, those harbouring such feelings, those giving utterance to such sentiments, cannot partake of the Lord's Supper without incurring His displeasure. Entertaining such a spirit and such feelings causes them to be unworthy, and they have need of repentance. Those who eat the flesh and drink the blood of the Lord should always remember Him and should be filled with perfect love for Him and for their brethren, and upon no other principle can they expect to have His Spirit to be with them. We feel satisfied that there is a feeling of apathy and carelessness upon this subject which should not exist among the Saints. . . .

To partake of the sacrament often and in a proper spirit is a very great safeguard against apostasy, because the Saints who will do thus will always remember the Lord and, as a consequence, according to His promise, shall have His Spirit to be with them. But to partake of it unworthily involves terrible consequences. No Elder can do his duty and permit persons who he knows are not feeling and doing right to partake of this ordinance. (February 23, 1861, MS 23:120-22)

FOLLOW REVEALED ORDER. It is a safe rule for us to follow in all things that which the Lord has revealed for our guidance; and where He has condescended to reveal any set form of prayer or order of procedure, those words should be used and that order should be followed with due strictness. We cannot improve on the ways of the Lord. The world has been trying to do so ever since Adam fell, and signal failure has characterized all their attempts. We, the Latter-day Saints, should not fall into the same quagmire. The ways of the Lord are perfect, and all His laws are righteousness.

On the other hand, the Lord will not make a man an offender for a word. If we through a slip of the tongue, or a sudden lapse of memory, fail to follow word for word the form given, that will not invalidate the ordinance or make the prayer of non-effect. In all these things the Spirit has to be considered, and the question that should be answered in our hearts is, "Are we doing this (whatever it may be) with an eye single to the glory of God?" If we are administering the sacrament, we may ask ourselves, "Are our hearts aright before God and are we officiating in this holy rite fully realizing and conscious of the importance of that supreme sacrifice which we commemorate and with the desire to keep in active remembrance the infinite benefits it has brought to us and to all mankind?"

When we have this spirit, we shall not be negligent in minor matters connected with the observance of the ordinance. Then, anything savoring of uncleanliness or disorder will be repugnant to our feelings, and we shall approach the table of the Lord with reverence, respect and love.

DEVIATIONS SOMETIMES PERMITTED. There are times and places where the Lord permits, on account of the condition and surroundings of His people, a slight deviation from established customs. For instance, on some of the small islands of the South Pacific Ocean there is no bread, and all the water is salt, and the fruit of the coconut tree is the chief food of man. If the members of the Church waited to solemnize the ordinance as their brethren do in more favored lands, the native Saints would seldom, if ever, partake of the sacrament. But in these strange conditions the Lord accepts instead of bread and wine, or bread and water, the meat of the coconut as the emblem of the body and its milk as the emblem of the blood of our crucified Lord. This is the best the people there can do; therefore, it is accepted of God; but, if we, with our advantages, inspired by some whim or fanciful notion, were to make such changes, we should expose ourselves to the displeasure of the Lord, because we could present no justification for such a change.

Any wilful departure from that which the Lord has commanded is dangerous in the extreme. It is by such departures the Church of Christ has in past times left the true path; little by little they went astray. The Lord accepts water as the sacrament instead of wine; when there is no bread, He accepts that which is used in its stead; but the ordinances of God's house cannot be deviated from. (August 15, 1897, JI 32:530)

OBSERVE THE FORM AS REVEALED. Where the Lord has condescended to give us a form of words or a manner of procedure in the performance of any ordinance in His Church, we should esteem it a pleasure and a duty to observe strictly what the Lord has revealed and neither add to nor diminish from His expressed wishes and commands. Where no exact formula is given of Him, we are safest in following the usual practice of the Saints, sanctioned by the presence or teachings of "those who hold the keys." Then, for the rest, let the Holy Spirit guide us to the details and the exact language to be used. If we are living our religion as faithfully as we should be, there is little fear of our going far astray while we thus officiate as His servants. (November 15, 1899, JI 34:705)

THE SACRAMENTAL BREAD. The officiating Elders or Priests should endeavor not to break much more bread than is needed; in other words, they should adapt the amount broken to the number present to whom it is to be administered. If any remains over it should be returned to the care of the brother who provides the bread for the ordinance, and he should be admonished to see that it is not used for improper purposes. . . .

We learn from the writings of the early Christian fathers that it was the custom in the ancient Church in the days of the Apostles and their immediate successors for the Deacons, after the sacrament meeting was closed, to carry the bread to the homes of those Saints who from sickness or other justifiable causes were prevented from being present at the assembly of the Saints. Those thus kindly remembered partook of the bread with gladness. We have known this to be done in these days and believe such action, whether by the Deacons or others, to be justifiable and praiseworthy, but in the organized wards of the Church, it should be done with the knowledge and consent of the Bishop.

The Lord has not commanded that the emblems of His infinite sacrifice should only be partaken of at a public meeting or on a certain day. . . . Neither the revelations of the Lord nor the practice of the Saints justifies such a conclusion. We have had the pleasure of partaking of this ordinance in the House of the Lord on other days than Sunday when the proceeding was sanctioned by the presence and participation of all the General Authorities of the Church, and was under the immediate direction of our Prophet, Seer and Revelator, God's earthly mouthpiece, both him who now lives and those who have gone before. (November 15, 1889, JI 34:704)

THE LAST SUPPER. At the Last Supper, at which the Savior Himself was present, the bread and the wine were not passed as is the custom now among us. It was an actual supper. In our Church numerous instances have occurred where the Sacrament has been administered, in certain places, in the same way—that is, bread and wine (or water) have been partaken of as a meal and not, as is usual when the Sacrament is passed in our general meetings, in the shape of small pieces of bread and a little sip of water.

The Savior, as recorded in the Book of Mormon, after breaking the bread, "gave unto the disciples and commanded that they should eat. And when they had eaten and were filled, he commanded that they should give unto the multitude." [3 Nephi 18:3-4.] Afterwards "he commanded his disciples that they should take of the wine of the cup and drink of it, and that they should also give unto the multitude that they might drink of it and were filled; and they gave unto the multitude, and they did drink, and they were filled." [3 Nephi 18:8-9.]

It seems from this that in partaking of this ordinance they satisfied their appetites—that is, they ate and drank until they were filled.

This would be the proper manner to administer this ordinance now if circumstances permitted; but situated as the Church is, it is not convenient to administer the Sacrament in this manner, and, therefore, our present mode is the one that is sanctioned by usage and by permission of the Lord through His inspired servants. (January 15, 1897, JI 32:52-53)

Chapter 13

Fasting and Fast Days

THE FAST DAY AND FASTING. Probably the most explicit definition of fasting as acceptable to the Lord is given in the fifty-eighth chapter of Isaiah, where the Prophet, reproving hypocrisy and comparing a counterfeit with a righteously-observed fast, says:

> Behold, ye fast for strife and debate, and to smite with the fist of wickedness: ye shall not fast as ye do this day, to make your voice to be heard on high.
>
> Is it such a fast that I have chosen? a day for a man to afflict his soul? Is it to bow down his head as a bulrush, and to spread sackcloth and ashes under him? wilt thou call this a fast, and an acceptable day to the Lord?
>
> Is not this the fast that I have chosen? to loose the bands of wickedness, to undo the heavy burdens, and to let the oppressed go free, and that ye break every yoke?
>
> Is it not to deal thy bread to the hungry, and that thou bring the poor that are cast out to thy house? when thou seest the naked that thou cover him; and that thou hide not thyself from thine own flesh? [Isaiah 58:4-7.]

We see that in the sight of the Lord the ostentatious display of humility, such as would be indicated in the wearing of sackcloth and the strewing of ashes about the body, does not of itself constitute an acceptable fast. Something more than the outward show is needed. It is not enough to bow the head in seeming humility while within there is strife and hard-heartedness. We may not understand that even the going without food or the giving of alms to the poor is of itself a passport to divine favor. The idea is that with the outward sign of humility there shall also be the contrition of heart, the charity, the love of fellowman that produce in the worshiper a desire to see and correct his own shortcomings and to strengthen and build up himself as well as his fellowman in faith and excellence. True fasting causes one to put away worldly-mindedness, to feel his weakness as compared with God's might, to draw near to Him in earnest supplication. The humiliation of the flesh leaves the spirit less trammeled in its appeals to heaven. And every one who has tried its efficacy in time of sorrow and distress will acknowledge the spiritual support that has followed. . . .

It would not seem that fasting can be construed under any circumstances to mean feasting. It is true that in the book of

Doctrine and Covenants the Lord, speaking of the Sabbath and commanding that the food for the day shall "be prepared with singleness of heart," adds, "that thy fasting may be perfect, or, in other words, that thy joy be full. Verily, this is fasting and prayer, or in other words, rejoicing and prayer." [D&C 59:13-14.] But rejoicing in the outpouring of the spirit and feasting upon spiritual things does not imply worldly merry-making. . . . Humility, contrition, charity—these things constitute rejoicing far beyond anything that the festal board can yield.

FAST DAY INSTITUTED BY BRIGHAM YOUNG. The observance of a fast day, when donations for the support of the poor are to be given to the Bishop for distribution, was instituted at an early day in these valleys by President Young. It was in a time of scarcity, when no one had any too much, and some did not have enough. He gave instructions that a general fast should be regularly observed throughout Israel and that the food which would have been eaten, or its equivalent, should be given to the poor. The occasion became a time of spiritual refreshing, when in their assemblages the Saints were moved to the exhibition of sincere brotherly love and to the expression of strong testimonies of the truth of the Gospel, accompanied in many instances with powerful manifestations of the spirit and the giving of precious experiences and instructions.

It also came to be a custom that children should be blessed at these meetings, where a record of births could be kept in the Ward books. And by a natural process, where faith, charity and humility were so strongly manifested, fast day prayers for and administration to the sick came to be a feature of the exercises. All this is in accord with the old definition of a fast—a time for denying the carnal appetite and building up and satisfying the spiritual nature, not with a woe-begone face and hypocritical prayers but with a cheerful countenance and true, heartfelt devotion.

It is to be regretted that in some quarters there is a disposition to belittle and ignore the fast day. We consider it one of the most important of our Church services and cannot too strongly urge the benefits and blessings that follow its correct observance. (April 15, 1892, JI 27:248-49)

ORIGIN OF FAST AND TESTIMONY MEETINGS. It has always been a custom in the Church of Jesus Christ to meet together for fasting and prayer and, no doubt, bearing testimony also. . . .

It is recorded that the baptized believers on the day of Pentecost "continued stedfastly in the apostles' doctrine and fellowship, and in breaking of bread, and in prayers." [Acts 2:42.]

An account of the labors of Paul and Barnabas among some of the branches of the Church reads as follows:

> And when they had ordained them elders in every church, and had prayed with fasting, they commended them to the Lord, on whom they believed. [Acts 14:23.]

Moroni says:

> And the Church did meet together oft, to fast and to pray, and to speak one with another concerning the welfare of their souls. [Moroni 6:5.]

It is evident from these records and from Moroni's that the same practice prevailed in the Church of Jesus Christ in those days that now prevails among the Latter-day Saints. The members of the Church met together in their local meetings as we do now in our Wards, and they met fasting and for the purpose of praying and bearing testimony one to another concerning their faith.

And wherever there is a Church of Christ organized, this has been, and is, and will be the practice among them. (June 15, 1898, JI 33:438)

WORKING WHILE FASTING. If the ordinance of fasting always required the abstaining from all work, many would be unable to take part in it. Besides the usual fast day, which occurs on the first Sunday of the month, and which for that reason can be accompanied by the laying aside of labor, many persons have the habit of fasting regularly once a week or oftener. Such persons omit in no respect their customary labors—they cannot do so. In like manner a special fast for the sick, or for any other purpose, can be observed.

It would be no doubt desirable for such as were able to do so to meet together and unite their prayers for the object desired. But those who cannot do this can still fast with as much sincerity and faith while performing their usual labors as if the other course were followed. Their prayers, even, can be offered while pursuing the every-day duties of life whether in office, workshop or field, with as much earnestness and faith as in the meeting-house or the closet.

AN AFFAIR OF THE HEART. Fasting is intended to be an affair of the heart rather than an outward manifestation, just as secret prayer is recommended by the Master in preference to the display of the Pharisees. One who fasts need not by a long face, or by a pained expression of countenance, or making a virtue of abstaining from his customary work, give public notice in this manner of his observance of the fast. The main thing is to bring the heart and being into a condition receptive to the influences of the good Spirit and to approach in prayer the throne of the Father with a soul filled with praise, humility and faith.

Whether one works with his hands or lays aside all his labor while observing the fast has far less to do with its efficacy than the lowliness of the spirit and the purity of motive which should accompany it. And there is no reason why a person cannot enjoy these latter while engaged in his necessary labors on a week day just as well as and have his offering received with even greater favor than if he tried to make too much of a display of it. (August 15, 1900, JI 35:535)

ABSTINENCE FROM WATER IN FASTING. There is nothing in the shape of a commandment upon this point, but to be a proper and perfect fast it is quite necessary that water should not be used any more than food. . . .

A notable illustration of this kind of fasting is found recorded in the 3rd chapter of Jonah. After Jonah had proclaimed to the people of Nineveh the word that the Lord gave him, to the effect that He would destroy Nineveh unless the inhabitants thereof repented, the people believed God, and a fast was proclaimed. The king himself and the nobles humbled themselves before the Lord, and the decree they published was:

> Let neither man nor beast, herd nor flock, taste anything: let them not feed, nor drink water: but let man and beast be covered with sackcloth, and cry mightily unto God: yea, let them turn every one from his evil way and

from the violence that is in their hands. Who can tell if God will turn and repent, and turn away fom his fierce anger, that we perish not? [Jonah 3:7-9.]

It will be seen that the animals as well as the people refrained from drinking water. This was a fast which the Lord accepted, and Nineveh was spared. (April 1, 1891, JI 26:218)

WORD OF LORD CONFIRMED. Again, we see it stated in a medical journal that the free use of cold water as a beverage is an excellent remedy for many ailments. The experience of the Latter-day Saints who have observed the counsel of the Lord has proved to them that it is the best of all beverages, when it is pure. There are many places, however, where the water is of so impure a character that it ought to be boiled before drinking. . . . We have no doubt that the health of the children, and grown people, too, would be greatly promoted if greater pains were taken to secure pure water for drinking purposes.

Another remedy for acute diseases has been brought to our attention. We see it stated in a medical journal that an eminent physician has proved in his practice that fasting is an excellent thing for patients who have acute infections. By fasting, he says, the alimentary canal is cleansed, so that germs do not acquire virulence and produce serious complications. His extensive experiments establish the fact that animals, and also men and women, who are kept fasting recover far more rapidly from acute infections than others in the same condition who are fed as usual, or even much less than usual. He has won for himself the name of "the starving doctor," because he forbids all food to his patients in acute infections, especially in pneumonia if there is any reason to suppose that the digestion is not in good order.

Observations of 140 cases of pneumonia are said to have confirmed the wisdom of this course. In every case it was noted that during the prolonged fast the patient partially regained the strength he seemed to have entirely lost before. Latter-day Saints are recommended to fast and pray; and no doubt there is true philosophy in this command. The Lord, who created us, does not require us to do anything that would be injurious to us. It appears plain from this doctor's experience, that fasting may be of great benefit physically to all who practice it.

In this connection it is interesting to note the remarks of men eminent in the profession of medicine. They state that it is a great mistake to suppose that doctors can cure people, when attacked with disease. All they can do is to help nature. It is nature, or the recuperative power of the body of the sick patient, that effects the cure. The doctors may alleviate pain, but they cannot cure disease by any of their remedies. When this view is taken of the profession of medicine, we can see how beneficial the administration of the ordinance of laying on of hands can be for those who seek relief through it, and who strictly comply with the counsel which the Lord has given to His people concerning their food and their beverages. (June 30, 1898, MS 60:412-13)

Chapter 14

Prayer—The Bulwark of the Saints

EVEN WICKED MAY ENJOY GOD'S BLESSINGS. The men and the women who do not pray to Him are of course protected and preserved by God; they are fed, clothed and furnished by His bounty; He sends His rain upon the just and the unjust, and even those who blaspheme and deny His goodness and mercies, and those who even deny His existence receive kindnesses at His hands. All this does not cause Him to withdraw His care entirely from them, and it is this mercy and compassion which the Lord has for His children that causes many of them to think that there is no God.

They see the wicked enjoying every blessing, and, reasoning as poor, human, ignorant beings are apt to do, they say: "There can be no God, or if there be a God, it is no use to pray to Him, because see those people who do pray to Him; do they fare any better than those who do not? Aren't those who do not pray to Him prospered? Do they not have riches and the good things of this life just as much as those who do pray to Him? What is the use of praying to Him, where there is no sign that anyone has been benefited by it?" In this way these people reason and think their reasoning is sound. But they know not the thoughts of the Lord nor His purposes. They do not even know the thoughts and the feelings of those who serve Him and of those who pray unto Him. They are incapable of judging any of these things. (January 1, 1895, JI 30:17)

THE IMPORTANCE OF PRAYER. It is a bad sign for those making our professions to be neglectful in seeking to the Lord for that strength which He alone can give and which is so necessary for Saints to possess. . . .

There can be no true spiritual vitality about a man or a woman who does not pray. They know nothing about the power of their religion. They have not any conception of its height, its depth or its breadth. Without prayer, also, no one can truly realize that feeling of humility which the people of God should possess, for it is by prayer that a knowledge of our imperfections and weaknesses is brought home to us. It is by prayer that the most correct conceptions can be obtained of the majesty of our God and of His purity and holiness. No man or woman can be in a proper condition to withstand temptation or be properly on his or her guard who does not pray. It is a direct command from the Lord, often repeated in His word, constantly declared by His servants, that it is the duty of His children to pray to Him without ceasing. When they do not bow the knee, it is still their duty to pray in their hearts.

A SAFEGUARD AGAINST EVERY EVIL. Prayer is an unfailing source of happiness. It is a continued cause of relief to those who offer it in a proper spirit to the Most High. The burdened and afflicted soul who goes to the Lord in prayer never comes away without relief. Those who are tempted and tried do not seek Him in vain, when they bow themselves before Him. How anyone calling himself a Latter-day Saint can neglect this duty, which is so productive of benefits, which brings so much comfort and increases joy so materially, which is a source of strength and a safeguard against every evil, is most strange. Whenever prayer is neglected, it is evident that faith is lacking; either the person who neglects it has never known the blessings which result from it or, if he has known them, has so far forgotten the goodness of God as to be in a most dangerous condition.

However faithful men and women may be, they still are required to watch and pray; for they are commanded, "Let him that thinketh he standeth take heed lest he fall." [1 Corinthians 10:12.] But the man or the woman who does not pray is positively unsafe and is liable to be overcome at any moment and to become an alien to all the covenants and promises of the Lord. . . .

EVEN RESURRECTED SAVIOR PRAYED. If it were necessary that He, so perfect and so pure, should seek for strength and consolation and power through this means, how much more necessary is it that we, who are so weak and fallible, should seek through the same means for that help which we need?

But not only did our Savior pray to His Father while He was in this mortal condition, but the Book of Mormon informs us that He prayed, while among the Nephites, to His Father after His resurrection. Even then, in His exalted state, having triumphed over death and the grave, having ascended on high and let captivity captive and having been received at the right hand of the Father, He still bowed Himself down in humble prayer before His Father in heaven. What a beautiful example He has left for us! And how diligent we should be in following it. (May 1, 1891, JI 26:278)

A GUIDE FOR DOING RIGHT. Let us ask the Lord at the appointed times to bless us in all that we may do, say or think all the day long, and then let us guide our life by this prayer and not do anything but what we are sure would be consistent with our requests to Heaven. And if we have our doubts about any thing being right or wrong, let us leave it alone until we can inquire of the Priesthood or of our parents.

That which we cannot ask the blessing of God upon is almost sure to be wrong, and if we have none of His servants at hand to appeal to and dare not approach Him humbly in prayer, rest assured that that thing had best be left undone or that word unsaid. If, on the other hand, we can go with full confidence and with all our hearts and ask the blessings of Heaven on any action, we may feel certain it is not far wrong; for no boy or girl, whose heart is right before the Almighty, dare ask His blessing while doing those things which he or she knows the Lord has forbidden or in leaving undone those things that He has revealed unto us it is His will we should perform. (October 22, 1869, JI 4:172)

THE EFFICACY OF FAMILY PRAYER. Is it any wonder that people get in the dark concerning spiritual things when they neglect this important duty? Is it strange that children of parents who thus neglect so plain and necessary a duty as family prayer should grow up indifferent to and ignorant of the principles of the everlasting Gospel? How can love for our Heavenly Father and for the truth exist in the minds of parents who are thus unmindful of their duty? Or how can this love be fostered in the minds of children when their parents are so careless and ungrateful to the Almighty as they must be when they neglect to pray in their families?

No family that fails to attend to family prayers in the proper season can keep up with the progress of the Kingdom of God. Such families fall behind in everything. They become dark in their minds, dull in their spirits and lose what little faith they may possess. They are guilty of gross ingratitude, and this is a great sin. The Spirit of God is grieved and will withdraw itself from every person who does not appreciate the goodness of God to him and who fails to render Him that worship and thanksgiving which are due to Him as our Creator and Protector.

As human beings we can judge by our own feelings, to some extent, of the manner in which our Heavenly Father views such conduct. Take the case of a kind and loving father and mother here on earth. They have children whom they love and for whose benefit, advancement and prosperity they labor without ceasing. They are continually planning for their good. They watch over them, provide food and clothing and shelter for them and bestow upon them various gifts. But if these children receive all these benefits without entertaining any feeling of gratitude toward their parents, paying no respect to them and not showing in any way that they value the gifts or appreciate the kindness which are bestowed them, what effect does this conduct have upon the parents? They are hurt and grieved and feel that their kindness and provident care are wasted upon those children and that they are unworthy of all that has been done them.

If this be the case with earthly parents, how much more is it with our great Creator and Author of our being, the Fountain of all our blessings and happiness!

PRAYER A BULWARK. Prayer is the bulwark of the Saints. It shields and protects those who offer it in sincerity and faith. Without prayer man is exposed to wicked temptations and to every evil. When he goes unto the Lord in humility, he shows Him his weaknesses and the dangers by which he is surrounded. This prompts him who prays to seek unto God for strength to overcome his weaknesses and to resist every temptation. His faith is strengthened by having his prayers answered. He has communion with his Heavenly Father through the Holy Ghost, and that Spirit becomes his constant companion and guide.

God is with him, and He reveals to him those precious things that belong to His Kingdom. The man who observes the command of God concerning prayer feels more and more the necessity of crying unto the Lord for help. He sees the danger in which he is placed, and he is guarded against that danger.

Children in seeing their parents pray are impressed by the

example. When they, therefore, are in trouble, they seek relief through prayer unto God. They know that He hears and answers them, and this is a testimony to them that God lives. It is a constant comfort in the hours of temptation and trial and in the midst of the afflictions with which all have to contend.

PRAYER IS SPIRITUAL NOURISHMENT. To live without prayer is to live a mere animal existence. It is to leave the best part of our natures in a starving condition; for without prayer the spirit is starved, and men dwindle in their feelings and die in their faith. If anyone is disposed to enquire into the truth of this and satisfy himself upon this point, let him visit the families of those who observe their prayers in the season thereof. The effect upon the household is very marked. Children grow up in an atmosphere of faith. A reverence for God, for truth and for everything holy and pure is developed within them. They are more easily controlled. Their consciences are more tender. They have a higher conception of that which is right.

If a family where prayer is neglected be visited, the children will be of a different type and disposition. What influence is there to hold them? If the parents do not honor God, what grounds have the children for honoring their parents?

We trust that every reader . . . will make it a fixed rule to attend to secret and family prayers. Better go without a meal than to neglect this duty. If your stomach is empty, you will feel faint and be reminded that you must give it food. Remember that the spirit also needs food, and make it your business to attend to supplying it in the way that God has appointed. Then your spirit and your body will be developed alike, and strength will be maintained. (January 15, 1892, JI 27:58-59)

TEACH CHILDREN TO PRAY EARLY. Children should be taught in early life to pray to God. They should be taught that there is a God who will hear and answer their prayers. When they are sick, they should be taught to ask their father or the Elders to lay hands upon them, and if neither the father nor any Elder is near, to have their mother lay her hands on them and pray for them; this is not sinful; it is not wrong. Women do not have the Priesthood like men have, but they can pray for their children, and their prayers are heard just as much as the prayers of the men are heard, though they may not have the authority to rebuke disease as men who bear the Priesthood.

Children should be brought to their mother's knees and taught to pray and be brought up in a way that they will understand the nature and the power and the efficacy of prayer. If you will do this with your children, you will fortify them against the days of trial and temptation which will come to them when they grow older. Where this is done, you will have boys and girls that will be a blessing, a comfort and an honor to you, because their faith will be developed in early life, and they will know for themselves that there is a God.

It is very delightful to witness the faith of children and to hear their expressions concerning these matters when they are properly taught. I am sure that if mothers would take this course with their children, they would have much more comfort from their children, their children would be easier governed, and they would develop in the children the best qualities of their minds; for every child is open particularly to these good influences, and children can be governed by appealing to their better natures, especially when they have been taught in the way I have spoken. . . .

LET CHILDREN PRAY IN FAMILY CIRCLE. We ought to make our religion attractive to our children, and one way to do that is to have every member of the family pray. Some men seem to think that their prayers alone are heard, that the prayers of their wives or their children are not listened to. If any entertain this idea, they are much mistaken, because the Lord hears the prayers of women just as much as He does of men, and He hears the prayers of children just as much as He does of grown people.

Every child should be taught to pray in the family circle. As soon as he can lisp or talk or be taught to frame a prayer, he should be asked to pray in the family circle; and the Lord hears the prayers of these little children, and they take interest then in family worship, because it is a great part of their service as well as their parents.

When a child can ask a blessing, if he or she can only say,

"O Lord bless this food, for Jesus Christ's sake, Amen," it is better to let them commence even with these few words than not to have them pray. It is pleasing to see the interest children take in asking blessings. They feel as though they were honored and they take pleasure in it. So in prayer. It is not the multitude of words that the Lord pays attention to. He does not listen to our fine, flowery sermons and our fine, flowery prayers; He looks at our hearts and the sincerity of our desires.

MAKE PRAYERS BRIEF. We ought to worship Him with our hearts and not with these long, flowery sentences. Another thing: If we pray in secret, we will not want to make such long prayers in public as some do; we shall have relieved our hearts in our secret prayers to a very great extent. We can pray by ourselves and we can take as long time as we wish to, and we do not wear anybody out unless it is ourselves. It is not probable that those who listen to us are wearied by our devotion.

When others are kneeling down with us, we ought in our prayers to be direct and brief and not pray about everything there is on the earth and imagine that we must mention everything in detail or the Lord won't know about it. He does know, and we do not need to mention everything as though He had forgotten and would not take notice unless we mentioned it. If we pay attention to the Lord's prayer that he taught His disciples, we will see the beauty of that, how simple it was and direct; it contained no superfluous words, but it was to the point, asking for that which they needed. . . .

PRAY IN OUR HEARTS. It is a good thing to know how to pray; and we are not heard for our much speaking in prayer. It seems to me we should be full of the spirit of prayer, and we should pray in our hearts as well as with our lips and on our knees and cultivate the habit of praying in our hearts. We cannot stop always to get down on our knees to ask for that which we need; but we can ask the Lord in our hearts, no matter what we are engaged in.

We may be going to meet somebody that is of importance and have not time to stop to pray, but we can ask God to give us wisdom. If we are going to transact some business, we can ask

God to be with us in the transaction, to give us His Holy Spirit to enlighten us and enable us to do the right thing. I do not know how I would have got along in life if I had not done this, because there are many times we are thrown in circumstances where the wisdom of heaven is needed, and it is a good thing to cultivate the habit of asking the Lord for that.

I believe if I was going to break a horse or do some work in my field as a farmer or anything of this character, I would want to ask the Lord's blessing upon it. It would not probably be convenient to kneel down and ask Him right then for that special occasion; but I would ask Him in my heart. Of course, in our family and secret prayers we ask the Lord for these special things.

You are called on to speak suddenly or to do something suddenly; it is a good thing to ask the Lord to be with you when you are doing that, to guide you. When we have a decision to make, we should ask the Lord to enlighten our minds that we decide aright and come to a correct conclusion.

A mother going to have an interview with a child that is unruly should ask the Lord to give her His Spirit to talk to the child and to pour out His Spirit upon the child that it may be softened. When I have anything disagreeable to do, I always feel to do this, to pray that the Lord will soften the hearts of those with whom I am brought in contact, give their hearts the right feeling and give me the right feeling. I believe a great deal of the success of my life has been due to the Lord hearing this kind of prayer, for I know he does hear such prayers. (January 1, 1897, DW 54:290-91)

SAYING AMEN. There is another practice that ought to be maintained among us; it is the saying of "Amen" in an audible voice after prayer has been offered in the congregation.

The Church in early days was taught that this was an acceptable practice in the sight of God. It was expected that every member of the Church, when prayer was offered, would in an audible voice say "Amen" at the conclusion of the prayer—in effect saying to the Lord that the prayer that had been offered was their prayer. . . .

Our children should be taught to say "Amen" when a blessing is asked at the table or when prayers are offered in the Sunday school or in the family circle; and the same should be done in the public congregations. In this way we can witness unto the Lord that we are interested in having the prayers that are offered heard and answered; and we may rest assured it will be more acceptable to the Lord, because in doing this we display an interest in the objects that are prayed for. (February 15, 1896, JI 31:117)

Chapter 15

The Word of Wisdom—God's Law of Health

AN AID IN PHYSICAL REDEMPTION. On the 27th day of February, 1833, the Prophet received the revelation known as the Word of Wisdom, warning the people to abstain from impurities and grossness in their food and drink, and promising them rich blessings of physical strength and protection from the power of the adversary as a reward for their obedience. The requirement of bodily pureness, to be gained by clean and wholesome living, was not more directly made upon the children of Israel anciently than upon the Latter-day Saints through the Prophet Joseph.

This revealed Word of Wisdom embodies the most advanced principles of science in the condemnation of unclean or gluttonous appetites; and if it were implicitly obeyed by the human family, it would be a power to aid in a physical redemption for the race. Its delivery to Joseph marks another step in the divine plan for man's eventual elevation to divine acceptability—a plan which had already proved itself of heavenly origin by its sublime character. (1888, LJS 142)

HOW TO CHECK DISEASE. While the Latter-day Saints have not been promised exemption from the sickness and pestilence that will yet afflict human beings, they are promised that if they observe the commands which the Lord gives them they shall have a goodly degree of health and shall have wisdom and shall escape, to a certain extent at least, the power of the destroyer. Death is in the world, and righteous people must die as well as unrighteous. There is no escape from this, because the word of the Lord has gone forth concerning men's days. . . .

Pestilence and woes of various kinds will come upon the inhabitants of the earth in our day according to the word of the Lord, and the rising generation should be taught the necessity of living pure and temperate lives so that they may not fall victims, but live the full measure of their days. . . . Living as we do in the world we can not reasonably expect to escape all the evils which afflict mankind; the promises made to us as a people do not extend that far; but they do assure us that we shall not suffer to the same extent as those will who break the commandments of God and despise His counsel. And it is that our children may have the full benefit of these promises that they should be taught correct methods of life. (March 15, 1891, JI 26:173-74)

LONG LIFE AMONG GOD'S PEOPLE. "Temperance in all things" is a portion of the law of God. The reception of the Holy Ghost undoubtedly lengthens the years of men and women, and its happifying, peaceful influence causes them to both look younger and feel younger, as days and years creep upon them, than do those who have not received of this priceless gift through obedience to the commands of heaven. . . .

With us, many a one who has passed the seventy years allotted unto man is still hale and vigorous, filling the daily duties of his calling with energy and promptness, and he would be surprised if it were hinted that he was growing old. . . .

Long life, with health and peace, has ever been considered a mark of God's favor. To the young He promises, if they will obey their parents, this reward of lengthened life—their days are to be long in the land which the Lord their God gives them. . . .

This promise of long life, like all other blessings is predicated on law. We must observe the laws of God that bring about these results, or they will not be ours to enjoy. Formal acceptance of God's word will effect little. We must live it, and live it honestly and thoroughly if we reap the reward. (November 15, 1899, JI 34:715)

NO HIDDEN MEANINGS. The Word of Wisdom should be taken in the spirit in which it was given. It is not difficult to understand. There is no hidden meaning, beyond the reach of the capacity of a child. The Lord has given us excellent counsel concerning our food and drink, and the testimony of those who have observed it is that it is attended with the blessings that He has promised. . . .

There have been various opinions as to whether it is now a commandment or not. But what difference is there, in a case of this kind, whether it is a commandment or only counsel? The man who would not take the counsel of the Lord in regard to matters of this character, would not be likely to obey a commandment. Every parent can ask himself the question how he would feel towards his children if he gave them good counsel and they declined to obey it, because it did not come in the form of a command. He would think they had very little respect for him. Each one can reflect upon how our Father in heaven must feel to have His kind counsel concerning their food and drink and health disregarded by His children who profess to be His Saints.[1] (April 1, 1891, JI 26:219)

HOT DRINKS NOT GOOD FOR MAN. We are told, and very plainly too, that hot drinks—tea, coffee, and all drinks of this kind—are not good for man. We are also told that alcoholic drinks are not good, and that tobacco when either smoked or chewed is an evil. We are told that swine's flesh is not good, and that we should dispense with it; and we are told that flesh of any kind is not suitable to man in the summer time, and ought to be eaten sparingly in the winter. (April 21, 1867, JD 12:221)

DRINKING CAUSES WITHDRAWAL OF SPIRIT. Now I tell you, as a servant of God, that no man who is an habitual drunkard can have the Spirit of God dwelling with him. The spirit of intoxication and the Spirit of God will not co-exist in the same bosom. I do not mean to say that there are not times when alcohol may be used with profit as a medicine. I have never taken that ground. But the habitual use of alcoholic drinks is contrary to the law of God and to the law of the Church.

I do not speak for all upon this matter, but I cannot, as one, fellowship in my feelings an habitual drunkard. I know that the Spirit of God will not dwell with him, and sooner or later he will be led astray and do things that will carry him out of the Church if he should live long enough. (April 8, 1883, DNW 32:258)

WORD OF WISDOM MUST BE TAUGHT. The writer does not wish to say anything . . . that can be viewed as extreme

[1]"It was not given, at that time, by way of commandment or restraint but by revelation. . . . Subsequently, years afterwards, from this stand, it was proclaimed from the mouth of the Prophet and President of the Church of Jesus Christ of Latter-day Saints, Brigham Young, that the time had now come when this word of wisdom—then given not by commandment or constraint—was now a commandment of the Lord to the Church of Jesus Christ of Latter-day Saints and the Lord required them to observe this word of wisdom and counsel, which is the will of God unto the people for their temporal salvation." (President Joseph F. Smith, *Conference Report*, October 1908, p. 4.)

upon this subject of the Word of Wisdom. He has never felt to find fault with aged or infirm people who have contracted the habit of using drinks that we are told are not good for man, and he does not wish to indulge in any censure of those who have formed these habits. But he is very desirous that the rising generation shall grow up free from them and that every pains shall be taken, by parents and by teachers, to impress upon the minds of the children the great advantages which they will possess by never acquiring these bad habits.

We would like to see such a feeling grow up in all the families of this Church that every parent will take pleasure in having children who have never acquired the habit of using these articles and who have never even tasted them. If every parent will take this view and have satisfaction in training his children this way, the effect upon the rising generation will be very marked, and we shall have before very long a race of people who will be free from every habit that the Lord points out as hurtful to us. (February 1, 1898, JI 33:124)

THE LORD'S PROMISES. Many of the Saints do not seem to be alive to the importance of those laws which pertain to well-being and preservation of health and strength of the body. Their old traditions cling to them, and it appears to be difficult for them to shake them off. Yet the day must come when the people of God will be superiors, physically and mentally, to every other people upon the face of the earth. Before this day shall come, however, the ignorant and the neglectful will either have reformed or have passed away. Pestilences of various kinds, which we are led to expect through the word of the Lord are yet to break forth, will have their effect in calling the Saints' attention to those laws of life and health which, to be a strong and vigorous people, we must observe. . . .

If pestilence should stalk through the land, it will doubtless have this effect also upon the Latter-day Saints and their habits and surroundings. Many who are now careless respecting the words of the Lord contained in the Word of Wisdom will be likely to reform their habits and pay attention to the counsels which He there gives. So also in regard to the care of their persons and of their habitations.

We are promised greater safety than other people are likely to enjoy, but the promises are based on certain conditions which must be observed. If these are observed, then the promise begins to operate. We are not told whether the word of the Lord to the children of Israel in Egypt, wherein He told them to sprinkle the lintels and the door-posts of their houses, was universally observed or not. If there were any who neglected that precaution, the record does not inform us. They were told that every house thus marked with blood should be exempt from the visitation of the destroyer; he should not enter there, and the first-born in those houses should escape the dreadful fate that was to befall the firstborn of other households in the land.

Suppose the children of Israel, after receiving that direction from the Lord through the Prophet Moses, had either refused or neglected to sprinkle the doorpost and lintels with blood, could they have reasonably expected the promise to be fulfilled to them? Certainly not. And why should people in our day expect to enjoy health and an exemption from the visit of the destroyer when he goes forth as he did in Egypt if they do not comply with the conditions which the Lord has prescribed.

It is the Lord's design made apparent in His word to have a healthy, vigorous, intellectual, long lived people. He is gathering those who love Him from the various nations for this purpose. If they will obey Him, He will make them the progenitors of a race that shall fill the earth with men and women of pristine vigor. The old days will come back, and men will live to an extraordinary age. And all this by obedience to the laws of our nature, which God has revealed and will continue to reveal to those who receive His word. In our case will be illustrated that phrase, "the survival of the fittest"; and this phrase will not only apply to our own people. Those who obey the laws of life and health as God reveals them will have advantages over those who neglect them. (November 15, 1892, JI 27:689-91)

WORD OF WISDOM PROMISES. Those who observe the Word of Wisdom will be distinguished among this people because of the wisdom that God will give them. God will give them the blessings that He has promised, and He will preserve them. When you go as Elders to administer in a family that observe these words of God, you will have faith to lay hands on the sick and to ask the blessings of God in their behalf and to heal them through the power of God; whereas, if they are living in violation of these words, the faith of the Elders and of the persons themselves will be weakened, and they will not have enough to claim the promises that God has made. This la grippe and other diseases that are going through the country are merely precursors of the pestilences that will yet sweep through the nations of the earth, and we are required to stand in holy places that we may escape these destructions; and God has given unto us these counsels that we may be fortified so to speak, against these scourges. . . .

We should have faith in God in these matters, believe that which He says, and claim the promises. Not that we can altogether escape death, for death is in the world; but we may escape these pestilences and judgments that are going forth among the nations of the earth. (June 20, 1892, DW 45:258)

GREAT TREASURES OF WISDOM. It is true, probably, that there are many points concerning our welfare that may not have been touched upon by our Heavenly Father in the Word of Wisdom, but in my experience I have noticed that they who practice what the Lord has already given are keenly alive to other words of wisdom and counsel that may be given.

I would consider that for a person who was in a profuse perspiration to go into the wind without being properly clothed would be more foolish and injurious than to eat meat or to drink tea or coffee to excess. There are a thousand ways in which we can act unwisely; our attention has been directed to some few points, and if we observe them, the Lord has promised us great treasures of wisdom, which will enable us to see a thousand points where we can take better care of our bodies, preserve our health and which will enable us to train our children in the way of the Lord. (April 21, 1867, JD 12:44-45)

NON-OBSERVANCE A DISGRACE. It is now upwards of fifty years since the Lord gave to His people the revelation known as the Word of Wisdom. It is a disgrace to Latter-day Saints that it should not be observed. We cannot understand how they can excuse themselves, either before their brethren or before their God, for allowing themselves or their offspring to cultivate habits of this character—using these articles which God has told us are not for our use and are injurious to our bodies. One would think that after what He has written upon this subject no man or woman who loves God and desires to keep His commandments would have any other feeling than one of shame and condemnation before the Lord if he was guilty of disregarding the kind and fatherly counsels which He has given to His people upon these points. . . .

It may be said, however, that these are small matters. This is true, to a certain extent. But behold the condescensions of our God in speaking to us upon these small matters! He deemed them of sufficient importance to give us His word concerning them; and shall we say that they are small and unworthy of notice when our Eternal Father considers them of sufficient worth to give us His written word upon the subject? If we despise His counsel upon these points, we are likely to despise it in other matters that may appear to us of graver importance, and by degrees the Spirit of God may be grieved until it will leave us. (July 1, 1887, JI 22:200)

SHOULD NOT NEED TO PREACH WORD OF WISDOM. What a shame it is that a portion of the time of our Conferences has to be occupied in dwelling upon this theme and others of a similar character! We should be above these things, my brethren and sisters. We should live so high above them that there would be no necessity to mention them and that our children in seeing it would feel that there is indeed some virtue in the revelation of God concerning the Word of Wisdom and will themselves refrain from the practices it counsels us to avoid. (DEN, March 4, 1895)

HABITS ARE EASILY FORMED. I know it is not encouraging to see how little has been accomplished by the Prophets and Apostles who, from the Prophet Joseph down to this day, have urged the people to observe the "Word of Wisdom." But there will be a people raised up, I am assured, who will respect and obey the counsel of the Lord; and while it is evident that what we have done so far has not been the success that has been desired, we must keep on trying until we do succeed. . . .

There is danger that even drinking a cup of coffee may weaken the child through his life, so that it would always be a temptation to him to drink it. There may be cases where children can taste such things and have no strong inclination to use them to overcome; but in the most of instances a taste of this kind can easily be awakened, and it becomes a difficult matter to afterwards resist the temptation to indulge the taste.

Some persons may think this an extreme view to take of the effect of tasting stimulants; but experience furnishes abundant reasons for believing that as long as children are permitted to taste and drink these articles the habits of using them will be formed and frequently cannot afterwards be controlled. (January 1, 1898, JI 33:37, 68)

WORD OF WISDOM BREAKERS NOT TO TEACH. Persons who do not keep the Word of Wisdom should not be selected for these positions [as presidents and teachers.][2] Better to leave them vacant, if no one can be found who would be suitable to act, than to put persons in charge of the children who indulge in these habits. It is felt that it is of the utmost importance that those who are brought in contact with the children should be able to set the very best example, and that it was more important for this class to be correct in their habits than almost any other class of officers in the Church.

Children notice the habits of older persons. . . . If we permit men who smoke, or drink hot and intoxicating drinks, to teach the children or to stand in authority among them, it naturally leads children to think that it is not important whether the Word of Wisdom is observed or not. (February 1, 1898, JI 33:124)

---

[2]"We expect all the general officers of the Church, each and every one of them, from this very day, to be absolute, full tithe payers, to really and truly observe the Word of Wisdom. And we ask all of the officers of the Church and all members of the general boards, and all stake and ward officers, if they are not living the gospel and honestly and conscientiously paying their tithing, to kindly step aside unless from this day they live up to these provisions." (President Heber J. Grant, *Gospel Standards,* p. 72.)

Chapter 16

Administering to the Sick

THE ORDINANCE FOR THE SICK. Among the blessings promised by the risen Savior as signs which should follow the believers in His Gospel, He said, "They shall lay hands on the sick, and they shall recover." (Mark 16:18.) The . . . "laying on of hands to cure human sickness," then, was practiced and taught by the Savior of mankind. And it became an established ordinance of the Church under the direction of His Apostles. [See James 5:14-15.]

. . . When the true Church of Christ was re-established on earth through the ministry of Joseph Smith, the restoration of this ordinance was one of its marked characteristics, distinguishing it from the ecclesiastical systems established by men. Hands were laid upon the sick, and they did recover. In thousands upon thousands of instances, in all kinds of diseases, in every country where the Elders have ministered, the sick have been healed by the power of God through the laying on of hands. And there is no "quackery" about it. Those who administer lay claim to no extraordinary sanctity or personal supernatural power. They simply act as ministers of Christ, carrying out His commandments and relying upon His promise.

The question may be asked, "Does the laying on of hands cure in every instance, and if not, why not?" The answer is no, and the reason is because faith is necessary to effectual administration, and faith does not always accompany it. James says, "the prayer of faith shall save the sick." Jesus always declared that it was faith which caused the healings that attended His ministry. Said He, "Go thy way: thy faith hath made thee whole." [Luke 17:19.] "If you have power to heal the sick," exclaims the skeptic, "why don't you exercise it before the world and make everybody believe you?" Gently, wise scoffer. Faith does not come by seeing signs, but signs come by faith. The healings are not the cause but the effects of faith. They are not given to make people believe, but they follow them that do believe. In his own region of country Jesus did no mighty work, "and he marvelled because of their unbelief." If signs were to create faith, that was the very spot where they were most needed.

If the power to heal in every case was given to men, out of

sympathy for the suffering they would continually exercise it, and there would be, as a consequence, no sickness and no death. By this means the divine plan would be frustrated, and this earth would be no place of probation or sphere of trial. If objection is raised against the laying on of hands because its effects are not uniform in every case, the poet's advice, "Throw physic to the dogs" should be followed, for there is nothing more uncertain than the results of medical treatment, and we should therefore use no drugs and fee no doctors.

The most remarkable cures have been effected through the laying on of hands, both in ancient and in modern times. The Bible bears abundant testimony to the former; the Latter-day Saints in every country are witnesses of the latter. And if in these times of unbelief it sometimes happens that relief does not follow administration of the ordinance, it should not be any matter of wonder, because the Apostles of the early Church, amid the wonders wrought under their hands, could not always obtain the faith necessary to heal. Therefore, Paul gave advice to Timothy in regard to his "often infirmities" [1 Timothy 5:23], and in relating an account of his travels, had to say, "Trophimus have I left at Miletum sick" [1 Timothy 4:20]. Yet Paul counted himself not behind the chiefest of the Apostles, in "signs, and wonders, and mighty deeds." [2 Corinthians 12:11.]

All have not faith. And those who are able to exercise faith at one time may not be able at another time. Some men have faith to heal; others have only faith to be healed. But the ordinance should be administered to the sick to fulfill the law and to give them the benefit of all the faith that can be obtained in their behalf. The power to heal alone does not prove the possessor to be a man of God, nor that his doctrines or principles are correct. Neither does the absence of the faith to heal or be healed prove the non-possessor a bad or unconverted man. But wherever and whenever the Church of Christ is upon the earth, the gift of healing through the prayer of faith will be exhibited, and any Church from which that blessing is entirely absent lacks one of the characteristics of Christ's Church, and therefore cannot be His, but is destitute of His authority.

The provision made for the sick in this Church, is given in the book of Doctrine and Covenants, section 42:43-44, 48-52.

THE POWER OF FAITH. Faith is a force. Those who have experienced its influence and seen its effects know this to be an incontrovertible fact. But faith does not come by the will of man. It is not the child of hope nor the offspring of desire. The laws by which it acts are not fully known to mortals. But by its power the sick have been instantaneously healed, the blind have been made to see, the deaf to hear, the lame to walk, the apparently dead to come to life, the elements to obey the voice of man, and the heavens to open to his gaze and disclose the secrets which are veiled from unbelieving eyes.

He who is Omnipotent works by faith. He calls light out of the darkness; He brings order out of chaos; He calls worlds into being and quickens inanimate atoms with the breath of life; and faith is the force by which He wields His sceptre of power, directs the creative energy and fills the universe with beauty and glory.

It is a dormant faculty of every human soul, because the spirit of the children of men are the off-spring of God. Every seed brings forth of its kind. Earthly life is not the period for its perfect exercise. But when the redeemed sons and daughters of the Eternal One come up to the measure of His fulness, faith will be developed in them with all its strength and potency, and they will follow in the footsteps of their Great Head, and pattern after His mighty works among inexhaustible elements, in illimitable space, throughout a ceaseless eternity. (October 15, 1877, MS 39:675-76)

EXERCISE FAITH IN HEALING ORDINANCES. Many of us have not faith enough even to send for the Elders of the Church when any one of our family is sick; but the first thought is, "go for a doctor," as though the gift of healing had been lost in the Church. How many of you feel as if the gift of healing no longer existed in the Church of Christ but that doctors must be sent for and drugs administered? And this among the Latter-day Saints, a people who profess what we do and to whom such glorious promises have been made!

I am scarcely ever called in to administer to a sick person without being told what the doctor is doing and what he says. To me, it is an evidence of a want of faith in the ordinances of God's house and in His promises. To think of a people with the promise made to them that their sick shall be healed, if they will only exercise faith, neglecting this and treating it as though there was no certainty to be attached to it!

It is the same in other directions. We fail to set a proper example before our young people. If I were to send for a doctor, what would be the effect upon my children? Why, they would say, "That is the course my father took, and he is an Elder in the Church and a man of experience; he sent for the doctors, and why should not I? My mother was a good woman, but when one of the children was sick, she sent for a doctor; she did not trust to the ordinance alone; and shall we not send for a doctor? Must it all be faith and no works?" How often do we hear this sort of reasoning?

I believe in works; I believe in nursing, in taking care of the sick and in doing all that is possible for them; but I believe also in the ordinances of the house of God. God has made precious promises to the Latter-day Saints concerning the health of their families, and I tell you, in the presence of the Lord, that if the Latter-day Saints would observe the Word of Wisdom there would be less of this disposition to send for doctors and more faith in the ordinances that the Lord has established. . . .

And let me tell you, there will be pestilences, and there will be diseases; for the Lord has said that there shall be an overwhelming scourge pass through the nations of the earth; and if the Latter-day Saints do not keep His counsel on this as well as other matters, how can they expect to enjoy immunity or receive deliverance? (August 26, 1894, DW 49:450)

TRUST MORE IN GOD. Speaking about faith-cures, I have felt deeply impressed with the idea that the members of our Church do not value as they should the means which God has placed within their reach for the relief and healing of the sick.

There is too great a disposition, when sickness enters a household, to send for a doctor. Occasional appeals will be made to the Elders to come and administer, but the two methods are too frequently united—the doctor on the one hand and the Elders on the other.

The experience of those who put their trust in the Lord, and who with careful nursing unite the administering of the ordinance, goes to prove that the Lord has not forgotten His promises. Instances are very common among the faithful Saints of the gift of healing being manifested in a very wonderful manner.

In the breasts of our children, especially, the greatest care should be taken to inculcate faith in this healing ordinance. Where children are thus taught, it is remarkable how strong their faith becomes. . . .

God has not forgotten His promises, and He has not withdrawn Himself from His people. But the Latter-day Saints should make use of these means more frequently than they do, and put more trust in God and less in man's skill. (March 26, 1888, MS 50:194-95)

HEALING BY FAITH. The laying on of hands for the healing of the sick is an ordinance of the Gospel. One of the signs which the Lord Jesus Himself promised His disciples in ancient days that should follow them that believed was, "they shall lay hands on the sick, and they shall recover." [Mark 16:18.] In our day the promise has been renewed, and we can claim it. . . .

Many, however, fail to avail themselves of these promises, and excuse themselves for doing so by saying that faith without works is dead. They seem to think that works consist in sending for a doctor and using what he may prescribe, having apparently more faith in man's skill than in God's power to heal through the ordinance which He has appointed.

SICK SHOULD BE NURSED. In saying this we would not wish to convey any wrong idea. We believe it to be the duty of those who have sick in their households to do all in their power for their comfort, to nurse them with the greatest possible care and to use what skill they may have in that direction, asking the Lord to bless the means which they use and also to inspire those who may have to wait upon the sick to do the very thing for them that will be of the greatest advantage. In this way works can be united with faith, and the ordinance of the Gospel can be used. . . .

It is only reasonable to think that the Lord knows better that which is good for us than man does. His power to heal is without limit. He desires His children to exercise faith. By its exercise great blessings can be obtained. The more it is exercised and the oftener the results which are desired are obtained the stronger does faith become.

TEACH CHILDREN TO EXERCISE FAITH. Children who are taught by their parents to desire the laying on of hands by the Elders when they are sick receive astonishing benefits therefrom, and their faith becomes exceedingly strong. But, if instead of teaching them that the Lord has placed the ordinance of laying on of hands for the healing of the sick in His Church, a doctor is immediately sent for when anything ails them, they gain confidence in the doctor and his prescriptions and lose faith in the ordinance.

How long would it take, if this tendency were allowed to grow among the Latter-day Saints, before faith in the ordinance of laying on of hands would die out? Little by little the practice of using drugs and resorting to men and women skilled in their use would grow among the people, until those who had sick children or other relatives who did not send for a doctor when they were attacked with a sickness would be looked upon as heartless and cruel. Perhaps they would be taunted for not sending for some skilled person and perchance be condemned for trusting entirely to the ordinance of the Gospel and the proper nursing and kind attentions which every person who is sick should receive.

There is great need of stirring up the Latter-day Saints upon this point. Faith should be encouraged. The people should be taught that great and mighty works can be accomplished by the exercise of faith. The sick have been healed, devils have been cast out, the blind have been restored to sight, the deaf have been made to hear, lameness has been cured and even the dead have been raised to life by the exercise of faith. And this, too, in our day and in our Church by the administration of God's servants in the way appointed. All these things can again be done, under the blessing of the Lord, where faith exists. It is this faith that we should seek to preserve and to promote in the breasts of our children and of all mankind. (November 1, 1893, JI 28: 669-70)

FAITH TO BE HEALED. A cheerful and buoyant mind as well as a sound brain are all important in both the prevention and the healing of disease. Many doctors realize the importance of keeping the mind in a proper condition during sickness, and they do all they can to inspire confidence in the patient. . . .

Those who have had numerous opportunities, as many of our Elders have, of administering to the sick must be fully conscious of the effect that the will and the determination of the sick have upon their own health. This is really faith. How many times have the sick been healed by the administration of the Elders through arousing within them faith in the promises of the Lord. The cheering and comforting words of the Elders, the promises they are led to make, have a tendency to strengthen the sick in their power to resist and overcome disease.

Men may ridicule the laying on of hands and the prayer of faith, but faithful Latter-day Saints know that the gift of healing is in the Church of Jesus Christ and that the promises made by the Lord concerning the administration of the ordinance which has been established in the Church for this purpose are fulfilled. The more the gift of healing is exercised the stronger it grows. The more the Latter-day Saints depend upon this ordinance and seek relief through it the greater are the benefits and the more frequent are the instances of recovery through the administration of the Elders in the appointed way.

When not appointed unto death (for death is passed upon all), there is no ailment that afflicts humanity that cannot be reached by faith and the administration of the ordinance of the Gospel. Miracles have been performed and are of frequent occurrence in the Church where the Saints rely upon the promises of the Lord. . . .

When children are taught the importance of this principle, they naturally, when anything ails them, seek relief through the laying on of hands, and when they have hands laid upon them by the Elders, they are healed in a great majority of cases. Faith is like every other principle; it can be cultivated and can become a strong power in the man or the woman who possesses it. (August 1, 1896, JI 31:450-51)

ADMINISTERING TO SICK BY PRIESTS. A Priest holds the authority of the Aaronic Priesthood, and while that Priesthood does not give him the power to lay hands on baptized believers for the reception of the Holy Ghost, it undoubtedly gives him authority to lay hands on the sick, if it be necessary. Indeed, members of the Church can lay hands on the sick and pray for their recovery, though they have no right, if they rebuke the disease in the name of Jesus, to say they do so by the authority of the Priesthood. (March 1, 1898, JI 33:186)

ADMINISTERING BY MOTHERS. Even sisters can do this, and there is no impropriety in it, though it would be better if one holding the Priesthood could be obtained to attend to this ordinance. It is frequently the case that mothers find it necessary to administer to their sick children at times when no one is at hand who bears the Priesthood whom they can secure to administer the ordinance of laying on of hands for the restoration of sick. There have been repeated instances of such administration by mothers being attended with healing effects.[1] This, we suppose, no one of experience in the Church will question. (January 15, 1896, JI 31:60)

ADMINISTERING AND CONTAGIOUS DISEASE. A well and healthy person has as much right to be considered in matters pertaining to the preservation of his health as a sick person has to be considered in matters pertaining to the restoration of his health. To prevent sickness is no less to be desired than to cure sickness. While it is true that those who are well do not need a physician, it is also true that no correct sense of duty requires a physician or any one else to jeopardize a healthy person in seeking to aid a diseased one. That the sick may be healed is the proper desire of every right-minded person, but that in seeking to aid them, others who are not sick shall be also brought down in illness, is a requirement of neither humanity nor common sense. And this view of the case is greatly emphasized when a disease so loathsome and so highly contagious as small pox is believed to be, is under consideration; for then it is not only a question of perhaps helping one while perhaps harming one—it is a question of desiring to aid one at the serious risk and danger of perhaps the whole community.

[1]"Respecting females administering for the healing of the sick . . . there could be no evil in it, if God gave His sanction by healing; . . . there could be no more sin in any female laying hands on and praying for the sick, than in wetting the face with water; it is no sin for anybody to administer that has faith, or if the sick have faith to be healed by their administration." (*Teachings of the Prophet Joseph Smith,* pp. 224-25.)

Now, no one will feel like saying to a Bishop or an Elder that when called upon to go and administer to the sick he must not do it. He may have abundant faith that through his administration the afflicted ones may be healed and he himself escape unharmed. Many Elders have manifested this faith in instances of the most frightful plagues, and the results have justified them. But if one have such faith as this, having no fear for himself, let him at least be warned against exposing others to such plagues as have been named. He ought to complain of no proper regulation adopted as a precaution for the safety of the neighbors and the community, submitting if need be to restraint of liberty to come and go at will and manifesting thus a consistent interest not alone in the sick but in the well also. (January 15, 1900, JI 35:63)

ADMINISTERING TO NONMEMBERS. It is always lawful to do good. We say this on the authority of the Savior of mankind. If a person has faith to seek health through the ministrations of the Elders in the name of Jesus, even though he have not the greater faith to accept and obey the fullness of the everlasting Gospel, he should not be deprived of the lesser blessing of bodily soundness by any lack of willingness on our part to magnify the name of God.

We nowhere read in the scriptures that when the sick came to Jesus Himself and sought His healing blessing that He first asked, "Have you been baptized?" He did not inquire of the blind or paralytic, "Are you a member of the Church?"

It is true these gifts of the Holy Spirit are to follow the believers; they were not placed in the Church to make converts. But the man or woman who asks for the administration of the Elders (we are not now talking of sign-seekers) is, to certain extent, a believer, though not yet a member of Christ's holy Church, and is not doing wrong by seeking the blessing. That God is not offended at this manifestation of faith is evident from the fact that He often honors these ministrations by healing the subject. (March 1, 1894, JI 29:144)

The rule generally adopted by all Elders under such circumstances, as far as we understand, has been to require the sick person, before being administered to, to make a covenant that he or she would obey the ordinances of the Gospel, and upon this promise being made the Elders felt justified in administering the ordinance for the healing of the sick. (January 1, 1896, JI 31:25)

Chapter 17

Virtue, Chastity, and Love

MODESTY IN DRESS. Every modest girl should set her face against any fashion that would for a moment identify her with those of her sex who have no claim to modesty. Loud dressing leads to loud manners and loud manners to all kinds of evils. There is no virtue in a woman more appreciated by good and sensible men than true modesty. This reaches even to the dress we wear and the way we wear it.

Can any of our young lady readers tell us the estimate people are apt to put on them if they see them dressed in the extreme of a fashion, no matter how outrageous or even disgusting? Neatness and cleanliness are always becoming, but many a fashion has been introduced into the world to hide the deformity or sin of some one, who being a "lady of high degree," was very apt to be copied by those wishing to flatter her, for imitation is the sincerest kind of flattery.

The modes that first see the light in the midst of the corruption of Paris and other great cities of Babylon are no more worthy of being copied by the pure and innocent daughters of Zion than other follies and frivolities of the Gentile world. We should make our own fashions of which neatness, comfort and adaptability should be the distinguishing traits. (February 6, 1875, JI 10:30)

ADULTERY GREATEST SIN NEXT TO MURDER. The adulterer commits the greatest sin next to murder that can be committed by a human being, according to the word of the Lord to us. The man who commits sin with his neighbor's wife, the man who seduces the innocent, who takes advantage of the unwary, who by his fascination or attraction or by persuasion or by the power which God has given him for a righteous purpose, the man who uses that to degrade his sister, the daughter of God, commits the next greatest crime in the catalogue of crime in the sight of God to the shedding of innocent blood. (April 8, 1883, DNW 32:258)

VIRTUE THE FOUNDATION OF GREATNESS. I would rather see men punished with death—which we believe is a law that should be put in force against any man who ruins women—than that there ever should be a time in our country when corruption and wrongs of this character should run riot and be unchecked. Virtue lies at the foundation of individual and national greatness. No man can amount to much who is not a virtuous man, who is not strong in his virtue, I do not care who he is. He may be as talented as Lucifer; but if he is not a virtuous man, his greatness will not amount to much. Virtue lies at the foundation of greatness. (June 20, 1883, JD 24:224-25)

VIRTUE THE CHIEF CORNERSTONE. God has established this Church, and He has told us from the very beginning that the chief corner stone, it may be said, of this great edifice that He has reared and is rearing is virtue. Early in the history of the Church the Prophet Joseph received revelations to this effect, that he who looked upon a woman to lust after her should deny the faith, and unless he repented, he should be cast out. What an amount of purity is embodied in this statement of the Lord to us in this revelation!

A man must not only refrain from doing that which is wrong with the opposite sex; he must not only refrain from carrying his lust into the actual commission of crime, but he must be so pure in heart that he shall not look upon the other sex with a lustful eye and a lustful desire. If he does so, we are told by the Almighty that he shall deny the faith. . . . The frequent apostasies from this Church, the many who have left the Church, denied the faith, lost the Spirit of God, the most of them, no doubt, are traceable to the commission of this sin. It is, as I have said, the crying sin of the age. . . .

TEACH CHILDREN IMPORTANCE OF VIRTUE. Therefore, it is of the utmost importance that we, in training our children, should lay deep and solid in their minds the importance of virtue. They should be taught that their whole lives as Latter-day Saints depend upon the cultivation and preservation of this principle and that if they are guilty of wrong in this direction, unless there is sincere and heartfelt repentance before the Lord, He will undoubtedly withdraw His Holy Spirit from them and leave them to themselves to become a prey to those wicked influences that are seeking constantly to take possession of the hearts of the Saints of God.

Now, we can best do this in childhood; we can teach our children in childhood and in youth, and as they grow to manhood and to womanhood, we can fortify them against those evils. . . .

A GREATER STRICTNESS NEEDED. There should be greater strictness enforced among our people. There has been a growth of wrong-doing in many quarters that has been most painful to all those who have the welfare of the Saints of God at heart and who desire the prosperity of Zion. . . . Now, such a condition of things if permitted to continue in our midst, unchecked, would be productive of the most terrible consequences. The Spirit of God would undoubtedly be so grieved that it would forsake not only those who are guilty of these acts, but it would withdraw itself from those who would suffer them to be done in our midst unchecked and unrebuked; and from the President of the Church down, throughout the entire ranks of the Priesthood, there would be a loss of the Spirit of God, a withdrawal of His gifts and blessing and His power, because of their not taking the proper measures to check and to expose their iniquity. (January 18, 1885, JD 26:138-39)

PURITY THE STRENGTH OF ZION. Impress the minds of the children with the great importance of purity, of avoiding everything vulgar, of keeping clear from all who are inclined to vulgarity and to anything that would lead to evil and unchastity. The purity of our people is the strength of Zion. Their love of virtue, the chasteness of their conversation and their associations constitute the strength of the Latter-day Saints. We who have children in our charge can do much towards perpetuating this love of purity by fortifying the rising generation against the evils of the world.

The consequences that will follow the violation of the laws of virtue are dreadful to contemplate. The Lord will root out an impure generation, just as He has declared. Any generation that indulges in practices by which virtue is trampled under foot is sure to bring the displeasure and anger of God, and His destroying power will fall upon them. It is the great evil of our day and generation, and we are in the midst of these temptations. (February 1, 1901, JI 36:81)

THE GREAT SIN OF THIS GENERATION. The great, crying sin of this generation is lasciviousness in its various forms. Satan, knowing how powerful an agency this is in corrupting men and women, and in driving the Spirit from them, and bringing them under condemnation before the Lord, uses it to the greatest extent possible. It requires an incessant warfare to check its spread and to prevent the people of God from becoming its victims.

No people who practice or countenance these sins can be accepted of the Lord or find favor in His sight. His anger will fall upon them unless they thoroughly and heartily repent of every such evil. When we take into consideration the teachings we have received upon this subject, the holy covenants into which we have entered, and the professions which we make, unchastity should have no existence among us. It is sorrowful to contemplate that Satan finds those among us who are willing to yield to his temptations, and thus bring misery upon themselves and all connected with them.

We solemnly call, as we have done so often before, upon all the officers of the Church to set their faces like flint against practices of this character. Those who indulge in them must be dealt with according to the laws of God, and they must be made to feel that if they do indulge in this wickedness they cannot have the fellowship of the Saints nor a standing in the Church of Christ. If men and women would only profit by the experiences of those who have fallen, they would resist the allurements of sin and walk in the path of righteousness. "The wages of sin is death." The misery which it brings upon the guilty, and upon all connected with them, furnishes some idea of the dreadful condition of the wicked who die in their sins and do not obtain the forgiveness of their God.

Oh, that men and women could be warned, and that they would turn to the Lord and seek unto Him, humble themselves before Him, put away their sins, and obtain His Holy Spirit to be their guide and their companion, then no matter what the circumstances might be in which they were placed, they would have the peace of heaven, the joy of the Holy Ghost, and a conscience void of offense towards God and man! And this is the condition in which every Latter-day Saint should live. (October 6, 1886, MS 48:706)

Now, my brethren and sisters, what is the great and damning sin today of this generation? What is it that is causing the inhabitants of the earth to rush on the broad road to destruction? . . . It is the impurity of mankind. It is the corruption and licentiousness that have grown up in the world, until virtue has become almost a matter of ridicule. . . .

THE MOST FRUITFUL CAUSE OF APOSTASY. There has been no more fruitful cause of apostasy in this Church than this. Those who have been familiar with the Elders who have fallen and know the cause of their fall will agree with me, I am sure, in saying that this sin has been the most fruitful cause of the overthrow of Elders in this Church. . . . The Spirit of God will dwell only in holy and pure tabernacles. To have it, therefore, we must be pure, not only in our acts, but in our words and our thoughts; for by the medium of thought we can corrupt ourselves and indulge in lust, which will drive the Spirit of God away from us, leaving us in darkness. (May 19, 1889, DW 39:17-18)

UNVIRTUOUS TO LOSE FAITH. The testimony that we bear is that the Latter-day Saint who indulges in sexual sin will be damned, if he does not repent. There has been no greater cause of apostasy in this Church than the want of virtue. You can predict the future of a man who is guilty of sins of this kind, unless he repents, as sure as you can predict that darkness will follow the setting of the sun.

God will have a virtuous people, and those of you who are not virtuous will go the way that others have gone unless you repent; you will lose the faith, for the Spirit of God will not dwell in an unholy tabernacle. The man or the woman that is unvirtuous cannot retain the Spirit of God. They may be members of the Church today, in full fellowship, unsuspected by their fellows, but if they do not repent, their wickedness will produce its fruits and the result which God has said would attend it.

Think of what the word of God is. In two revelations that He has given to the Church, He has said that "he that looketh upon a woman to lust after her shall deny the faith . . . if he repents not." [D&C 42:23.] He that "looketh" upon a woman, remember—not lay his hands upon her—but "he that looketh upon a woman to lust after her, shall deny the faith." Therefore, we must not only be pure in deed but be pure in thought, in order to retain the Spirit of God and to have it dwell in our tabernacles. It will not dwell in those who are lustful.

This is the standard that God has raised for His people. He wants us to come up to this standard—to be pure as angels are pure. And why should not we be? If we are going to dwell with God and Christ and with the holy angels, why should not we emulate on the earth the purity that they possess, which makes heaven the blest abode that it is?

I am thankful that this standard has been raised among us. It gives hope for the future of humanity. Otherwise, the fate of this generation is sure. They are going the downward road, and nothing can save them except thorough repentance. The Elders wonder why it is that they do not gather out more from the nations of the earth than they did formerly. The reason is obvious. The people are corrupt. They are full of lust and abominable evils. Abortion and foeticide and kindred sins are practiced almost universally. (October 5, 1890, DW 41:650-51)

Many times we wonder how men fall away. We look around and see if we can define the cause. What is the cause? The man was a good, faithful man, strong in the faith, and yet how weak he has grown. He is careless about his duty and indifferent. He is spiritually sick; he exhibits the evidences of spiritual disease, and if he examines his own heart, he is conscious of it, but blinded by the spirit that has taken possession of him he will not repent. If he could only be made to realize the dreadful condition which he is in, he would be stirred up to repentance and would put all his sins far from him. (April 21, 1895, DW 51:290)

EXAMPLES FROM CHURCH HISTORY. Oliver Cowdery, who stood side by side with Joseph, who was ordained by an angel from heaven, who was the second Elder in the Church, who beheld the Son of God himself, who saw many wonderful things and was blessed of God as was Joseph—this man whom one would think would have stood if any man in the flesh ever could—indulged in sin. Joseph warned him against that which he did, but he persisted in it, and the result was his Priesthood was taken from him, and the crown that he would have had was given to another. Hyrum Smith received the blessings that Oliver Cowdery had had bestowed upon him and which he had forfeited by his impure conduct.

Ought not this to be a warning to all of us? What man is there in the flesh who can calculate upon being secure from committing sin if he could not? This is the fate also of other men who received great gifts from God. Apostle Lyman Johnson had great manifestations. Angels ministered unto him, and he was the first man in this generation to be chosen one of the Twelve Apostles. Yet he apostatized, denied the faith and became an enemy to the Kingdom of God. These are illustrations of the truth of what God has said, and our history is full of such illustrations. You see men of great promise—I have watched them in my life—all at once wither up, lose their power. They lose the life that was in them. What is the cause? Why, they have committed sin. (June 20, 1892, DW 45:258)

BETTER TO DIE THAN LOSE VIRTUE. We should teach our children these principles. Every daughter, as soon as she is old enough, should be taught that it is better for her to lose her life than her virtue. Every boy should be taught that it is better for him to die than to be guilty of unvirtuous conduct. Impress it upon them in their childhood. And then, when you have done it all, you may find some of them going astray and doing wrong. Still, it is the duty of parents to acquit themselves by teaching their children these things. (DEN, March 4, 1895)

MEN MORE ACCOUNTABLE THAN WOMEN. Men ought to be held, and I believe the Lord does hold them in such cases, to a far stricter accountability than he does women. The woman has her own passions to contend against; but when she has the man's importunities added to these, shall not the woman be viewed with mercy and be looked upon differently to that vile creature who, possessed of strength and power, adds his importunities to her weakness and overcomes her, and makes her the victim of his unholy lust? I say, Yes, Yes! Such men will be damned; and if there is any deeper damnation than another, they will be consigned to it. (October 6, 1897, CR 67)

THOSE WHO PRESIDE HAVE GRAVE RESPONSIBILITY. Oh, ye Presidents of Stakes and ye Bishops, you must be on the watchtower about these things, for God will hold you accountable. The sins of the people will be found upon your garments in the day of the Lord Jesus, if you do not cleanse impurity from the midst of your Wards. If you recommend men who are unworthy, through tenderness of heart and through sympathy, when they are wicked, I say to you, in the name of Jesus Christ, that the condemnation of God will rest upon you, and He will hold you to a strict accountability. For God has not chosen men to preside without laying upon them responsibility of a very grave and weighty character. He holds us accountable for these things. (October 5, 1884, JD 25:327-28)

PURE AND CORRECT THOUGHTS. There is no temptation which it is more necessary to guard against, because there is probably no practice which is more injurious in its tendencies, than that of giving way to evil surmisings. It is very true that "As he thinketh in his heart, so is he." [Proverbs 23:7.] Words and actions are but the external fruits of the inward thoughts of the soul; they must be conceived there before they find their birth from the lips or the hands of the corporeal frame. Hence, we can see the necessity of properly governing our thoughts and of cultivating a habit of pure and correct thinking.

If a man be pure in thought, he will be correspondingly pure in action; but if he allow his mind to roam in unrestricted freedom through the various avenues of evil or to dwell unchecked upon the contemplation of forbidden indulgences, it will not be long before his feet tread those paths and his hand plucks the tempting but deceitful fruit. When once the tempter gains the citadel of the heart, his power is very great, and there is no knowing to what excesses of folly and crime he may incite his unhappy victim.

Our first and chief efforts, therefore, should be directed to having our hearts cleansed from all evil by the sanctifying and purifying influences of the Spirit of the Lord, and then, the tree having been made good at the root, its fruit will be sure to be of a corresponding character. Hence, the Lord says, "My son, give me thine heart." [Proverbs 23:26.] Not thy lip service, thy money, or anything else that may be possessed as an inseparable adjunct of life, but thine heart, knowing, as He does, that where this is given all else will follow. (February 13, 1864, MS 26:105)

A DISTINGUISHING FEATURE OF MORMONISM. There is one thing that distinguishes the Latter-day Saints from every other people that I know anything about—and I have traveled considerably—and that is they love one another. It is not in name; it is not a profession of love; but they are a people who love one another so strongly that they are willing to die for each other if it is necessary, and it is that deep and abiding love that binds them in union.

Travel among the "Mormons" wherever you will, north or south, east or west, at home or abroad, in the United States or in foreign lands, this love is a distinguishing characteristic of the people; you behold it everywhere. Men may never have beheld each other's faces and yet they will love one another, and it is a love that is greater than the love of woman. It exceeds any sexual love that can be conceived of, and it is this love that has bound the people together. It has been a cement that all the persecution, all the tribulation and all kinds of trial could not dissolve or break; and the extraordinary feature of it all is, as I have said, that this people who are thus bound together are not a people of one township, not a people of one nation, not a people of one language, but they are as diverse as it is possible to get the human family to be.

It would not be so strange if all were Americans, or all eastern men, born in New England, brought up with the traditions of New England; it would not be so strange if all were men of the middle States, or of the northern States, or of the western States. But who is there that asks among the "Mormons" or Latter-day Saints as to a man's nationality? Who is it asks where a man or a woman came from? No one. Here are Danish, French, German, Italian, English, American—northern, southern, eastern and western men—all living together as brothers, full of love for each other; none of that rancorous feeling that exists between different nationalities is to be witnessed. (July 24, 1881, JD 22: 365-66)

THE POWER OF LOVE. There is one power which the Latter-day Saints in their history have had experience in exercising—the power of love. The Savior's teachings impress upon those who receive them the potency of love. It is much more effective than violence.

It is grander in its results. It is happier in its effects. It wins the wrongdoer. It softens the heart of the offender. It disarms the anger of the violent. It expands the heart and produces the most delightful results upon the person who exercises it and who restrains himself and instead of yielding to anger and to resentment repays the one who wrongs him by kindness and love. Let anyone try this, if he has not done so, he will see how true the saying is that has come down to us in the scriptures, that "A soft answer turneth away wrath." (March 1, 1895, JI 30:147)

LOVE AND ITS POWER. The principle of love lies at the foundation of all true religion. Children should be taught to love God. If they love Him, they will obey Him; they will never do anything to offend Him or to grieve His Holy Spirit. Where love is absent, true and acceptable worship cannot be rendered for the heart is not in it. We can see this in our daily life. The child who has true love for its parent will not fail to obey him. Such a child will do all in its power to please its parent; and if it should at any time do anything that would offend, it will readily ask forgiveness and humble itself before its parent.

Where love does not exist, and the obedience of children is only obtained by threats and fears, there is but little real respect and reverence manifested. Children should obey their parents not because they are forced to do so by fear of punishment or by threats but because they take delight in doing that which their parents ask them to do. Both receive pleasure in this way. The children take pleasure in pleasing the parents; the parents receive pleasure in witnessing the willingness of the children to comply with their requests. Really good government in the family cannot prevail in any other way. . . .

Members of the Church of Christ should not base their obedience to the Lord and His commands upon the fear of punishment that will follow if they do not comply with His requirements. A far better way is to obey the Lord because we love Him and because we take delight in doing His will. How good and kind and long-suffering and merciful He has been to us. . . .

A Being so beneficent, and who shows such wondrous kindness to us, is worthy of our worship and of our love. When we feel as we should do, our hearts are filled with love and adoration for Him; and if we have this love within us and remember all that He has done for us, can we not worship Him with all our hearts? Can we not obey Him in all things? Is it not our delight to listen to His counsel and take pleasure in doing that which He asks? Remember, it is for our salvation that He makes requirements of us and gives unto us His laws. Some may imagine that they are doing our Father in heaven some great service by obeying Him. It is those who obey who receive the greatest benefit from their obedience. . . .

Every man, woman and child should cultivate love; for "God is love." [1 John 4:8.] We should love one another. We should love our parents. We should love the Lord our God and everything that proceedeth from Him. By cultivating this heavenly principle, we shall be prepared to dwell in His presence, where love abounds. (September 15, 1890, JI 25:562)

Section 3

ASSORTED GOSPEL THEMES

The Gospel has been revealed for the purpose of enabling mankind to comprehend saving truths. It contains the laws which men and women must obey to prepare them for that higher society which exists in heaven. It is by observing these laws and precepts that angels have attained to their glory, and by which also He who is greater than the angels has reached His high and exalted position—our beloved Savior and Redeemer, Jesus Christ.

—George Q. Cannon
Juvenile Instructor
29:680

Chapter 18

Habits—Good and Bad

THE VALUE OF SELF-DENIAL. Undoubtedly self-denial is an excellent quality, and one that all should practice. Our natures, appetites and inclinations should be controlled. A child should be taught self-denial in many directions besides these that have been mentioned. In fact, to be pure in the sight of the Lord great self-denial is required throughout life, in order to bring everything into proper subjection to the law of the Lord and the requirements of His Gospel. The body and its appetites and desires must be brought into subjection to the spirit.

It is for this purpose that a probation is granted to us on the earth, so that we may by obedience to law make our bodies fit tabernacles for the Holy Ghost to dwell in, and in this manner prepare it for a glorious resurrection and a residence, in an immortal condition, in the presence of the Lord. (December 15, 1894, JI 29:769)

ANGER AND THE SPIRIT OF GOD. The Spirit of God produces peace and quiet and good-temper. Men and women who have the Spirit are amiable, are kind and loving one towards another. They control their tempers, because the Spirit of God will not dwell where the spirit of anger and hatred and violence exist.

We should, of all people upon the face of the earth, be the best tempered, the kindest, the most forbearing, the most loving, the least disposed to quarrel. (June 15, 1882, JI 17:190)

THE EVIL OF UNCONTROLLED ANGER. It is very difficult to be angry and sin not. The anger which is not unto sin is that which God and his servants feel against the wicked and their evil ways; but the anger of children one with another is not from God, but from that source from which all evils flow and sorrows rise. It is the temptation of the wicked one to lead us astray.

We have all to learn to govern our tempers and passions. It matters not if we be big or little, old or young, we must not let them control us. If they do, they will destroy us. A man with passions he cannot govern is like a run-away locomotive engine;

no one knows where it will go or the injury it will do, but it is sure to come to destruction at last.

How sad a sight is a passionate child, one who disputes and contends, who quarrels and fights. What good can we prophecy of such a child if these angry passions are not checked while it is young. That feeling grows in many into the spirit of shedding blood and has made many a man a murderer, as it did Cain, who in his wrath slew his brother Abel. Sorrow waits on all those who do not strive to conquer this burning, choking, death-dealing feeling of anger that so quickly and uncalled for rises in our hearts and fills for a short time our whole souls. It is not of God. He abhors it, and men fear and hate it.

The passionate man is a foe to himself. Anger plows more furrows on the forehead and spoils more pretty faces than age itself. The passionate man carries in his bosom a never-dying fire that burns to his destruction and consumes the vital powers of his being. Many men shorten their lives, not for weeks or days but for years, by giving way to anger. It is like an earthquake is to the ground; it overturns and displaces, disorganizes and destroys, and throws all of the hidden machinery of a man's body into disorder. And thus a man brings evil on himself.

Perhaps you may think it strange that anger should hurt the body; but it is so. The spirit and body are so united that all the feelings of the mind act upon the body. Love and hatred, joy and sorrow, hope and fear, cheerfulness and gloom all work for good or harm on this outward clothing of the spirit. Even the fact, small as it may seem, of our asking a blessing on our food and thanking our Heavenly Father for it has a good effect on our bodies. That is, if the heart rises with the lips in gratitude. That feeling of gratitude or thankfulness fits the stomach to receive the food, while gloom or anger unfits it for its work. A crust of bread eaten with a cheerful heart will do us more good than the choicest food partaken of in sullenness or wrath. Thus, in so small a thing as this may appear, while we honor God, we bless ourselves.

The spirit we should bear is peace, meekness and love. Jesus said, "Blessed are the peacemakers: for they shall be called the children of God." [Matthew 5:9.] What a glorious title! Let us try and remember it. Remember also that a wise man has said, "A soft answer turneth away wrath: but grievous words st[illegible] up anger." [Proverbs 15:1.] Boys and girls who fancy that they have received an insult or suffered a wrong should think twice before they speak once, and think that "a soft answer turneth away wrath," then act upon this thought and give a kind word with a smile, and peace will dwell in two hearts where, had a cross word been given, anger would have reigned.

There is one thing more, never vex a companion to anger by taunts or unwise jests. Such a course is also wrong; it produces the evil we have been talking about. But let your intercourse be in kindness and love, and you will grow up to be indeed "the children of God." (April 15, 1868, JI 3:60)

PUNCTUALITY A DESIRABLE TRAIT. One of the most desirable traits in a man's or woman's character is punctuality. The word covers a great deal of ground. We call a man punctual when he keeps an appointment at a given minute or hour; and this is the most common use of the word. But it really means much more than this. A man is punctual who, whenever he gives his word, keeps it, who never neglects to fulfill his promise at the time and in the way he has said he would. The punctual man, therefore, is the truthful man; while the man who is unpunctual is apt to mislead and perhaps deceive others and is guilty of conduct closely akin to untruthfulness.

Punctuality is a virtue that every juvenile should cultivate. Much of the success and happiness of life depends upon its observance. Boys and girls who are punctual are sure to secure confidence. People learn to rely upon them. They trust them. They always have good credit. If they wish to obtain a favor, their character for punctuality secures it for them. If they are in a position where it is necessary for them to borrow, their punctuality is trusted, and they get what they want. And it is frequently in what are called small things that this quality is best shown. Certainly it is in such things that it should be cultivated.

One form of this virtue is shown in the answering of letters. In this respect many otherwise very worthy people are neglectful. They are neither punctual nor courteous. They receive letters of love, letters of friendship, letters of business, letters of inquiry; but instead of answering them when they are received, they lay them aside till some other time, which they think will be more convenient, and they are perhaps never answered. Such conduct is not only unpunctual; it is rude; it is very bad manners and is a lack of good breeding. Of course, there may be times when other pressing business may prevent the most punctual people from answering letters. Under such circumstances such neglect can be excused. But, as a rule, the best time to answer a letter is immediately upon its receipt or as soon thereafter as possible. The one who receives it has the spirit of it then and usually can better answer it then than at any other time. If it be put off, every day that passes makes it more difficult to do, until it is forgotten altogether, in which event the writer feels slighted and perhaps offended. Not only does the writer feel that he has been shabbily treated, but the one who has failed to reply feels ashamed and condemned at his own neglect.

One of the most punctual men we ever knew was President Young. Yet he was a busy man. But he was punctual at his meetings. He was punctual at his meals. However crowded he might be he did not feel that it was proper to keep others, not even his family, waiting for him. His family met for prayers at a certain time of an evening; he would break away from the most engrossing business, from the most interesting conversation, to be punctual at family prayers; he would not even keep his children waiting for him. (April 1, 1883, JI 18:104)

PROCRASTINATION. Another bad habit akin to want of punctuality is that of procrastination. The meaning of procrastination is the act of putting off till tomorrow or a future time.

Children should be taught to avoid this and not suffer a habit of this kind to fasten itself upon them. They should be made to understand that whatever should be done ought to be done promptly and at the time that it is expected. Work is always done best and quickest and with the most satisfaction at the proper time. To put off till tomorrow that which should be done today is a bad habit to fall into.

Young people frequently have an inclination of this kind. If not watched and reminded of what they have to do, they are likely to neglect work and put it off, especially if the duty or the labor is not pleasant. If they are not well trained on this point in early life, when they become men and women they find it difficult to do unpleasant things, and because of this duties are frequently neglected. Observing people find by experience that it is always more satisfactory and attended with better results to perform a duty at the time it ought to be done, especially if it should be something unpleasant. (December 1, 1892, JI 27:726)

HAVE NOBLE ASPIRATIONS. The man or woman that lives the most fruitful and interesting life is the one that has wholesome, vigorous aspirations. Without these a person's life may be commonplace or even a failure, though his abilities are great; possessing them he must attain influence and success, whether his abilities seem at first great or small. Aspirations, if they are real, create a need for abilities to carry them out. If abilities are present, they are put to use; if absent, they are cultivated. . . .

Political eminence is not the only goal to which we may aspire. Vocations should be chosen according to tastes and opportunities. The effort should be to make oneself most useful in his occupation and thoroughly the master of it. Our life plans should be carefully made and should always be subject to reasonable change. The most prominent thought in them should be excellence and combined with this determination to work. . . .

But aspirations are not complete if they do not lead to moral strength and spiritual activity. Without these qualities the character lacks true greatness. The Savior never led an army, never held position in any state, but how incomparably does His divine personality surpass that of the mightiest conqueror or of the most illustrious ruler! Joseph Smith, His chosen servant in latter days, was not college bred nor trained in any political school, but yet how much more keen was his insight into national conditions than that of the men who ruled the nation during the latter part of his life, and how much better would humanity have been if his advice had been followed and the fratricidal war between North and South averted!

"Aim at the stars; you may attain the mountain tops." Human beings cannot reach perfection, but we can think of it and can strive toward it. And the more clearly we conceive what is true and perfect and the more sincerely we strive the closer will we approach it and the better will be our lives. (September 1, 1898, JI 33:600-601)

AVOID THE EXTREMES. There is a disposition evinced in many individuals to follow up some favorite idea or some particular theory and stretch it to undue bounds, attaching to it an importance far beyond what it is legitimately entitled to. . . .

The Gospel has been revealed to elevate us above these narrow, contracted notions and teaches us that one truth is not entitled to such paramount importance above another but is chiefly valuable by its connection with kindred truths, all blending into each other and forming a whole calculated to exalt man in every condition of existence. Still, many men who have had sufficient opportunities in the Church to obtain a more liberal and extended understanding of the truth permit themselves to be governed by this one-sided principle and, seizing upon some favorite doctrine, make it their hobby and invest it with all the importance due to the entire scheme of salvation. . . .

The Priesthood are sent forth as saviours of men, and it devolves upon every one who is called to minister among the people to divest himself of illiberal and contracted ideas and to teach the great truths of salvation whereby man can be made free, ever pursuing a course to win the love and confidence of the honest among men and dealing by them in a spirit of charity and kindness. . . .

Hence, to be effective ministers of salvation, the Priesthood ought continually to keep in their minds and teach, by precept and example, the importance of all the principles of truth with which they have become acquainted, ever carefully avoiding extremes, that the Saint may increase in knowledge and understanding and power before God. . . .

And if they permit that hobby-riding spirit, so dominant in the world, to govern them, intelligent men and women will be repelled instead of attracted by the influence which accompanies them; whereas, liberal views and charitable teachings in consonance with the spirit of the Gospel will possess an irresistible charm for all who love freedom of thought and purity of life. (July 6, 1861, MS 23:424-26)

CORRECT SPEAKING AND WRITING. There is too little regard paid to the elementary principles of education. . . . Every child should be taught to write a good hand. The greatest care should be taken in teaching them this art. The forming of figures, also, should be taught with care; and, of course, reading and spelling ought to be considered of the first importance as the foundation of an education. There is too great a tendency to having our children study the higher branches of education and to look upon reading, writing and spelling as of little importance. This is a great mistake. No matter how educated a man or a woman may be, if the handwriting is poor, it gives a bad impression to those who see it of the writer's education; and if bad spelling is added to bad writing, of course no one reading it can suppose that the person is anything but a dunce. (March 15, 1897, JI 32:186)

BE CAREFUL WHAT YOU WRITE. Among the many wise counsels which the Prophet Joseph Smith gave to his brethren and to the world, one was never to commit anything to paper in correspondence that could be communicated orally or that if written would not bear publication. This counsel the Elders of our Church and our people generally should follow; in fact, it would be better for everyone to remember it and never put in writing that which they would be ashamed to see in print.

There has been no end of trouble through carelessness in these respects. When a person has committed to writing that which should not be said, it is difficult and in some cases impossible to recall it. Words spoken are heard and sometimes remembered in a way to produce unpleasant results; but that danger is insignificant compared with that which attends the committing of things to writing that should not be said. (April 1, 1896, JI 31:199)

An improper word or a wrong idea, when spoken indiscreetly and without any evil intention by a servant of God, may be removed from the memory and mind of the hearers or be so modified as to lose its hurtfulness, by the influence of the Spirit of God; but, when they are once written, their effects cannot be so easily corrected. . . .

A man who to-day may not attach much importance to his

opinions might possibly be disagreeably surprised in the great day of accounts, were he, while he lived, to write much and be careless as to its agreement with truth, to find how much evil had been wrought out by his indiscreet and irresponsible writings. An importance is frequently attached to the utterances and acts and position of a man who has lived a generation or two previously which his contemporaries would be quite unwilling to accord to them. When it is truth which has been written by a faithful servant of God and thus been perpetuated, it produces great good; but when it is error, it will readily be perceived that its effects are increasingly hurtful.

PAUL'S WRITINGS GIVEN UNDUE PREEMINENCE. There is an amount of deference paid to the writings of Paul at the present time which he possibly never anticipated would be when he penned them, or he might have written differently on some points; that is, if we accept the present version of his writings as not very, very incorrect. With his contemporaries they did not weigh so very much. Even among his brethren and the Saints—though they, doubtless, attached far more value to them than anybody else—they did not receive the consideration which the writings of others obtained, who are considered now-a-days his inferiors. He either wrote more than many of his brethren, or what he did write was much better preserved than their writings, and posterity have therefore assigned him a preeminence among his brethren which, when alive, he did not possess.

EVERY WORD SHOULD BE CAREFULLY WEIGHED. If we take the past as a guide, posterity will be considerably influenced by our ideas and views. The Elders can scarcely conceive, at the present time, of the weight which will be attached by future generations to their words and acts, as they may find them recorded; how exceedingly careful we ought to be, then, that we should not be the means of perpetuating error or anything that would be likely to lead to evil!

We should consider it far preferable to have everything that we had ever written destroyed and blotted out of earthly existence than to have our writings be the means of perpetuating error or imparting improper ideas. Let our every word, then, as servants of God and speaking by His authority, be carefully weighed that when it is sent forth, whether its circulation be limited or extensive, it may accomplish good. (August 6, 1863, MS 26:505-506)

AVOID THE USE OF SLANG. Children are imitative; they are quick at learning and seizing new or odd expressions. If they hear swearing or vulgar language, they are apt to pick it up, so with slang. For this reason, parents and teachers and all who are in frequent contact with children should be careful in their speech. Good style in speaking is learned early in life and is rarely, if ever, forgotten. So with a careless, bad style.

The style of language used in the family circle should not only be for home purposes and every day wear, but should be that which can be used in other society and upon state occasions. By being thus trained young people will feel at ease among all cultivated and well-bred people, an advantage which all of them will, sooner or later, learn to appreciate. (October 1, 1893, JI 28:602)

IMPORTANCE OF ACCURACY. Every young person should be particular to cultivate the habit of exact truthfulness in all his words, whether in conversation upon trivial matters or in the relation of events of importance. It is remarkable how easily a habit of carelessness can be acquired in this direction. . . .

Children should be taught in early life to state everything exactly as it occurs. Their consciences should be developed in this direction, and they should be made to feel how wrong it is to be inaccurate in their statements of what has occurred. They should be taught to repeat conversations as nearly as possible in the spirit as well as the words in which they have been uttered; for though the same words may be repeated, they may convey an entirely different impression unless they are repeated in the same spirit in which they were originally spoken.

There should be a love of truth developed in every human breast, and everyone should be made to feel the great importance of truthfulness. Too great care cannot be taken in relating occurrences or conversations which are likely to affect the opinion of the person to whom they are related concerning other parties who may be absent. If one person conveys an incorrect impression to the mind of another concerning an absent one, a great injury is done, and sometimes serious consequences follow. . . .

It should be the aim of all to obtain such a character for telling the truth that every acquaintance will know that, when such persons make statements, they can be thoroughly relied upon. It should be understood that they would not deviate the breadth of a hair from a correct statement of facts concerning any transaction to which they may have been a party. A character of this kind secured by a young person is invaluable to him or to her throughout life. We should be as reliable in our sphere as the angels are in their sphere, and never, willingly, make any statement that will not bear the strictest scrutiny. (January 15, 1890, JI 25:50-51)

DISRESPECT FOR AGED A GROWING EVIL. Let every child be taught to respect and reverence not only their parents but old age. Let us endeavor to raise up a generation who will respect age. One of the great and growing evils that exists to-day in our land is the disrespect that is manifested by the young to age. Let us train our children to be respectful and to honor the gray hairs of the aged, to honor their parents that the great promise that was made in olden times may be bestowed upon them—namely, that their days may be long in the land. (June 27, 1880, JD 22:58)

TAKING LORD'S NAME IN VAIN A SERIOUS OFFENSE. "Thou shalt not take the name of the Lord thy God in vain; for the Lord will not hold him guiltless that taketh his name in vain." [Exodus 20:7.] This was one of the commandments that the Lord gave to the children of Israel when He led them out of Egypt. All the people were required to observe it, and if they did not, the penalty was very severe. . . .

The Lord required not only the children of Israel to observe this commandment, but the stranger also who should be living in their midst. The penalty for breaking the commandments was

. . . death. It is a terrible punishment, but then the crime was a great one. Suppose that every one were punished with death now who took the Lord's name in vain. A great many would have to die. Even among those who call themselves Latter-day Saints a great many would fall victims to this penalty.

If it was wrong in the days of Moses to take the name of the Lord in vain, is it not wrong now? If a man were stoned to death for blaspheming the name of the Lord at that time, what should be the penalty now? Moses did not punish that man until he had asked the Lord what he was to do with him. [Leviticus 24:10-17.] He was killed by a command of the Lord. This shows that the Lord wants all men to honor His holy name.

When we hear boys and men speak lightly of our Father in Heaven, cursing or swearing, we think of the punishment that this man received. For Latter-day Saints, or their children, to take the name of the Lord in vain is a dreadful crime, because they have been taught better. They know it is wrong, and yet are there not many who are guilty of this?

USE HIS SACRED NAME INFREQUENTLY. We have sometimes heard Elders telling some story or some joke in which the name of the Deity has been taken in vain, and they would repeat it. Now, this is very wrong. It is just as great a sin for the man who repeats what another man said, in taking the name of the Lord in vain, as it was for the man who first said it, to do it. Therefore, if a man takes the name of the Lord in vain, we should not repeat it nor think ourselves justified in doing so because we merely quote his language.

There are some Elders who use the name of the Deity very frequently in their preaching and in their praying; they make the name altogether too common. In praying the Savior taught His disciples to say, "Our Father, who are in heaven." "Our Father!" How Sweet this is; how near it brings us to him! What better or more endearing title can we use? Children, when you pray, address Him as Father, and when you speak of Him, do so as our Heavenly Father, or Lord, and do not use His sacred name lightly or frequently, neither in praying nor speaking; and remember that He "will not hold him guiltless that taketh his name in vain." (September 1, 1877, JI 12:198)

AN INEXCUSABLE VICE. To profane the name of God is a heinous sin—one that the Almighty proclaimed against in a very early age and many times since. It is one of the sins mentioned, of which the Lord said "even the souls that commit them shall be cut off from among their people." [Leviticus 18:29.]

Of all the vices we can think of that of profanity admits of the least possible excuse or palliation. It gratifies no sense nor appetite; it benefits no one; it does not even commend the person indulging in it to the estimation of anyone. It is a most senseless and unreasonable practice, that can be accounted for only on the score of depravity.

Our language is certainly rich enough in expletives to allow any person to express his feelings with all the emphasis necessary without using profanely the name of the Deity for such a purpose. . . .

If a person believes in the existence of the Creator, how wicked, how irreverent, how ungrateful in him is the practice of profaning His name! If a person does not believe in the existence of such a Being, how foolish, how unreasonable it is for him to swear by that name! (September 1, 1881, JI 16:198)

A SAFE RULE TO FOLLOW. It is a safe rule that it is not wise to adopt any habit in this life that must be given up before we can enter into the joys of the next, or, we should never encourage on earth that which will not be permitted in heaven. Every one of us is willing to admit that good men do not swear; do we expect they will do so when they enter the presence of God? Do angels take the Lord's name in vain? The idea is so ridiculous that we scarcely like to ask the question. But then there is another question which this leads to of great importance to the blasphemer. It is this: How dare we do that which angels dare not do? Is it possible for us to argue that that which is forbidden in heaven is praiseworthy on earth? . . .

Though we are sure no boy can tell us any advantage that can arise from the abuse of God's holy name, yet we can tell him many evils that arise therefrom. To begin, it is unnecessary and consequently foolish; it lessens our respect for holy things and lead us into the society of the wicked; it brings upon us the disrespect of the good who avoid us; it leads us to other sins, for he who is willing to abuse his Creator is not ashamed to defraud his fellow creature; and also by so doing we directly and knowingly break one of the most direct of God's commandments. (September 27, 1873, JI 8:156)

MORAL COURAGE. Moral courage is a gift which every man should highly prize and which our young readers should cultivate. Physical courage is a quality not uncommon among men and animals—the courage to face danger, to grapple with tangible obstacles and to incur the risk of death. In the excitement of battle, or under the influence of passion, men perform daring feats of valor and lose all sense of fear. Under the influence of stimulants, too, men will face danger and have no fears as to results. This kind of courage is rather common among men and is frequently called brute courage.

But moral courage is a quality of a different character. It requires moral courage to be a Latter-day Saint. It requires moral courage to do the right thing and say the right word when it is unpopular to do so. No man can be a truly great man who does not possess this quality. A man possessed of moral courage never shrinks from telling the truth. Such a man is never a liar or a deceiver or a hypocrite; he is never untrue to his principles. To use one of the phrases now common in our day, such a man has the courage of his convictions. A man or woman possessed of true moral courage always excites admiration and compels respect. Moral cowards especially respect such persons, for the reason that it is natural for mankind to admire the good in others that is lacking in their own characters. (November 15, 1882, JI 17:344)

EVIL OF FALSEHOOD. The man who frames a lie is a great sinner; but the one who loves a lie, and who circulates a lie after it is told, is also under condemnation. Many stories go from mouth to mouth concerning the truth of which those who repeat them know nothing. But it seems as though the constant repetition of a falsehood impresses many people as though it were a fact.

Where Latter-day Saints, so-called, are found telling that which is untrue, they should be called to an account. It is written that whosoever loveth and maketh a lie shall not be permitted to enter into the Holy City, nor to have a right to the tree of life, but they are to be without, with dogs, sorcerers, whoremongers, murderers and idolaters. The Lord has said, "He that telleth lies shall not tarry in my sight." [Psalms 101:7.] Latter-day Saints should be warned upon these points, that they may not grieve the Spirit of the Lord, nor do injury to their friends and neighbors, by indulging in this pernicious habit of repeating and attaching credence to every slander and false rumor that may be put in circulation.

But every one should be careful, when they hear a story about their brethren and sisters, to refrain from repeating it until they know it to be true, and then not to do so in a way to injure the person about whom it is told. The reputation of our neighbors and the members of our Church should be as dear to us as our own, and we should carefully avoid doing anything to another or saying anything about another that we would not wish done or said about ourselves. (October 6, 1886, MS 48: 713-14)

COWARDS TELL LIES. Always tell the truth. He is a coward who does not tell the truth; she is a coward who does not tell the truth. You would not like to be called cowards, but recollect that if ever you feel tempted to tell a lie, it is cowardice which prompts you to do it. You are cowardly when you do not tell the truth.

Says a boy, "If I do tell the truth, I may get whipped." It is better to be whipped for telling the truth than to save yourselves from it by telling a lie, although no wise parent or teacher would whip a child for telling the truth. But do you not see that if you tell a lie to avoid a whipping, it is fear which causes you to lie? The boy or girl who is afraid to tell the truth for fear of a whipping is a coward.

Always remember that it is cowardly to tell a lie but brave to tell the truth. Everybody admires the truthteller. If, when you do wrong, you frankly and bravely own, "I did that," your parents will feel thankful that they have a son or a daughter who is brave enough to tell the truth, and though they will disapprove the wrong committed, they will feel in their hearts to bless you for telling the truth. (July 19, 1873, JI 8:116)

AVOID ALL EVIL SPEAKING. Latter-day Saints cannot speak evil of their neighbors or their brethren and sisters without coming under censure and grieving the Spirit of the Lord. Such examples before children are attended with very bad effects. Children hear their parents or others speak lightly about absent friends or relatives, and it encourages them to do the same; they think they are at perfect liberty to comment in the most familiar manner about everyone whom they may know. In many cases neither age nor standing nor sex is respected; young people criticise the words and acts of others with the utmost freedom, and because of the example of their parents perhaps, or of others with whom they associate, they do not think they are doing anything improper in being thus flippant with the reputation of those whom they may know. . . .

Children can be trained to avoid speaking evil of anyone, and they should be taught to exercise the greatest care in this direction. The Gospel of the Lord Jesus Christ and all the teachings of the servants of God are of such a character as to check this inclination in the human mind. . . .

The person who speaks evil of another injures himself or herself more than the person concerning whom the remarks are made. It should be understood by the Latter-day Saints that doing wrong in any form injures the person who commits it, whether it be in word or in act, to a far greater extent than it does the person whose injury is sought.

The truth is, no righteous person can be permanently injured by anything that may be said or done about him. It may seem to do him harm for the time being, but the Lord overrules all these things and controls them for the good of those who serve Him. Therefore, it is not only contrary to the commands of God to speak evil and to tell falsehoods concerning others, but it is bad policy. The injury falls not upon the person for whom it is intended, but upon the one who indulges in it. (May 15, 1895, JI 30:305-306)

EXERCISE TRUE CHARITY. Charity would prevent us from speaking unkindly of the weaknesses or faults of our brethren and sisters and would enable us to treat them leniently and refrain from gossiping about them or magnifying them in speaking of them to others. There is enough good in every human character, especially in those Latter-day Saints, to permit us to dwell lovingly upon the good traits and qualities of those with whom we associate, and then with proper charity we can cover and hide from our view any weaknesses that they may have.

But when Latter-day Saints are guilty of wrongs which amount to clear violations of the law of God, it is not right to cover over those wrongs by exercising charity. There is a way to correct them, and it is true mercy to a man or a woman who thus violates a law of God to bring that to his or her attention and to make him or her conscious of the fact that it is a violation of God's law. A true friend to such parties will not hesitate to speak the truth plainly to them upon questions of this kind and take the necessary steps to have them checked in the commission of wrong and to repent truly and sincerely of it and forsake it.

Herein many officers in the Church have erred. They have exercised mistaken clemency towards sinners. They have supposed that they were exercising charity by bearing with those who were transgressors of the law of God. A Bishop or other officer who takes a course of this kind is as unwise in his sphere as the parent who suffers his child for it. (June 1, 1887, JI 22:168)

PRACTICAL JOKING. At no time should we do anything that can be avoided which would chagrin, inconvenience or pain our fellowmen, and no word or sentence should ever pass our lips, even in a joke, which will not bear the strictest scrutiny under the searchlight of truth. If our surplus energy must find vent in some way, let it be utilized in providing surprises in the shape of blessings for the widows and the fatherless or in doing something that will contribute to the happiness and well-being of our fellowmen. (September 1, 1895, JI 30:527)

RAFFLING NOT APPROVED. Speaking in general upon the practice of raffling, we wish to say that it is not approved of by the authorities of the Church. We think it ought not to be encouraged among our people, no matter how worthy the various purposes or persons that may be urged as beneficiaries from its profits or proceeds. We regard it an especially bad practice to introduce among children. It comes very close indeed to a form of gambling; it at least teaches those who engage in it to build hopes on mere chances, the great majority of which, of course, cannot help but be futile in the very nature of things. . . . It is sufficient to say that it is not regarded as a good practice; it is not attended with good results and ought not to be encouaged among our people. (January 15, 1899, JI 34:48)

CARD PLAYING—A TOOL OF THE ADVERSARY. There is no language of ours that will too strongly condemn this growing evil among the young people of Zion. We look upon it as a dangerous amusement and one which every self-respecting man and woman ought to avoid, and especially those who profess to be Latter-day Saints. We have watched the course of some boys and girls who have persistently followed this habit and have yet to see the first case where good has resulted from this game. On the other hand, instances without number might be named where great evil has followed the playing of cards. . . .

Cards are the tools of the adversary, and even though there may be, as some claim, no evil in the game of cards itself, such amusement frequently leads to bad results.

It should be the rule of young people never to go upon the devil's ground, in other words, never to place themselves in the way of temptation. They will then be better able to resist evil when it does come to them, as it most assuredly will do to each individual who maintains his integrity and retains his place among the people of God. (February 1, 1895, JI 30:97.)

GAMBLING AN EVIL. There are many evils in the world which young folks need to be guarded against. One of these is gambling. There are various forms of this evil but they are all bad and should not be indulged in. Such games of chance as appear most innocent are liable to lead to others that involve greater risks, and they ought to be avoided. When one indulges in a game of chance of any kind, it presents before him a great temptation to continue the practice. In this way many have been led to ruin. . . .

Every boy and girl should keep in mind that the proper way to gain wealth is to work for it—to earn it by legitimate labor. It should also be remembered that such labor is always honorable and that there is no occasion for any one to feel ashamed or humiliated because he has to work for his living. (August 15, 1898, JI 33:572-73)

THE SIN OF INGRATITUDE. There are some sins which are greater than others. To sin against the Holy Ghost, or to shed innocent blood, is a most dreadful crime, the worst a man can commit and one that cannot be forgiven. Judas Iscariot was guilty of this, and many other apostates have been guilty of the same crime. Next to this is the sin of adultery. Those who indulge in this great sin fall under heavy condemnation, and unless they thoroughly repent, their punishment will be severe. Many more sins might be mentioned which are of a very grave character; but we will only mention one now. It is the sin of ingratitude, a sin that is far too common.

Probably some of our readers may not understand what this sin is. We will explain. God, our Heavenly Father, blesses his children with His Spirit and health, food, raiment and other favors. Those who receive these and do not feel thankful to Him for them are guilty of ingratitude. (May 27, 1871, JI 6:84)

BE HONEST BECAUSE IT IS RIGHT. "Honesty is the best policy." This is a very old and true maxim and one that is often quoted. But is there no higher and better reason why people should be honest than because policy suggests that they should be so—than because it pays to be honest? We think so. A person should be honest from principle—because it is right to be honest. If a person is honest merely because there is a prospect of his losing something by dishonesty, he is very likely to change his tactics when the prospect changes. If a person observes the law and does right from fear of punishment only, he is liable to do wrong when the penalty of wrong-doing is not before his eyes. . . .

We believe that "honesty is the best policy." We believe that honesty will pay. But suppose it wouldn't pay; would that fact justify us in acting dishonestly? Not by any means. (May 15, 1880, JI 15:66)

DEBT—A TERRIBLE SLAVERY. Extravagance is the sin and peril of the age. Either from the example of others or the laxity of their own principles, people are prone to live beyond their means. Whatever they earn, they spend more. Debt is easily fallen into, but its slavery is terrible. It discourages ambition; it is a drag upon high endeavor; it is a slow but consuming death to an honest and sensitive soul. War hath slain its thousands, but debt its tens of thousands. It makes of him whom it catches in its toils a serf and either a coward or a scamp. It gnaws like canker; it burns like caustic; it grinds on and on till the grave closes over the unhappy victim. It eats relentlessly away at his substance not only while all the world is awake and active, but also while all the world sleeps. No lock or bar can keep out its blight; in no clime or concealment can the debtor escape its iron clutch.

"To earn a little and to spend a little less" means contentment, courage in facing one's fellows, incentive to braver struggles with the world's adversities and honor and reputation of the most priceless sort. Peace of mind is a jewel beyond compare, whether it be associated with wealth or poverty or be found in that genial middle zone where contentment with a little holds sway. But debt is a tormentor and a mill-stone about the neck, and is the natural and sworn enemy of happiness. Shun it, reader, as you would a serpent! (September 1, 1899, JI 34:529-30)

MASKED AND CHARACTER BALLS. There are decided objections to masked balls among the Latter-day Saints, because they can so easily be made agencies of evil. It is difficult to understand how one's interest or pleasure can be increased by concealing his or her face at a social party. Of course, not all who do this have any improper motives whatever; but the opportunity for the evil-minded is there, and innocent persons are frequently thrown into close contact with others as partners whom they would scorn to meet or associate with under other circumstances. A masked ball, as such, is therefore entirely disapproved of.

As to character or costume balls where the face is not masked, much of the objection above referred to would be removed. There is of course the item of expense in dressing in character, and sometimes there is a tendency to indecency in costume; in other words, those who take part sometimes feel that properly to present the character they have in mind they must wear clothing . . . they and their friends would be ashamed of under other circumstances. Such a feature as this is, of course, to be criticized. But, on the other hand, character balls can frequently be made very entertaining and even instructive where thought is bestowed upon the costume and it represents truthfully the person or the time that the wearer has in mind. . . . They, however, are only enjoyable when characterized by good taste, and, like all other amusements of the kind, should be managed with great prudence. (March 1, 1899, JI 34:139)

MODERATE AMUSEMENT IS PROPER. We have no fault to find with anybody for seeking amusement. It is proper that it should be indulged in, moderately, of course. We may go to the extreme in almost everything, and it is very easy to do so in pleasure-seeking. But while we would condemn that, we would not commend the example of the over-industrious person, who is as absorbed in business and the cares of life as to find no time for amusement. And still more would we condemn that fakir-like class of persons, who, in their religious zeal, consider it necessary to spend their lives in the practice of austerities and stifle the pleasure-desiring attributes of their natures.

Mankind represents the only species of all the creations of our Father, so far as we are aware, which is provided with the faculty of indulging in laughter. We are not endowed with that faculty without a purpose. Though we are taught in the revelations of the Almighty that loud or excessive laughter is not pleasing to Him, we have no reason to suppose that we can please Him by stifling the inclination to laugh or to indulge in pleasurable emotions. Seeking passing pleasures is right, but it is not the sole, nor indeed the highest object of life by any means. . . .

Many, very many avenues of pleasure are open to those who are cultivated intellectually, that are closed effectually to others on account of their ignorance. Among these may be mentioned the innumerable and varied pleasures which the reading of books affords, the practice of literary composition, music in its various branches, and intelligent, instructive and elevating conversation. Ignorant, illiterate people are not qualified to indulge in any such sources of enjoyment as these and are almost forced in their pleasure-seeking to resort to those of a baser kind. . . .

A clear conscience and assurance that our course is approved by the Almighty and, above all, the presence of the Holy Spirit, will tend to afford us pleasure, and without we live to enjoy these, our seeking for pleasure is like chasing our own shadow or grasping at bubbles that vanish at our touch. (January 15, 1882, JI 17:24)

SOCIAL ENJOYMENT AND AMUSEMENTS. We have given the religious world a lesson upon this point. We have shown that social enjoyment and amusements are not incompatible with correct conduct and true religion. Instead of forbidding the theater and placing it under ban, it has been the aim of the Latter-day Saints to control it and keep it free from impure influences, and to preserve it as a place where all could meet for the purpose of healthful enjoyment. . . .

Our social parties should be conducted in a manner to give gratification to all who attend them, however delicate and refined they may be in their feelings. Rude and boisterous conduct and everything of an improper character should be forbidden at such assemblages. . . .

Pleasure and relaxation, which in themselves may be not only harmless but really beneficial to mind and body, are often rendered evil in the extreme, because of their surroundings and associations. The thoughtless and inexperienced are frequently oblivious to the harm thus attending something in which there is no essential wrong, and are led to look with allowance, if not actual approval, upon things that would shock them under other circumstances. The indiscriminate commingling of the Saints with persons not of their faith whose habits, history and purposes are bad or unknown to them is fraught with evil and to be strongly deprecated. To expose our youth to the contaminating influence of vile men and women such as often congregate in places of public amusement, where they are thrown together in social intercourse, is more than folly; it is wickedness. It is proper that strangers should be treated with courtesy and respect, but intimacy with them is not desirable, and our young people should be cautioned and guarded against casual acquaintanceship and the society of persons whose intentions and influence may be of the very worst character. . . .

Order should be maintained in the midst of merriment. Indecorous language and conduct should be frowned down. All excess is deterimental. Temperance should govern in everything. Amusement is not the purpose of life; it should be indulged in only by way of variety. When people accustom themselves to constant and oft-repeated rounds of pleasure, the true objects of human existence are forgotten and duty becomes irksome and detestable. (April 8, 1887, MS 49:297-98)

DON'T DESTROY ANIMAL LIFE. Our religion teaches us that human life is most sacred and should not be wantonly taken. The Lord also has spoken with great plainness concerning the animal creation. The beasts, fowls and fishes are all the creation of His power and their lives are precious in His sight. No properly constituted person will lightly take the life of any creature; and every girl should be taught that it is wrong to adorn herself with feathers obtained from the slaughter of birds. Animals, fowls and fish are created for the use of man; but their lives should not be wasted. They are to supply the wants of man, not to be slaughtered for mere amusement or for the gratification of vanity.

It is strange that there should be such a desire on the part of human beings of our race to kill birds for the mere pleasure of shooting them. The first impulse with many boys and men, when they have guns in their hands and they see birds flying or wild animals running, is to shoot, though they have no use whatever for the animals or fowl thus killed. Probably, after they have shot, their victims are left to rot on the ground. Such a practice is murderous, and we think that our boys should be taught by their parents that it is wicked to take the life even of the humblest animal or the most insignificant bird. They should not shed blood, only when it is necessary to produce food. To merely go out "gunning" for pleasure is wrong. (November 15, 1893, JI 28:712)

WANTON KILLING. There is a great difference between wild beasts and birds and human beings; but, nevertheless, all derive their life from our Great Creator. He has bestowed life upon man and upon beasts, birds, fishes and insects, and no one has the right to take that life, except in the way and under the conditions which the Lord prescribes. . . .

The Lord has given animals, fowl and fish to man for his use. They are placed under man's control, to be used for food with prudence and thanksgiving and not wastefully. . . . When people can use game of any kind for food, and they stand in need of it, the Lord is not displeased if they kill it. When, however, they hunt it for the mere pleasure of killing, then sin is committed.

The time will come when man and animals which are now wild and ferocious will dwell together without hurting each other. The Prophets have foretold this with great plainness. But before this day comes men will have to cease their war upon the animals, the reptiles and the insects. At the present time every one of these flee from his presence with fear; they feel that if he can reach them by his weapons, he will kill them. The Lord gives them knowledge enough to take care of the lives which He has given them, and He, doubtless, teaches them to shun man. But when man becomes their true friend, they will learn to love and not to fear him. The Spirit of the Lord which will rest upon man will also be given to the animal creation—man will not hurt nor destroy, not even tigers and lions and wolves and snakes, and they will not harm him—and universal peace will prevail. (December 1, 1889, JI 24:548-49)

KINDNESS TO ANIMALS. Every child that is brought into contact with animals should be taught, by parents and by all who attempt to instruct the young, that it is a very great sin in the sight of the Almighty for the dumb creation to be treated with cruelty or even with neglect. A merciful man is merciful to his beast. A good master will see that his animals are fed and cared for, if they have been performing labor, before he himself sits down to food or to take rest. A merciful man who loves the animals which he owns and uses would not be contented to sit down to eat if he knew his horses or his cows were hungry and uncared for. He would see that they had food and water and were protected from the inclemency of the weather as much as they possibly could be before he could enjoy his own food and drink and comfort. This same feeling should be impressed upon the minds of all children so that no animal that is in their care may be neglected. (February 15, 1899, JI 34:113-14)

TREES ARE SACRED. The poet tells us "the groves were God's first temples," and we know that early religious observances of nearly all pagan peoples were associated with trees. The first and greatest incident in the world, so far as concerns the human family, is directly associated with trees by the sacred writer: "Of every tree of the garden thou mayest freely eat; but of the tree of the knowledge of good and evil, thou shalt not eat of it; for in the day that thou eatest thereof thou shalt surely die." [Genesis 2:16-17.] And then, when the parents of our race had disobeyed the divine command, again a tree is prominently mentioned: "Lest he [the man] put forth his hand and partake also of the tree of life, and eat and live forever, therefore I, the Lord God, sent him forth from the Garden of Eden, to till the ground from whence he was taken. . . . So I drove out the man." [Moses 4:28-31.]

"The tree of life," "the tree of knowledge," how vast the significance of such terms! Is it any wonder that early peoples, even though pagan, worshipped trees and under their shade, that the poet was moved to exclaim, "the groves were God's first temples," and that every sensitive and right-feeling soul today regards a growing tree as something almost sacred? . . .

For my own part, I consider the life of a tree so sacred that I am reluctant to destroy it, even when the tree is no longer useful where it is, and even when it is in the way of better improvement; and I cannot understand the temper and disposition of people (nor can I have much friendship for them) who needlessly and ruthlessly go hacking about with axes or knives destroying tree life without purpose.

I would like to see our children taught to respect tree life as they do bird life and animal life and human life. All are parts of the great creation of our Father—and none of the workmanship of His hands should we presume to tamper with, wreck or destroy, except as our needs may justify or our intelligence suggest as necessary for the welfare of those concerned. (May 1, 1899, JI 34:264-66)

Chapter 19

True Education—Literature for the Saints

SELF-DEPENDENCE NECESSARY. It is necessary that every man and woman and child connected with this work should learn as rapidly as possible the habit of self-dependence, to exercise faith before God for themselves, so that each one in his place or in her place will be able to perform his or her part to the acceptance of our God and in such a manner as to bring to pass their own salvation. This is much more easy at the present time than it was in the past from the fact that doctrine is becoming better understood, the principles of the Gospel are more thoroughly disseminated by the aid of all the various agencies that are at work in our midst. . . .

This work is spreading to so great an extent that responsibility must rest upon individual members. The Presidency of the Church, the Twelve Apostles, the various presiding authorities, can no longer do as they have done in years past—carry the people along. The people themselves must learn to walk, to bear their own burdens, to perform their own duties, and to take such a course as will result in their own development and in the advancement of this great work that God has established upon the earth. . . .

INTELLIGENCE NEEDED. It would be an impossibility for this work to achieve the high destiny in store for it and concerning which we have indulged in so many glowing anticipations upon any other principle than this. We are told that intelligence is the glory of God, and it certainly is the glory of man. And with the obstacles that have to be overcome, that confront us every step in our progress, there must be knowledge developed among this people; there must be the highest attainment and grade of intelligence developed among us. Upon no other principle can we stand. Upon no other principle can we progress. Upon no other principle can we accomplish the great results that we have before us. (July 15, 1883, JD 24:181-82)

A FOUNDATION FOR TRUE EDUCATION. It is of the utmost importance to us and to our children and to the work of God which is entrusted to us that we should give our children every advantage of education, including the training of them in the principles of the Gospel, for it is of the first importance that all should have laid the foundation in their hearts of faith in God and confidence in the Holy Priesthood and in the ordinances of the house of God. This is of the first importance, more important than anything else, more important even than teaching them to read and write. Train them in the faith of God and in the knowledge of God, so far as it can be imparted to them, until they can find out God for themselves, seeking him in earnestness in their closets and private places.

And when we have laid this foundation in their hearts, then impart to them skill in education to read and write perfectly. (June 27, 1881, JD 22:287)

No system of education can be perfect which does not teach the principles of righteousness and faith in God. Learning has not saved the world, neither can it save it. No man by wisdom ever found out God, and men may study all their lives and acquire all the knowledge and worldly wisdom that is within the reach of the human mind and yet be utterly destitute of the true knowledge of God.

It is of the utmost importance that our children should, in the first place, be taught faith in God. This cannot be left out of our system of education. Every child in our midst should be taught how to obtain a knowledge of God. This should be made the corner stone and the foundation of all education. (April 15, 1890, JI 25:243)

TEACH CHILDREN THE GOSPEL. Our children should be indoctrinated in the principles of the Gospel from their earliest childhood. They should be made familiar with the contents of the Bible, the Book of Mormon and the Book of Doctrine and Covenants. These should be their chief text books, and everything should be done to establish and promote in their hearts genuine faith in God, in His Gospel and its ordinances, and in His works. But under our common school system this is not possible. . . . In no direction can we invest the means God has given us to better advantage than in the training of our children in the principles of righteousness and in laying the foundation in their hearts of that pure faith which is restored to the earth. (October 6, 1886, MS 48:715-16)

RELIGION SHOULD BE TAUGHT. There is no good reason why the biographies and writings of pagan philosophers should be admitted into our schools, while the life, teachings and works of the Son of God are denied admission there. As our schools are now managed, the infidel has every advantage. Infidelity is almost sure to follow the use of many of the text books. The books which are opposed to true religion and to imparting a true knowlege of all that is holiest, best and most valuable for men to know are rigidly excluded from the school-room. This is wrong.

No people in the world ought to have a deeper interest than we Latter-day Saints in the question as to whether religion should be taught in the school-room. Our very existence is wholly dependent upon our religion. The most deadly blow that could be struck at our organization would be to deprive our children of instruction in our religion. The prosperity and permanency of our society depend upon the thorough instruction of the rising generation in its principles. (August 15, 1886, JI 21: 252)

DESTINY OF ZION DEPENDS ON TRUE EDUCATION. Our destiny is assured; the Lord has spoken so plainly concerning it that no doubt remains upon it. Zion must be at the head. The struggles that we have to encounter are the training intended to qualify us to occupy that supreme position among the nations which the Prophets have predicted. But before Zion can achieve her true position, her sons and daughters must be educated in the highest and best sense of the word—not the education of worldly wisdom, but the education which has for its basis a true knowledge of God and of the glorious principles revealed by Him in these days. Taking this for the foundation, we can build a superstructure of knowledge upon it that will be grand and glorious.

It should be the aim of every parent, of every teacher, and of every public man in our land to furnish the rising generation with every facility to make them so intelligent that they can appear with credit in the midst of the high and the noble among the various nations of the earth. (August 1, 1882, JI 17:232)

TRUE SEEKERS OF KNOWLEDGE. As a people the Latter-day Saints are ardent friends of learning, true seekers after knowledge. They recognize in a good education the best of fortunes; it broadens the mind, creates liberal and noble sentiments and fits the possessor for a more successful struggle with the obstacles of life. No matter how rough the path or how hard the labor, intelligence helps to make it easier. On the other hand, the pleasures of life are heightened by knowledge; one appreciates more fully the beauties of art and enjoys with supreme zest the wonders of nature. The possession of knowledge is of itself the highest pleasure, indispensable and satisfying to those who are thrown among cultured people and comforting to the solitary and the recluse. (April 1, 1892, JI 27:210)

STRIVE FOR GOOD EDUCATION. The value of a good education is beyond price. This is especially so with the Latter-day Saints. We have to meet the world; we have to show it that the Lord has given us a system of government, of religion and of morals superior to any other.

The world is educated. The people pride themselves upon their knowledge gained through education. They despised the Elders in former days because they were unlearned; but those Elders had the power and blessings of God to attend them. They met the learned and the educated and gained victories over them. They also reached the honest and, under the blessing of the Lord, convinced them of the truth and brought them into the Church.

The Lord is still with His Elders. He still helps them whether they are educated or not. But times have changed. We are now in circumstances where we can gain education. All the boys and girls in our land can now get a good education if they will strive for it. . . .

The Church is growing and spreading. It is gaining influence. Our Elders can now reach people of a different class to those to whom they preached in the beginning. This will be more and more the case every year. We shall be able before long to get access with our doctrines to the leading people and the ruling classes in every land. To accomplish the Lord's purposes in this direction the Elders should be educated. They should know all that the world knows and, in addition, have the wisdom and knowledge which God bestows upon His true servants. . . .

Seek for education. Learn to be good writers. Learn to read properly. Learn to spell correctly. Learn to put to use the rules of grammar. Learn every useful branch. Read the best books. . . . Learn good manners. Practice good manners at home; speak politely and correctly at home. Then, when you go abroad into society, you feel at ease, because you are natural. You do there what you do everywhere, speak and act as a gentleman or a lady should. A Latter-day Saint, who lives according to the rules of his or her religion, is thereby made a gentleman or lady. Such persons cannot be anything else. (February 15, 1881, JI 16:42)

MORE THAN BOOK LEARNING NECESSARY. True education does not consist alone in a knowledge gained from books. A man may be very learned in book knowledge and yet be a great dunce in other respects and scarcely able to gain a living. We have seen men who could scarcely read and write who were far better educated in the true sense of the word than many so-called learned men. Their knowledge was of a true, every-day, useful character. They had educated brains and were well cultivated in other respects and were worth any number of educated book-worms. We place a high value upon education of the mind by means of book learning; but we would rather see our juveniles, if they must only learn one branch of education, well trained in the arts of life rather than to see them mere book scholars. But they need not be confined to any one branch of education.

Every child among the Latter-day Saints should learn to work with his hands, as well as with his head. In learning to work with the hands the head should not be neglected, for it is a well-established fact that men who have healthy employment for their brains and who keep their brains active live longer than those who work with their hands alone. (February 19, 1870, JI 5:28)

TEACH CHILDREN INDUSTRIOUS HABITS. Children should be taught industrious habits. They should be taught to labor; their bodies should be accustomed to toil, and skill should be imparted to them in the use of their faculties, their hands, their eyes, their brain and all the faculties of mind and body. Skill, also, in the use of tools should be imparted. . . .

Latter-day Saints should teach their children these things. Every child among us should learn to work. Every girl should acquire a thorough knowledge of cooking and housekeeping, and if she could make her own dresses and help make the clothes of her brothers or her sisters, it would do her no harm. To be a good milliner and dressmaker would be more valuable than a knowledge of some fancy accomplishments. A boy that could mend a wagon or help build a house or who could plough or help harvest would be a more useful citizen than if he did not possess that skill but understood Latin or Greek. (August 15, 1880, JI 15:186)

Our young people should be taught to employ their time to the best advantage and be made to see that to waste time is to waste money. They should be trained in such a manner that it would be painful for them to spend their time in "loafing." If they have no work to do, they should be studying, reading useful books and storing up knowledge. (March 15, 1891, JI 26:183)

TEACH CHILDREN TO TEST WHAT THEY READ. We should be exceedingly careful in the selection of books that we put in the hands of our children. . . . Teach the children not to accept that which they read in a book as true because it is printed; teach them to weigh for themselves, to examine for themselves and test for themselves the statements which may be made up on any and every subject that may be brought to their attention through the medium of books, whether scientific or otherwise.

The danger in indiscriminate reading on the part of young people lies in this: their impressions are vivid, and if what they read be incorrect, if, in point of fact, what they read is based on unsound premises and be entirely wrong but it is presented in an agreeable taking and specious manner, they are apt to accept it as being true.

GOSPEL TRUTH A STANDARD. Now . . . God has revealed certain principles which we know to be true, certain cardinal truths which are as finger-boards pointing the way of life. We should teach them to our children . . . and endeavor, by the help of God, to implant them in their hearts, so that they afterwards in their search for knowledge of any kind may be able to bring what they may read to this standard and test the same thereby. And if our children are taught thus to read, the danger of infidelity, the danger arising from superficial reading and the imbibing of incorrect ideas sometimes set forth in a scientific way will be, to a great extent, obviated; to my mind great care should be taken in these things by all teachers, by all parents, by every one, in fact, who has the care of young people or the direction of their studies. The same rule applies to every one, whether a child or an adult. Let us endeavor to cultivate this disposition in our children to investigate carefully, to weigh properly the statements which may be presented to them. (April 5, 1881, JD 22:274)

USE MEANS TO EDUCATE CHILDREN. A man who suffers his children to grow up in ignorance and without the benefits of education—that which pertains at least to a common school education—is guilty of a great wrong. We should take every pains in our power to instruct our children, to furnish them every facility for learning. . . . Spend [your means] wisely upon your children in your lifetime, and when you have educated them, when you have given them something which they can keep, when they lie down at night, without the slightest danger of burglars stealing it, they are equipped for the struggle of life.

Every child in our community should be educated, not in books alone, but to sustain himself, or herself, so that in case he or she be left alone, or otherwise, they will be able, from the elements around them, inasmuch as they possess the use of their own limbs and faculties, to earn a living and thereby aid somebody else to live. . . .

CHILDREN ARE LIKE UNPOLISHED DIAMONDS. I hope that we shall do everything in our power to furnish facilities for our children. Do not spare means in this direction. You do not know what future there is before your children. They are like diamonds. True, they may need polish, in order to bring out their brilliancy and best qualities; and education of the right kind will impart this lustre. . . . God has so distributed his gifts that He has not given them to any one family. I thank Him for that. He is not going to build up a dynasty in His Kingdom. He does not confine His gifts and blessings to any special class of men. He has distributed them like He has the air, so that all have them and all share in them.

A man and his wife may be an obscure couple, yet their children may make the brightest men and women. None of you know what your children are capable of until you give them proper opportunities. You should not think that because you have got through life without much education that therefore your children ought to go through in the same manner. Give your children opportunities, and do not work them to death and thereby stunt their minds; but give the boys a chance and give the girls a chance, bearing in mind that they will have more extended opportunities than you have had for the use of education, and you ought to train them accordingly. (April 5, 1881, JD 22:274-77)

PARENTS INDEBTED TO CHILDREN. I feel that when a child is born the parents are indebted to that child. To bring it into the world as a waif, to launch it upon the society without giving it a proper education and proper training and assistance, is a great wrong. If we did this, we would be like animals. It is the duty of every man and every woman who has a child to do everything in their power for that child, to qualify it to be a useful man or woman, and no pains should be spared in this direction. We live in our children. After we are gone, we will live in our offspring, and our good qualities will be perpetuated in them if we will take the right course. . . .

We should take pains to teach our boys and our girls everything that will make them useful and help to give them a knowledge of the principles that God has revealed. In this way we will be a blessing to our children. They will rejoice in us, and they will arise and call us blessed. What a glorious thing it is to think that our posterity will honor us and that they will say, "I know that my father was a good man, that he did all he could for me. I know my mother was a good woman; she loved me and did all in her power to give me a good start and to furnish me with all the knowledge that she could to make a useful woman," and to have those children quote the example of their parents to their posterity and let it go down as a heritage from one generation to another, until we shall arise up a generation that will be accepted of the Lord and upon whom His blessing and His power will rest.

LAY THE FOUNDATION NOW. We will soon enter upon the Millennium. God has told us this; and it should be the desire of every man and woman in this Church that their posterity may live, not only for a generation or two, but throughout the entire Millennium, and then throughout that period when Satan will be loosed again, that as long as time shall endure some of our posterity may be found among the friends of God, bearing the holy Priesthood, honoring God, keeping His commandments, not only through the Millennium, but during that period when Satan will be loosed again to go forth and tempt the nations, that even then some of our descendants will be found numbered among the righteous and continue to be numbered among them as long as time shall last. I think this is a desirable wish for every man. And let us lay the foundation now. Let us, as parents, influence our children. (April 6, 1891, MS 53:451-52)

STUDY DISCOURSES OF LEADERS. Where the people of God pay attention to the written word and cherish and observe the written word, they are always better prepared to hear the oral instructions of the servants of God; they are better prepared to receive those instructions; they have greater interest in seeking to obtain instructions than they have when they are careless about the written word of God. . . . How many of you read the Book of Mormon, the Bible, the Book of Doctrine and Covenants and the discourses of the Elders as they are published? How many of you make a practice of reading the word of God as it is in these records and as it appears in published discourses? . . .

If we talk about the living oracles and want to pay respect to them, how shall we do this? Shall we do it by never reading their words, by paying no attention to that which they say? That is a very poor way of doing. We ought to listen to their words. When we cannot hear their words, we should read them, for they are the words of the authorized servants of God. . . .

DANGER TO YOUNG PEOPLE. I have been impressed very much of late with the danger to which our young people are exposed. When the parents neglect to read the word of God, when they prefer novels, magazines, or any kind of light reading, and do not set the example by reading that which God has given to us, you may expect the children to do the same. They will not take up the Bible, the Book of Mormon and the Book of Doctrine and Covenants to read, because when they read these illustrated papers, these catchy prints, these light novels, everything of a serious nature loses its interest.

To people who are fed on highly seasoned food, a plain diet is not inviting; men who have been accustomed to stimulants crave stimulants. People who read the class of literature I refer to are in the same condition mentally; they desire the sensational, and reading which does not have some of this element in it possesses but little interest. The result is, our books and our discourses—that which God reveals—go without being perused. (October 5, 1897, CR 38-40)

A DUTY TO STORE UP GOSPEL KNOWLEDGE. The faithful servants of the Lord, in this dispensation, have the same promise extended to them which was given to the ancient Apostles and disciples— viz., that the Spirit shall bring to their remembrance all things that are necessary for them to utter when they stand up in advocacy and defense of the Gospel. But, if their minds are vacant and have never been stored with the principles of the Gospel and general, useful knowledge, there would be nothing for the Spirit of the Lord to operate upon; and, as it would be impossible for any being to bring to their remembrance that which they never knew, they would be very likely to be extremely disappointed in the aid which they expected to receive.

It is the duty of the Elders to constantly study the revelations which the Lord has given to His children in all ages and to make themselves thoroughly familiar with all the doctrines and principles of the Church and to store their minds with all the direct or indirect proofs, whether from sacred or profane history of the truths they are advocating. Then, they may, with confidence, ask and expect the Spirit of the Lord to aid them in selecting and bringing forth, from the store-house of the mind, those truths which are best adapted to the wants and circumstances of the people they are addressing. (September 26, 1863, MS 25:618)

WHAT DO YOU READ? From constant reading of fiction, the truth becomes tame and uninteresting. A realm of romance, or at least a world of extremes, is where he would choose to dwell; for his associates or ideals he would have either persons of strangely exaggerated attributes or impossible heroes.

On the other hand, the reader of sound, healthy literature is aided and strengthened by his reading for each day's struggle as it comes along. His heroes are real men, whom he or his parents or someone else has actually known, and the evidence of whose existence is found in the works they left behind them. He delights in the lessons of history as well as in the noble achievements of individuals. Those whom he admires have other things to recommend them to his fancy than abnormal traits of character and fictitious performances; and from studying their lives he is not made familiar with vice, either through direct description or by suggestion. His mind is clear; his head is steady; his tastes are earnest; his ambitions are worthy. He knows what it is to encounter difficulty, for he remembers the trials of others who have preceded him; but he is also encouraged to overcome it by recalling how they did the same. He loves truth, reality, nature and all that his senses and his conscience and his heart and his faith tell him is deserving of honest esteem. . . .

JUDGED BY BOOKS READ. A boy can not be judged half so correctly by the company he keeps as by the books he reads. In the former case he may not always be able to make his selection and may be unable to escape from company he really does not like. But the silent yet most influential companions, which we call books, these are matters of his own choice, and in his love for this one or that, he reflects his own inclinations as plainly and truly as a plate glass mirror reflects his features.

WASTE OF TIME A SERIOUS MATTER. If parents and children alike would realize that nothing is worth reading that is not worth remembering, hundreds of hours in each person's life might be saved and utilized that are now wasted—yes, worse than wasted, for in such pursuits the time itself is not only gone to no purpose, but the memory is weakened and the mind is more or less tainted. Waste of any kind is little short of crime; and worst of all waste—worse than waste of food, for more food can be grown or bought; worse than the waste of money or substance, for this can be perhaps again obtained—is the waste of time, which neither money nor influence nor prayers can regain—once gone it is gone forever. (January 1, 1899, JI 34:22-23)

PERNICIOUS LITERATURE. Those who constantly read falsehoods against the servants of God cannot help but be influenced for evil thereby. . . . It is a most pertinent case of "little by little." The man or woman who reads this ingeniously woven fabric of falsehood or venom at the first reading feels disgraced or angered. But curiosity, that potent cause of so much of this world's mischief, induces a desire for a second reading. An appetite for such pabulum is excited, and no matter how our nearest friends may be belied or the holiest things of our hearts' affections be traduced or ridiculed, we must read it. It is like eating the arsenic and other poisons, the appetite grows with that it feeds upon. And as has been said of vice by one of the poets, at first it is a monster of such hideous mien, we loathe, despise and abhor it,

> But seen too oft, familiar grows its face,
> We first endure, then pity, then embrace.

Little by little this transition takes place until the faithful servant or handmaiden of the Lord is like a ship on the ocean without compass or rudder when a storm arises, "tossed to and fro by every wind"; he or she knows not what to believe or disbelieve. Some it is certain, is false, but the ingenious argument is advanced that "where there is so much smoke there must be some fire"; consequently, some of the vile assertions may possibly have a foundation in truth, and an enervating condition of spiritual doubt is created, which throws a cloud over the life and unfits the man, as a Saint, for the duties of his calling. He becomes neither hot nor cold and is but ill fitted for the Master's use. . . . The danger increases as the days roll by, and eventually the doubter in his brethren becomes the denier of his God. (November 1, 1899, JI 34:656-57)

EFFECT OF IMPROPER READING. The continued reading of false reports and statements concerning the Church of Jesus Christ of Latter-day Saints and the character of its leading men have their effect upon the world. We have seen and had sorrowful reason for noticing the effect that this has had upon the minds of the people.

The Latter-day Saints themselves cannot read this class of literature without being affected by it. They may start out without lending the least credence to the statements that are made; but the lies oft repeated and oft read will have their effect; they will make their impression; they will leave seeds to germinate, which sooner or later will bear bitter fruit. Everything false, everything erroneous should therefore be shunned.

There is enough truth in the world to occupy men's attention, and especially children's, without bestowing thought or time upon that which is false. Everyone should shun books and periodicals of this character. No judicious parent would knowingly permit his or her children to associate with habitual liars, nor with persons who delight in untruthful statements. We should dread the effect of such contact. But this is no worse than permitting them to have access to literature of the same character, for their minds are sure to be poisoned by that which they read. (December 15, 1895, JI 30:766)

A SURE SIGN OF DANGER. The reader of any periodical, especially if it is a publication which sets forth positive views upon any subject, such as politics or religion, for instance, will, perhaps insensibly to himself, be impressed with those views. He will gradually fall into the habit of looking at questions in the light in which they are presented in the printed matter that he reads. Flakes of snow fall gently and silently, but they soon accumulate, and the earth and every other object is covered by them. In like manner the constant reading of newspapers, magazines, or books of a certain character has its effect upon the minds of those who read them; their views and all their conclusions respecting the questions that are discussed in those writings are influenced by that reading.

The effect upon Latter-day Saints of reading what are called anti-Mormon publications is always pernicious. Everyone who has had any experience in the Church has seen the bad results of this. The consequences of such a course of reading are quite as injurious as mingling in the society and making companions of apostates. It is a sure sign of a loss of faith when men choose the companionship of those who are opposed to the Gospel in preference to those who love and are devoted to the Gospel. It is an equally sure sign of danger and a certain precursor of the loss of faith and the Spirit of God when men or their families read literature that is opposed to the work of God or the influence of which tends to weaken reverence for God's word or God's authority. No one can take a course of this kind, and pursue it, without endangering his faith; it will inevitably lead to darkness and unbelief. . . .

A CAUSE OF APOSTASY. Faithful men and women do not fall suddenly without cause into a spirit of unbelief concerning the authority which the Lord has restored to the earth. There is always a reason for such a change, and especially so where the previous lives of those who fall into this way of thinking have been the very opposite in all respects to this mode of thought and action. That cause, if not entirely due to the neglect of keeping in touch with the spirit of the Gospel and of the times, is at least principally due to it. The Saints are in spiritual peril when the publications which are intended for their benefit, for their enlightenment and growth in everything pertaining to the Church of Christ, are neglected and other literature is substituted therefor.

In making these remarks I would not wish to convey the idea that it is absolutely necessary for the Latter-day Saints to confine themselves to our periodicals alone. I would, however, emphasize the feeling that those periodicals should occupy the first place in the reading of every man in the Church and of his family. The children of the Latter-day Saints should be taught to read Latter-day Saint publications, to draw their inspiration from them and thereby get broader, better and higher conceptions of the Gospel and its application to their daily lives. In other words, they should be taught to read the works and words of the Latter-day Saints. If they do not read those works and are not brought up in that spirit, it is easy to foresee the consequences—they will grow up unbelievers; having imbibed the spirit of the world, they will be of the world, and the faith of the Gospel that should be in and govern them will have no place in their hearts. (February 15, 1898, JI 33:143-44)

DANGERS IN MODERN EDUCATION. It is a difficult thing in the midst of the widespread unbelief and the false doctrines and theories which come to us and to our children in the guise of science to prevent the spirit of unbelief from influencing us. This also is one of the great obstacles in the way of the education of our children. The books which are in our schools, and from which our children are taught, contain theories that are unsound; they are based upon false premises that lead to wrong conclusions; and it requires the utmost care on the part of parents and teachers to prevent bad effects following education based upon such text books. . . .

We have all these things to contend with. The rising generation have to be watched over with a care that in former times was not necessary. There is danger in education of this kind. (October 7, 1894, DW 49:737)

Chapter 20

The Standard Works—Our Scriptures

STANDARD WORKS SUPERIOR TO OTHER BOOKS. The inspired books are superior to all others. No matter how good books may be nor how good the men may be who write them, they are not the standard works of the Church. The Bible, the Book of Mormon, the Book of Doctrine and Covenants and the Pearl of Great Price are the standard works. Others may be written under the influence of the Spirit of God, but they are not the word of God to the people. (November 13, 1900, JI 36:110)

OUR DUTY TO UPHOLD TRUTHS FOUND IN SCRIPTURES. I want to say here that there is a wave of unbelief sweeping over the land, and we can feel the effects of it among us. The leading magazines, or the popular magazines, are filled with ideas tending to unbelief, scientific hypotheses that are designed to destroy faith in the Bible, faith in the creation of the world, faith in the origin of man, and in the existence of God. Now these doctrines are being spread very insidiously. They are being taught in all the universities and colleges, speaking generally, of the land; with but few exceptions.

There is a generation growing up who do not believe in the cardinal principles of the Bible taught by our fathers before the Gospel in its fulness was revealed. These doctrines are being undermined, and it becomes the duty of the Latter-day Saints—it is the mission of the Latter-day Saints—to uphold these old truths and doctrines that have come down to us from God through the ages, to strengthen the faith of our children in them and, so far as we can, to neutralize the effect of these false doctrines that are being taught. . . .

WE HAVE THREE WITNESSES. We have the Bible but not that alone. They may indulge in their higher criticism and tell us that those whose names are attached to the various books of the Bible were not the authors of them, but we have something more sure than all their criticism. The Book of Mormon is of divine origin, divinely translated by the gift and power of God, and we know it is pure. It was not translated by man's ability; hence, we have a more sure word of prophecy, something to base our faith upon. We can call upon these testimonies because we know they are impregnable and cannot be destroyed.

In addition to this we have the word of God, the Book of Covenants, that has come from the Lord to us. It is the word of God to us who live now. Therefore, we have three witnesses. They may assail the Bible, as they do, and endeavor to prove that the writings attributed to different men were not written by them. We leave that to them. They can do as they please with their learning; we will cling to the Bible, because we know that whatever errors there are are errors of uninspired men who have done the translating. But they must not, and they cannot, tread upon other ground that we have.

They have assailed the Book of Mormon from an outside standpoint and claim that it was translated or, as they say, written by someone else than Joseph Smith. But we have disproved that, and the Book of Mormon comes to us pure, having been translated by divine power, and it contains incontrovertible internal evidence to those who read it and know anything about the power and spirit of God; it comes to them with internal evidence of its divinity, and they know it is true. Therefore, we have this, besides which we have the Doctrine and Covenants, and these three witnesses enable us to occupy a different position from any other religious denomination upon the face of the earth.

We should consider and teach our children all these things and fortify them against the pernicious doctrines being circulated and being taught in the institutions of learning in the land, and fortify them so that they will not imbibe the errors which will pass away, for they are not true. (October 6, 1897, JI 32:751-52)

THE VALUE OF THE BIBLE. A knowledge of the Bible obtained in childhood has its effect on the whole after-life. Unconsciously its grand truths are impressed upon the minds of children, and they are influenced by them. Children trained in the reading of the Bible, all other things being equal, are more likely to be truthful, virtuous and honest men and women than if they had been brought up without the knowledge of it. The decay of public morals, the breaking down of honorable methods among men, the increase of impurity of every kind, the growth of corruption and lax methods of administration and the indistinct ideas which are becoming so prevalent concerning honor are without doubt principally due to the neglect of the Bible. . . .

Now, as Latter-day Saints we do not set forth the idea that the Bible is a perfect book. Many errors have crept into it through translation. The men who have given us the translation that we use made no pretension to inspiration; they translated it as best they could. But, with all its faults, it still stands as a grand monument of God's dealings with the human family and of man's industry and zeal in preserving it. Our present civilization and the advancement which the world has made in the right direction are due more to the Bible than to any other book in existence. To prove this we have only to look at the nations which have never had it as a record in their midst and contrast their condition with the condition of the nations among whom it has been widely circulated. (April 15, 1895, JI 30:252)

THE BIBLE OF PRICELESS WORTH. This book is of priceless worth; its value cannot be estimated by anything that is known among men upon which value is fixed. . . . To the Latter-day Saints it should always be a precious treasure. Beyond any people now upon the face of the earth, they should value it, for the reason that from its pages, from the doctrines set forth by its writers, the epitome of the plan of salvation which is there given unto us, we derive the highest consolation, we obtain the greatest strength. It is, as it were, a constant fountain sending forth streams of living life to satisfy the souls of all who peruse its pages. (May 8, 1881, JD 22:260-61)

AN IMPLICIT FAITH IN THE BIBLE. The peculiarities, if such they may be called, which distinguish us from other people have their origin in our implicit faith in the Scriptures. There is no principle nor doctrine of our faith that we are not willing to have tested by the revelations and teachings contained in King James's translation of the Bible; and our Elders have gone forth taking that as their text-book, preaching from it the principles which those now called Latter-day Saints have embraced and which caused them to gather together from the nations of the earth. . . .

There is the great difficulty to-day; this is the cause of the diversity of beliefs in the Christian world. Instead of taking the word of the Lord as it is they wish to place their own instruction on that word so as to suit their own peculiar ideas and views; and having thus interpreted it they frame their belief in accordance with that interpretation. (August 15, 1869, JD 14:47)

BIBLE ERRORS. One of our Articles of Faith states "We believe the Bible to be the word of God as far as it is translated correctly." . . . As our duty is to create faith in the word of God in the mind of the young student, we scarcely think that object is best attained by making the mistakes of translators the more prominent part of our teachings. Even children have their doubts, but it is not our business to encourage those doubts. Doubts never convert; negations seldom convince. Falsehood cannot be overthrown by negative teaching but by establishing the opposing truth.

We are not called to teach the errors of translators but the truth of God's word. It is our mission to develop faith in the revelations of God in the hearts of the children, and "How can that best be done?" is the question that confronts us. Certainly not by emphasizing doubts, creating difficulties or teaching negations. It is the positive element of personal testimony in teaching divine truth that gives that teaching power. . . .

The clause in the Articles of Faith regarding mistakes in the translation of the Bible was never inserted to encourage us to spend our time in searching out and studying those errors, but to emphasize the idea that it is the truth and the truth only that the Church of Jesus Christ of Latter-day Saints accepts, no matter where it is found. (April 1, 1901, JI 36:208)

BIBLE NOT FOUNTAIN OF ALL TRUTH. If there is one thing for which we should be more thankful than for any other, it is this—that we have the knowledge that God has put himself in communication with men and revealed truths which will aid them in their onward course to the Celestial Kingdom of our Heavenly Father. Having this knowledge we have a testimony within us that we have embraced the Gospel, which we could never gain from the Bible.

With some men it is unpopular to say anything which may appear derogatory to the character of that book. Their affections and their faith are concentrated upon it; they almost worship it as a God. They reverence it as something so great, so sublime, so noble, so truthful, and so clear a reflection of God's countenance that to deprive them of it would be, they say, to deprive them of what they hold most dear and prize above everything they have besides.

I would not lessen their affection for the Bible. A certain amount of reverence for it is good. It is good to read here of the holy and good. It is good to have confidence in goodness, in holiness, in good and pure men. But, if we were to place all our confidence in this book, we should put something between us and that God, the light of whose wisdom illuminates its pages and gives it all its worth. To do this is to worship the book. I call it idolatry. . . .

I do not look upon it as the Creator nor as the fountain or source of all light. I do not look upon it as the Deity. I can read its pages and be instructed by the record of the teachings and sufferings of men who have, like myself, laboured and contended for the truth; and it strengthens me to persevere and faithfully exert myself, until I, like them, may obtain eternal life. Reading it thus, the Bible is valuable and should be appreciated and command love and reverence; but it should not be placed upon a pedestal and worshipped.

It is through the substitution of the book for God that confusion prevails through the religious world. They put it in the place of the revelation and truths and the gifts of God of which it tells us. It is through this substitution that infidelity marshals its hosts by thousands; for why should they adore a book that seems to split up the religious world and produce such confusion?

I want to teach you not to go to the book alone but beyond it—to the fountain whence it emanated—to Him who has filled us with noble and lofty aspirations, Who has brought us into intimate connection with Himself by revealing unto us His Gospel. We ought not to depend for our salvation and exaltation upon books but upon the Creator of the world, Who inspired the men who wrote this book. Possession of God's Spirit enables us to know whether this book is what it professes to be, and exalts us to the same level as the men whose narratives are here found.

In making these remarks it is not my wish to weaken your love for this book, but it is to give you to understand that it alone is not all that is necessary to build up the Kingdom of God. It is to induce you to look beyond it to that Being Who is the fountain of revelation and Who is the true source of all intelligence, so that if this book were burned and destroyed—if the millions of other books were all destroyed—there would still be a fountain of intelligence accessible to you from the life-giving stream, of which you might eternally drink.

It was not books alone that directed the ancients; the law of God was written in their hearts. They drank at the fountain of knowledge which God had opened up unto them as it flowed forth pure from himself and thus were enabled to write the records which we now so much venerate. It is our privilege to receive and enjoy this same Spirit and knowledge. This Spirit makes known unto us the object for which religion exists—for which the Gospel was revealed in ancient days—not to inspire blind reverence in books, or even in the men who have recorded their faith, their gifts and their endowments, but to lead men on in all ages to the exaltation God has reserved for them and to lead them to an acquaintance with their Father and God. (July 14, 1861, MS 23:513-14)

TESTIMONY OF BOOK OF MORMON. We do not believe it possible for any honest, unprejudiced soul to read the Book of Mormon in a prayerful spirit without being convinced that its words are the words of God. There is an influence which accompanies it, which the reader feels, if he will not reject it, that carries with it overpowering conviction and is a testimony that God is the Author, through His inspired servants, of that Book. So also with the Book of Doctrine and Covenants. (August 15, 1890, JI 25:500)

MANKIND PREFER DOUBT AND CONJECTURE. Had these records, which contain so much that is important and interesting to mankind, been brought to light by any other agency than that designated by the Lord, they would have been received with enthusiasm, and the discoverer would have obtained a world-wide reputation and deathless fame. But, because Joseph Smith attributed their discovery and translation to the power of God—because he testified that, in fulfilment of the Scripture, the Lord had brought to light another witness, written on another continent, of the truth of His dealings with the children of men, to corroborate the records already extant in their midst, they could not receive them. Mankind prefer doubt and conjecture to certainty and knowledge. (October 5, 1856, WS 220)

BOOK OF MORMON TO BE ACCEPTED. Beliefs change, and misrepresentation and falsehood fade away as time passes on and truth is received and accepted; and the day will yet come, and it is not very far distant, . . . when this Book of Mormon and all connected with it will be received and accepted —that is, all the truth, as the truth of the living God, for the reason that it is true and that God Himself is its author. For that reason, and for that reason alone, the time will come—and as I have said, it is not far distant, though it may seem very presumptuous to make such a statement—when this record will be accepted, as the Bible is now accepted, as a book of divine origin, and that it has been revealed through the ministrations and agency of holy angels. . . .

INTERNAL EVIDENCES. There are evidences in this work itself of its divinity. It is the internal evidence which the Book of Mormon contains that bears testimony of it. If Joseph Smith's claims as a Prophet of God had no other foundation than that which this book furnishes, then there is foundation enough for him to rank as one of the greatest Prophets that has ever lived upon the face of the earth. (September 18, 1881, JD 22:253-54)

It contains the internal evidence of its own divinity, that God wrote it through inspired men and that no one but an inspired man or men could have written the book. There is no book in the English language that compares with it, unless it be books which contain the pure word of God.

It has the advantage of the Bible in this, that it was translated by the power of God, not by the learning of man, and not selected from hundreds and thousands of versions as the Bible has been; for there is no end to the versions which exist of the books contained in the Bible. Of course, we have our version translated by learned men, but there is scarcely a passage of any importance in the Bible concerning which there is not some dispute among learned commentators.

But with the Book of Mormon it is different. God preserved those records for a purpose in Himself. They were hidden up. (April 6, 1884, JD 25:121)

So far as concerns the divinity of the Book of Mormon, the record itself bears the most abundant evidence of its truthfulness. No one can read it in a spirit of fairness without being impressed with it. As a child, I remember hearing the remark from one who, having been given a copy of the book, had read it through almost without interruption: "A good man would not have put forth such a book unless it were true, and a bad man could not have done it."[1] This is a peculiarity of the book. It carries its own testimony to every prayerful heart.

OUR DUTY TO USE EXTERNAL EVIDENCE. While this may answer for the Latter-day Saints, it cannot be expected to be convincing to skeptics and unbelievers. Those who are hostile to it will not only scoff at its claim to divinity, they will also tell all manner of falsehoods concerning it. Perhaps no amount of external evidence, no matter how strongly corroborative it may be, would satisfy such minds. The results of the effort to convince such people would not be worth the pains. And yet there is a duty to mankind which we as a Church cannot leave unfulfilled. If we can for them reconcile science with religion, it is our duty to do it, and thus leave without excuse those who are willing to accept science as the basis of belief and reject everything that runs counter to it.

Revelation has already made many things clear that have puzzled the most highly educated people. There is really no conflict between the true science and true religion. Truth cannot be opposed to itself; it is truth wherever it is found. And so

[1]George Q. Cannon's father made this statement.

those who have a foundation in revealed, and therefore undefiled, truth have the advantage of and can be of service to those whose accepted truths are more or less tainted with human theories and associated with errors. (May 15, 1900, JI 35:314)

THE BOOK OF MORMON WITNESSES. Fault-finders with the testimony of the witnesses to the Book of Mormon have urged as an objection to the reliability of their statements that of the eight witnesses four were of one family and three of another, while of the three witnesses one belonged to the same family that the four of the eight witnesses did. These objectors have seemed to think that because eight of the eleven witnesses belonged to two families they were too closely connected to make their testimony reliable.

But the circumstances which surrounded the translation of the Book of Mormon explain why so many of these witnesses were members of two families. It would be natural that the relatives of the Prophet Joseph who were with him and knew of the communication that he had received would make suitable witnesses, and also that the Whitmer family, whose house became his home while engaged in the labor of translating, should be the best witnesses of the divinity of the work, especially so when it is remembered that much opposition was manifested on every hand towards the Prophet and his labor.

COMPARED TO FOLLOWERS OF JESUS. In this respect, however, the resemblance between the immediate followers of the Son of God, when He was in the flesh, and the witnesses to the Book of Mormon is very striking. Geike, in his *Life of Christ*, in speaking of the Twelve Apostles whom Jesus selected, says they were his immediate neighbors and relatives. He says: "The Capernaum circle yielded him no fewer than seven of the twelve—Peter, his brother Andrew, James and John, James the Little and Jude and Matthew, while Philip belonged to the village of Bethsaida, in its immediate neighborhood, making in all eight of the Twelve virtually from the same favored place."

At least four of these Apostles—James and John, James the Little and Jude—seem to have been relations or connections of the Savior, so Geike says; and he adds that, if we accept the tradition which he quotes, he must add Thomas. This tradition is that "Thomas, whose Hebrew name was sometimes turned into the Greek equivalent Didymus, a twin, was the same person as Judas, the brother of Jesus, as if Mary had had a double birth after bearing her eldest son."

Speaking of the Apostles, Geike says: "We know nothing of the father of Andrew and Simon; but James and John were the sons of one Zabdia (Zebedee); and we know from comparison of texts that their mother was Salome, so honorably mentioned in the Gospels. Writers so acute as Ewald have seen in her a sister of Mary, the mother of Jesus; and if so, John and James were cousins to their Master." (September 1, 1891, JI 26:534)

THE BOOK OF MORMON GEOGRAPHY. There is a tendency, strongly manifested . . . among some of the brethren, to study the geography of the Book of Mormon. . . . We are greatly pleased to notice the . . . interest taken by the Saints in this holy book. . . . But valuable as is the Book of Mormon both in doctrine and history, yet it is possible to put this sacred volume to uses for which it was never intended, uses which are detrimental rather than advantageous to the cause of truth, and consequently to the work of the Lord. . . .

The brethren who lecture on the lands of the Nephites or the geography of the Book of Mormon are not united in their conclusions. No two of them, so far as we have learned, are agreed on all points, and in many cases the variations amount to tens of thousands of miles. These differences of views lead to discussion, contention and perplexity; and we believe more confusion is caused by these divergences than good is done by the truths elicited.

How is it that there is such a variety of ideas of this subject? Simply because the Book of Mormon is not a geographical primer. It was not written to teach geographical truths. What is told us of the situation of the various lands or cities of the ancient Jaredites, Nephites and Lamanites is usually simply an incidental remark connected with the doctrinal or historical portions of the work and almost invariably only extends to a statement of the relative position of some land or city to contiguous or surrounding places and nowhere gives us the exact situation or boundaries so that it can be definitely located without fear of error.

It must be remembered that geography as a science, like chronology and other branches of education, was not understood or taught after the manner or by the methods of the moderns. It could not be amongst those peoples who were not acquainted with the size and form of the earth, as was the case with most of the nations of antiquity, though not with the Nephites. Their Seers and Prophets appear to have received divine light on this subject.

The First Presidency have often been asked to prepare some suggestive map illustrative of Nephite geography but have never consented to do so. Nor are we acquainted with any of the Twelve Apostles who would undertake such a task. The reason is that without further information they are not prepared even to suggest. The word of the Lord or the translation of other ancient records is required to clear up many points now so obscure that, as we have said, no two original investigators agree with regard to them. . . .

For these reasons we have strong objections to the introduction of maps and their circulation among our people which profess to give the location of the Nephite cities and settlements. As we have said, they have a tendency to mislead instead of enlighten, and they give rise to discussions which will lead to division of sentiment and be very unprofitable. We see no necessity for maps of this character, because, at least, much would be left to the imagination of those who prepare them; and we hope that there will be no attempt made to introduce them or give them general circulation.

Of course, there can be no harm result from the study of the geography of this continent at the time it was settled by the Nephites, drawing all the information possible from the record which has been translated for our benefit. But beyond this we do not think it necessary, at the present time, to go, because it is plain to be seen, we think, that evils may result therefrom. (January 1, 1890, JI 25:18-19)

THE HILL CUMORAH IN NEW YORK. While on a recent visit to the States on business Brother Brigham Young, Jun., and I arranged to make a visit to the hill Cumorah—the hill where Mormon and Moroni secreted the records, by the command of the Lord, which were revealed to the Prophet Joseph Smith, and from which he translated the Book of Mormon. . . .

Undoubtedly great changes had occurred in the appearance of the surrounding country since the days when Mormon and Moroni had trod the spot where we stood; still, we could readily understand, even now, how admirable a position this would be for a general to occupy in watching and directing the movements of armies and in scrutinizing the position of an enemy. Around Cumorah is yet a land of many waters, rivers and fountains, as Mormon said it was in his day.

Our emotions on treading on this sacred hill were of the most peculiar character. They were indescribable. This was the hill Ramah of the Jaredites, and it is probable that in this vicinity Coriantumr and Shiz, with the people whom they led, fought their last battle. For this great battle they were four years preparing, gathering the people together from all parts of the land and arming men and women, and even children. The battle lasted eight days, and the result was the complete extermination of the Jaredite nation, none being left but the Prophet Ether—who warned the nation of the fate that awaited it unless the people repented and who lived to record the fulfillment of his own warnings and predictions—and Coriantumr who succeeded in slaying his mortal enemy, Shiz.

It is probable that the Prophet Ether, when he emerged from his hiding-place to view the destruction of his race, which he had been inspired to foretell, had ascended this hill and from its summit had gazed with profound grief upon the thousands of slain which lay scattered unburied upon the surface of the earth around. He and Coriantumr alone of all that mighty race which had flourished for upwards of fifteen hundred years were left. Who can imagine the feelings which he must have had on such an occasion?

From the summit of this hill, doubtless, Mormon and his great son Moroni had also witnessed the gathering of the hosts of the Nephites and the dusky and myriad legions of their deadly enemies, the Lamanites. Around this hill they had marshaled their forces, their twenty-three divisions of ten thousand men each, commanded by the most skillful of their generals—all to be swept away, except Mormon and Moroni and twenty-two others, in one day's battle, by the fierce and relentless foe whom God permitted to execute his threatened judgment. Stealthily, perhaps, for fear of exciting the attention of the Lamanites, Mormon and Moroni and their companions may have ascended this hill and gazed on the dreadful scene around them. What a picture of desolation and woe must have met their sight! How deep must have been their anguish at thus witnessing the destruction of the fair ones of their nation! No wonder they cried out in anguish and mourned with pathetic lamentations the rebellion against God which had brought this terrible destruction upon them.

Mormon's feelings must have been very peculiar. At fifteen years of age chosen to be the commander-in-chief of the armies of his nation, he had fought battle after battle until now, at seventy-four years of age, he witnessed the complete blotting out of what had been the most favored people on the earth. His reflections must have been peculiarly painful, because he knew that had they listened to him he could have saved them.

It was here that he hid the abridgment which he made of the records, and which is now known by his name, and it was here, thirty-six years after this tremendous battle, that his son Moroni also hid his abridgment of the Book of Ether and the record which he had made, from which we learn the fate of his father Mormon and his other companions, that sixteen years after the battle of Cumorah Mormon and all the Nephites except Moroni had been killed by the Lamanites. It was to this spot that, about fourteen hundred years after these events, Joseph Smith, the Prophet, was led by Moroni in person, and here the records, engraved on plates, were committed to him for translation.

Who could tread this ground and reflect upon these mighty events and not be filled with indescribable emotion? We were literally surrounded by the graves of two of the mightiest nations which had ever flourished on the earth. We stood in the center of their burial place. They had rebelled against God; they had slain His Prophets, disregarded His warnings and arrayed themselves against Him. (July 5, 1873, JI 8:108-109)

STUDY THE SCRIPTURES. In teaching the principles of the Gospel let us see that the children comprehend them. You have heard a great deal about the Bible, the Book of Mormon, the Doctrine and Covenants and the Pearl of Great Price. . . . We feel impressed to say to all of you, "Have no substitutes for these works." They are the inspired words of God. There is nothing you can refer to that is so good as they are. Make these books interesting to the children. I know that no better reading matter can be obtained than these books furnish.

We should instil into the children's minds a love for the word of God. Of course, there are other good books which may be used as auxiliaries and works of reference. I do not wish to depreciate them in the least; but I do not want to say one word in favor of any work in preference to the word of God. The word of God is not studied enough among us. . . .

I think you will find this feeling of indifference for the written word too general among our young people, and I take this opportunity of impressing upon you the importance of the study of these works. All other works, however well written they may be, cannot be compared with the word of God. The stories from the word of God are as interesting as any fairy stories that man ever wrote. (November 13, 1900, JI 36:267-68)

HOME READING FOR CHILDREN. Children should be encouraged to read the standard works of the Church at home. What they read at Sunday School is not sufficient. They are there but an hour or two once in the week, while in most cases they have many hours of leisure during the other six days. While children are young their minds are free and retentive. What they read they can remember, and they are lastingly impressed with it. . . .

It is a mistake to think that boys and girls from ten to fifteen years of age are too young to read and understand such books as the New Testament and the Book of Mormon. They are able to understand sufficient to be impressed with their truthful and sacred character and to be greatly benefited by their reading. Children who have learned the art of reading and take an interest in books will be sure to read something. If left to choose their own books, they may select those that are harmful in their character. (November 1, 1898, JI 33:728-29)

SCRIPTURE MEMORIZING. Children are fond of committing sentences to memory. It is a pleasure to them, and they take to it at an early age. This childish trait, if properly guided, can be turned to good service. By a little assistance in the way of suggestion they can be led to memorizing passages of scripture. If these passages are from the sayings of the Savior, or bear upon the principles of the Gospel, they will be of value to the children throughout life. Especially will this be the case if they are called into the mission field, or as teachers in the Sabbath School. . . .

It is a pleasing and profitable mental recreation for children to memorize. They will commit to memory something; if it is not good, it will be either bad or indifferent and useless. Their minds as well as their bodies must be active. It is no more difficult for them to commit to memory useful passages of scripture, even though they may not fully understand them, than to learn foolish nursery rhymes or current doggerel that has no meaning whatever. (December 1, 1898, JI 33:795)

KEEP ON SAFE GROUND IN THEOLOGY. There is no end to the questions that might be asked which would be very difficult if not impossible for any mortal to answer. It does not require much intelligence nor much thought to propound a query to which the wisest man can not make a satisfactory reply. A desire for information is of course to be commended; but a curiosity as to abstruse points in theology does not always indicate a real search for knowledge nor does it necessarily imply dearth of thought or diligent study. It is frequently an evidence of a quibbling mind, and in many cases that have come to our knowledge it suggests rather a desire to "show off" in argument and display skill in controversy than a desire for the real essence of truth.

However, there is much truth which all men cannot yet understand; and there are many things which are plain to some that are obscure to others. Where the plain word of God has been given, there is an end to dispute or controversy. Beyond this it is unprofitable for theological classes to venture; for when disputants follow their theories past the point where the written or revealed word extends, they are at once in a vast realm of uncertainty where one man's opinion is as good as another's.

We repeat, it is well for students in our theological classes to confine themselves to the written revelations and to the word of God as He has given it, not indulging in wild speculations and all sorts of fancies concerning things about which the Lord has not given His word. There are many things which He has revealed to His faithful servants that are unwise for them to teach, and they do not teach them. (April 1, 1899, JI 34:209)

LEAVE THE MYSTERIES ALONE. There are a great many things in connection with God's dealings with the children of men which cannot be explained fully to human understanding. Hence, faith is required. No man can please God who does not have faith. He must trust in God. It is not to be expected that men, in their mortal condition, can comprehend all the works and providences of our God. If they could, there would be no necessity for them to learn, for there would be nothing to learn. But because we cannot understand certain principles and give the reasons for everything that we see, it does not follow that those are not correct. It is because we are ignorant that we cannot understand or explain them.

The time will come, if we continue to progress, when we shall understand all truth; and the mystery that now surrounds many questions will be entirely removed by the light of heaven. It does not follow, because a matter cannot be explained, that it is false. There are very many features connected with the earth, connected with the religion of the Lord Jesus Christ, which are true but cannot be fully explained. And it is unwise for Latter-day Saints to be puzzling themselves over abstruse questions and matters that are of no particular moment at the present time that, if answered, would prove of no special benefit to them. (July 1, 1890, JI 25:404)

As "children of the light" [John 12:36; Luke 16:8], we have this great consolation, that the Creator has restored unto us every power of the Priesthood, blessed us with every ordinance of His Holy House and bereft us of no authority, key or endowment necessary for our eternal salvation and exaltation in His most glorious presence. This being so, what matters the rest? At best they are certainly not worth periling our immortal souls for, or by contention, which breeds disunion and ill feeling towards our brethren and mental darkness and sometimes spiritual death.

Most of the disagreements between brethren on doctrinal subjects arise from one of two causes. Either the disputants are contending regarding that which has already been revealed, but with which they, in their ignorance of the fullness of God's word, are unacquainted, or they are arguing with regard to questions which no man can answer because the Lord has not revealed them. The remedy for the former condition is an easy one. It is that we should make ourselves more fully acquainted with God's written word, a duty which too many, called by the name of Saint, woefully neglect. In the second place, it is labor in vain; it is a condition in which one man's opinion is as good as another man's opinion, and when the discussion is over and the reasons all submitted, the disputants are just where they started out, unless, unfortunately, hard feelings and coldness have arisen between members of the Church, then their last state is worse than the first. (April 1, 1897, JI 32:209)

TEACH ONLY SOUND DOCTRINE. There should be care exercised, especially when speaking in the presence of young, inexperienced men, in setting forth doctrine about which there is room for discussion. There is enough that is sound and true upon which Elders can converse without venturing upon topics concerning which there is liable to be disputation. Whenever contention or disputation arise among Elders, it may be accepted as a sure sign that there is something wrong; for the Spirit of God does not teach doctrines which are in conflict with each other, nor present opposing views concerning the plan of salvation. (October 15, 1891, JI 26:622)

Chapter 21

Apostasy from the Truth—Some Causes

APOSTASY AND ITS CAUSES. It has been truthfully remarked on many occasions that a man did not know himself or know his fellows until he or they embraced the Gospel in its fulness and purity. Then whatever good or evil qualities or dispositions he or they might have would be brought to the surface, and their true characters would be known. A man, under the influence of the Gospel, either becomes a very faithful, true man, or a very unfaithful, bad man. He cannot, while professing to be a believer in the truth and connected with the Church, stand still. He must inevitably progress or go backward, and the signs of his progress or of his retrogression have been made so familiar to the people by long experience that they have not the least difficulty in discerning his true condition.

There are certain rules with which experience has made the people familiar, that cannot be persistently violated without retrogression and apostasy following. They are as familiar as "household words" to all the members of the Church who have had any experience.

Experience has proved that the indulgence in whoredom. adultery and lust is fatal to faith in the Gospel. This practice is so antagonistic to the spirit of the Gospel that the two cannot co-exist in the same individual.

Experience has also proved that opposing or speaking against the Priesthood, or the authority which God has placed in His Church to govern it, is inevitably followed, sooner or later, by a loss of faith and by complete apostasy.

These are two rules, or they may be termed laws, which, during the experience of nearly forty years, have never been known to be violated without apostasy following, unless, indeed, the transgressor of them repented humbly and sincerely and succeeded in obtaining forgiveness. Position, knowledge or influence may be of advantage to a man under some circumstances; but they avail him nothing in averting the penalty which follows the transgression of either of these laws. It falls alike upon all, from the highest to the lowest, from the richest to the poorest, from the most learned to the most illiterate, and all are amenable to it.

Besides these, there are numerous other laws which must be observed. . . . When they are violated, it is quickly discerned, and frequently when least suspected by the person who is guilty of the violation. If a man is dishonest, grasping, greedy, taking advantage of his neighbour, neglectful of his duties as a Saint, not living up to his profession, delighting in the society of the wicked, and he persists in any or all of these things, confidence in him becomes weakened, it is seen that he does not possess a good spirit, and those who know him are prepared for what must inevitably follow, unless he repent, viz., a loss of faith, and, finally, apostasy.

Out of all who have lost their fellowship and standing in the Church from the beginning until the present, we never knew or heard of one who lost it when in the full and active discharge of his duty. Many have lost their faith and been expelled from the Church through their indulgence in the spirit of whoredom and lust. Many, also, through following the example of Lucifer, who opposed constituted authority and rebelled against it, and, like him, have been cut off from the society of the virtuous and the righteous; and many, also, for other sins; but when or where, in all the history of The Church of Jesus Christ of Latter-day Saints, was one ever excommunicated who was humbly and faithfully discharging his duties as a servant and Saint of God? There never was an instance of the kind.

We know that there scarcely ever was a prominent individual cut off from the Church that did not make the assertion that he was expelled without a cause. Such persons . . . have always been—if their statements were to be believed—exceedingly righteous. They were not wrong; oh, no, it was Joseph, or it was somebody else that had erred and was in the dark and had fallen. Frequently they have continued to assert that they were as strong believers in the doctrines of the Church as they ever were, that they knew them to be true, but the authorities were wrong; the man who held the keys had transgressed and was in the dark. . . .

It is a noticeable fact that apostates, as a rule, assume to be wonderfully pious. More self-righteous men could not apparently exist than some of the early apostates when cut off from this Church. In fact, while true religion is esteemed, hypocritical pretense to piety is viewed with suspicion by the Latter-day Saints, it being understood to be an evidence of apostasy.

Another evidence is that when men drink into that spirit they immediately become very popular among the wicked. Those who sought the overthrow of the Church and the destruction of Joseph in the neighbourhood of Kirtland, Far West and Nauvoo rejoiced when they heard of men apostatizing and proving false to him. While they were faithful and true the wicked hated them as they did him; but no sooner did they commence to operate against him, than they became the warm friends of this class and were welcomed to their society. This is a result which has never failed in cases of apostasy. (December 1, 1869, MS 31:779-80)

APOSTASY ALWAYS RESULT OF SIN. No man ever fell away from this Church without a cause. God does not deal with His children in that manner. He does not leave them to themselves; He does not desert them. This is the glorious feature connected with the service of God. In the hour of the greatest extremity, in the time when His children need help the most, He is always near to them; He surrounds them with His power, and He bears them off as on eagles' wings.

Therefore, no man ever fell into darkness; no man ever became weak in the faith; no man ever lost his standing in this Church without a cause, and that cause has had its origin in himself. Within himself the cause can be traced, and the all-piercing eye of God the Eternal Father has penetrated it. He knows it. The Spirit of God, from which nothing can be hidden, knows it.

The Holy Ghost is one of the Godhead, and when anything of this kind is done, He is grieved and withdraws Himself from the individual, who is then left to fall into the dark. The light of heaven withdraws itself from such an individual, and he no longer feels the testimony of the Spirit, and he wonders within himself how he could speak as he once did. This does not take place all at once. Rarely is the Spirit entirely withdrawn in a moment.

LOSS OF SPIRIT COMPARED TO SETTING SUN. It is like the sinking of the sun in our western horizon. We see the great orb of day disappear behind the mountains, and the heavens are still illumined with his glory; but gradually, and almost imperceptibly in our latitude, darkness spreads over the scene. So it is with the Spirit of the Lord. Being grieved and offended, and there being no repentance, it gradually withdraws itself from the soul, until darkness takes possession, and the man is left then to whatever influence and spirit he has yielded to. (February 17, 1895, DW 50:418)

APOSTASY A SLOW PROCESS. Everything that is impure will gradually be cleansed from the midst of the Saints. Adulterers and fornicators and liars and thieves may connect themselves with the Church and have a standing in it for a while; but sooner or later their deeds will be known. The Spirit of God will withdraw from them, and they will be left to themselves to deny the faith and separate themselves from the people of God. This cleansing process, though sure and steady, is not hasty. It sometimes takes years for men to entirely lose the Spirit of the Lord and their desire to be members of this Church. But sooner or later, if they live and continue to practice iniquity, they fall into this condition. Then, in the most of instances, they become bitter enemies to the work of God. (February 15, 1885, JI 20:56)

NONE TOO STRONG TO FALL. We live in a day when we cannot trifle with God. He has said that His Spirit shall not always strive with man; He will withdraw that Spirit from us if we do not follow out His commands, and we shall be left to ourselves. The most dreadful condition that I can imagine a human being to be in is this, for a man who has once tasted of the word of God, who has felt its power, who has had a foretaste of the powers of the world to come, and who has rejoiced in those blessings, to suffer the Spirit of God to depart from him through his own acts.

Whenever I have thought of it concerning myself, I have been filled with inexpressible horror. It has seemed as though a thousand deaths would be preferable, for to die is an easy thing;

it is a light matter compared with apostasy, the loss of the Spirit of God, the forfeiting of the favor of heaven, the loss of those blessings, promises and powers which God has bestowed, the loss of interest in the work of God, to have the Spirit fade and withdraw itself from us until we live without it. Can you imagine any worse condition?

Let him, the Apostle says, that standeth take heed lest he fall. There is no one so strong that he can be sure he will get through. It is only by the grace of God that we can expect to be faithful and to receive salvation. Think of the mighty men who have been in this Church who have fallen. . . .

ONLY FAITHFUL TO STAND. Can we expect to stand unless we keep the commandments of God and are faithful to the truth? No! There is only one way in which we can expect to do that which is right and to receive the glory of God; that is to hold out faithfully to the end, to walk humbly before our God, to walk prayerfully and circumspectly before Him and keep his commandments with all diligence, with all thankfulness day by day, hour by hour, seeking unto Him for strength, conscious of our own unworthiness, of our destitution in His holy sight, in the presence of His awful majesty. . . .

Let no man or woman deceive himself or herself and think they can sin and still retain the favor of God. God's Spirit will not dwell in unholy tabernacles, or with those who do not keep His commandments, who break their covenants and who do wrong either to Him or to one another. We should love one another with all our heart, keep ourselves from everything that would grieve the Spirit of God and live lives of Latter-day Saints in truth and in deed. (May 26, 1889, DW 38:710-11)

THE PRINCIPAL CAUSE OF APOSTASY. It would seem to persons who are ignorant of the ways of the Lord that if a man or a woman once knew the truth and received a testimony from God respecting it, they would never deny or forsake it; and to such persons the departure of men and women, who have testified of the truth, from the Church, is incomprehensible upon any other principle than that they have found out the errors of the Work. The experience, however, of those who have been for a long time connected with this Church has proved to them that the fault has not been with the Work but with those who having once known it have afterwards denied it. In ninety-nine cases out of a hundred, where men have known the truth for themselves and testified of it and have afterwards denied it, their apostasy is directly traceable to their violation of the following words of the Lord:

> And verily I say unto you, as I have said before, he that looketh on a woman to lust after her, or if any shall commit adultery in their hearts, they shall not have the Spirit, but shall deny the faith and shall fear. Wherefore, I, the Lord, have said that the fearful, and the unbelieving, and all liars, and whosoever loveth and maketh a lie, and the whoremonger, and the sorcerer, shall have their part in that lake which burneth with fire and brimstone, which is the second death. Verily I say, that they shall not have part in the first resurrection. [D&C 63:16-18.]

We confidently assert, and we believe that the assertion is capable of the fullest proof, that more persons have denied the faith in consequence of their flagrant disobedience to this revelation than from any other cause. . . .

It is the great and crying sin of this generation, and God's anger and fierce indignation will be poured out upon the inhabitants of the earth because of their wickedness in this direction. The most holy and godlike power that he could bestow upon them is abused and made the cause of the misery and degradation of the human family, instead of being used for their blessing and the glory of God.

This, doubtless, is one principal reason of Jesus saying that there will be few who will tread the strait and narrow path and attain unto such a position as will entitle them to hold the gift eternally which God has bestowed upon men for this short period of existence. If men will abuse the gifts of God here and trample them under their feet, it is madness for them to expect that he will bestow such upon them to be in like manner abused throughout eternity. . . .

It is utterly impossible for any man who loves or practices impurity to remain steadfast in this Church. If he looks upon a woman to lust after her, or carries into execution his lustful desires in any form, unless he speedily repents, he will deny the faith. This is inevitable, as the word of God and the entire history of his people abundantly prove. If men and women will be pure before the Lord in all things, to the extent of their ability, their progress in the Church of God and in the knowledge of God will be very rapid. Pure-minded people readily comprehend every principle that is advanced. They have no difficulty in understanding the truth when presented before them nor in obeying its principles. Such persons never apostatize. God is bound by His promise to preserve them, and they can put unlimited confidence in Him, knowing that He will deliver them from every evil. (March 14, 1863, MS 25:168-69)

NO PREDESTINATION TO FAITHFULNESS. What is there to prevent us all being faithful. Is there any destiny in this? Are any of us destined or predestined to be faithful and others not to be faithful? Certainly not; there is nothing of this kind in the providence of God. . . . There is no foundation in truth in any such assumption.

God has selected all of us to attain to this glory, if we will take the course that He has marked out for its attainment. He has pointed out the way as plainly before us as this aisle is before me now in which we should walk; He has told us what to do and warned us of the dangers that beset our pathway and which we must guard against in order to attain to the end in view.

We enter in a race, so to speak. We start out full of courage and hope, determined to run the race vigorously and continuously to the end. But something arises to render the race undesirable to us and to lessen in our estimation the high value which we placed upon the prize to be attained when we started out. There are causes which produce this; but they are not due to the predestination of God. The causes are to be found within ourselves.

How many members of this Church have felt that they would sacrifice everything that they had on earth, yes, and lay down life itself, rather than deny the faith and thereby lose the Spirit of God and the fellowship of their brethren and sisters? I suppose there is scarcely a soul to be found in the Church that has not had that feeling. How lovely the truth was in their sight when they joined the Church! How desirable salvation and exaltation appeared before them! Everything connected with the Church and with the authority of the Priesthood seemed to them to be of God, and they loved it. They loved every principle of the Gospel with intense love.

But after awhile that love fades away; they cease to value their standing, and by degrees these men and women, who at one time felt that they would rather part with their life than with their standing in the Church, cease to value that standing and let it go without any effort to retain it, not condescending probably to ask forgiveness for wrong done. . . . The hand of fellowship is colder and colder, darker and darker, until they lose entirely all the love they ever had for the work of God or for the people of God. . . .

A SURE SIGN OF APOSTASY. Now, there are certain things that we cannot do and remain faithful to the work of God. The first and foremost among these is, (and I dwell on it, I hope, in a spirit that will be understood even by strangers), speaking evil against the Priesthood of the Son of God. It is one of the surest signs of apostasy. You may think that you have cause for this; you may see things in men that may appear to you wrong and to justify you in indulging in criticism and censorious remarks, and perhaps you may even feel justified in uttering words of condemnation; but let me say to you—and I say it as the result of a life time's experience and observation—that this cannot be done by any man or woman in this Church, great or small, without incurring the displeasure of the Almighty and without grieving the Spirit of God.

Those who have entered into holy places have made covenants, which are sacred in the sight of God and of their brethren and sisters, not to speak against the Lord's anointed. . . . No Latter-day Saint can do it without grieving the Spirit of God and causing it to withdraw itself. Do you realize this, when you are tempted or aroused by anger to say evil things concerning your brethren or sisters? If you but think of the consequences that may follow the indulgence in such a spirit, I am sure that you will restrain your speech and you will not give utterance to anything of the kind. . . .

Leave those who do wrong to the Lord. He will see that His

servants are not permitted . . . to lead this people astray. If your brethren and sisters do wrong, take them out and talk to them yourselves and reason with them, but do not speak evil against them; do not backbite them and seek to lessen their influence with their neighbors. . . . I tell you as a servant of God that there is only one way to be saved and that is by keeping the commandments of God, and no man has any assurance that he will be saved unless he does this. (April 21, 1895, DW 51:289-90)

CONSEQUENCES OF TRANSGRESSION. Among the many truths brought to light by the revelation of the Gospel of Jesus Christ, one has been clearly proven in these days—that the man who practices iniquity cannot long maintain a standing in the Church of God. Men may obtain light and intelligence, may have the heavens opened to their view and enjoy the visions of eternity, may have seen the lame leap as a hart and the blind restored to sight through the exercise of faith and the power bestowed upon the servants of God; yet, after having witnessed and been the participants in all these blessings, if they pursue a course of wickedness, they will, sooner or later, fall into such darkness that truth and its accompanying blessings will no longer have any attractions for them, and they will be ready to forsake the Church of God, which they formerly prized so highly, and use all the influence in their power to oppose it. . . .

Because men have been in possession of knowledge and have experienced much of the goodness and power of God, it does not necessarily follow that they will always be in possession of the same feelings, irrespective of their actions. Lucifer, the son of the morning, holding power and authority, blessed with knowledge and experience, fell into transgression and became an angel of darkness, opposed to the Almighty and to all those who keep his commandments; and it is but reasonable to suppose that, if he could fall by indulging in sin, man, also, by taking a similar course, must be visited by similar consequences. The antagonism Lucifer manifests against the work of God is the same feeling that those who follow in his steps will have, in a less degree, towards that Work whenever it is established upon the earth. . . .

The loss of the Spirit of the Lord and a relapse into darkness are the inevitable consequences of a departure from or violation of the laws of God; and, so long as men are fallible and give way to temptation, so long will there be those who will be found fighting against the Lord and against His work and His servants. (July 19, 1856, WS 166-67)

DON'T LIFT VOICE AGAINST PRIESTHOOD. There are some things that are worse than others. One is to lift our voice against or in any manner assail the Priesthood of the Son of God. You may think this a trifling thing. You may say, "Why who are these men that I should not speak about them? I know they are fallible men; they are mortal; they are guilty of many weaknesses. I do not see why I should respect them, or why they should be shielded from criticism, or why I should listen to their counsel."

Now, judged by man's standard, this may appear to be true. There is not a man in the Church . . . that has anything overpowering about him, that we should render him any degree of obedience. It is not that. These are but the earthly vessels. . . . But while these men are but earthly vessels, it is the authority, it is the power, it is God . . . that is within them that causes them to do these godly works. Without God were in them, they could not baptize men for remission of sins; they could not lay on hands for the reception of the Holy Ghost.

It is the spirit and power which God gives to all who receive His Priesthood that makes them in the sight of God so holy that they ought not to be spoken against; they ought not to be belittled; they ought not to be disobeyed by the people of God. (April 17, 1897, DW 55:35)

A SYMPTOM OF APOSTASY. It is not for everyone to judge and condemn God's servants. It is against such a feeling that the warning is given, "Touch not mine anointed and do my prophets no harm." [1 Chronicles 16:22.]

We have been taught from the beginning that one of the most dangerous symptoms of apostasy from the Church is speaking evil of the Lord's servants; whenever a spirt of this kind takes possession of one who is called a Latter-day Saint, it is sure to grieve the Spirit of God; it invites darkness to enter the mind, and, unless it is sincerely repented of, it causes apostasy to follow. For this reason, if for no other, our children should be taught from the time they are old enough to comprehend that they are treading upon slippery ground whenever they venture to criticise, censure or condemn those whom the Lord has chosen to be His servants.

Many think it is part of their privilege in the exercise of free speech to do this and that it is a sign of independence. But there is none of the true liberty of free speech in it; it becomes license and is offensive to the Lord. . . . Respect for authority should be constantly taught. . . . The Saints honor God; they honor the authority which He bestows; and in honoring that authority they honor those who bear it. This is the spirit of true independence, and it does not take away the least particle from the true dignity of manhood and womanhood. The Lord says: ". . . them that honour me I will honour, and they that despise me shall be lightly esteemed." [1 Samuel 2:30.] (November 1, 1894, JI 29:668)

KNOWLEDGE ALONE NOT SUFFICIENT. To a person without experience in the work of God and in the operations of his Holy Spirit, it appears strange that men who have known the truth and who have testified to having received such knowledge should ever deny or forsake it. Such persons seem unable to comprehend how a man can become so utterly inconsistent as to declare that to be false, either by his words or by his actions, which he formerly declared to be true. Yet the history of the Work of God in these days abounds with instances of men who have thus acted.

The fact is, knowledge alone is not sufficient to save men. They must put their knowledge into practice and act up to that which they know. There must be united with the knowledge that the Gospel is true a desire to put its principles into operation and apply them to themselves. Men have not apostatized from the Church of God because they have lacked knowledge, (for God has always bestowed it upon those who have entered his Church in a proper spirit), but because they have not put their knowledge to a proper use.

The Lord has pronounced certain penalties for disobedience. He has threatened the transgressor of His commandments with the loss of His Holy Spirit, which loss should be attended on their part with the denial of the faith. Yet, though men have seen numerous instances of the infliction of this penalty, they will themselves go and deliberately commit the very acts which they have every reason to know will be followed by such terrible consequences. In this case their knowledge fails to save them from the loss of that salvation which, when they embraced the Gospel, they hoped to obtain.

No man can retain that knowledge of the truth which is necessary to save him, if he does not possess the Spirit of the Lord. There may be some truths of which he may have a knowledge and of which he cannot be deprived. There have been men connected with this Church who have received such a knowledge from God respecting the revelation of the Gospel to the earth, through the agency of angels and of the bringing forth of the Book of Mormon by His almighty power in raising up His servant Joseph to be a Prophet, as to be forever after incapable of doubting the truth of those things; yet, through grieving the Holy Spirit they have fallen into gross transgressions and fought against that work and that man which, but a short time before, they would have been willing, apparently, to have defended at the cost of their lives. The knowledge which they had respecting this being the Work of God, instead of being an aid to them after the Spirit of the Lord had withdrawn from them, was a condemnation, and they strayed as widely from the path of salvation as the most ignorant could have done.

APOSTATES CLAIM CHURCH TRUE UNTIL A CERTAIN TIME. The Saints should not imagine that because they know the truth and the Work of God at the present time that they will always know these things and therefore be able to stand. If they lose the Holy Spirit through their transgressions, from that moment their knowledge respecting the Work of God ceases to increase and becomes dead; a short time only elapses before such persons deny the faith. They may not deny that the Work was ever true or that the Elders were ever the servants of God, but they will place a limit and after that say, "Up to such a time the work was true and the Elders were right, but, after that, they went astray"—that very period being the time at which they themselves had committed some act or acts to forfeit the Spirit of God and kill the growth of that knowledge which they had had bestowed upon them. This has been the case in numerous instances in the past.

During the Prophet Joseph's lifetime, men who had lost the Spirit themselves through their transgressions would declare that he had gone astray, and in some instances attempt to point out the time when and the spot where his departure from the right path had commenced. Many of them were not in the least degree loth to contend that the work was of God and that Joseph had been the Prophet of God, but he had fallen, and they felt it to be their duty to deal with him and to rectify the errors and wrongs which he had committed. From his days until the present time numerous instances of this kind have occurred, and but few men have apostatized who have not been willing to affirm that the Work was all true and the servants of God were all right up to a certain point, since which everything had gone wrong.

The progress of the Work of God and the blessings which have rested upon His servants and people have given abundant proofs that the fault has lain with these persons who have been so loud in their talk respecting the transgressions of the servants of God. Indeed, if these were not sufficient evidences, their decrease in everything that pertaineth to godliness, and the miserable results which attend their efforts, would be quite ample of themselves to convince a Saint of God that His displeasure was resting upon such characters. It is plain that it is they who have transgressed and thereby driven the Spirit of the Lord from them; and at the very time they say the Church of God strayed, they themselves were guilty of transgression. (August 8, 1863, MS 25:504-506)

NO OBLIGATION TO PREACH TO APOSTATES. The Saints, and the Elders particularly, should never be in the least degree loth to advocate and defend the principles of their religion when they are in a position to warn the people and discharge the duty which they owe to mankind; and when they are in a position of this kind, if they are living near unto the Lord, they will have His Spirit to prompt and assist them; but they are not required to cast their "pearls before swine." [Matthew 7:6.]

They are under no obligation to preach to or hold controversy with those who have heard the Gospel an innumerable number of times and who have rejected and systematically opposed it, or with those who, having once known the truth and partaken of the Spirit of the Lord, have turned away therefrom. To talk to such individuals is time spent in vain; no good result can possibly attend such labor. There is enough work to be accomplished of a productive and satisfactory character in the world, to occupy all the time and attention of the Elders and Saints, without spending any in labor so barren of good results. There are thousands of individuals with whom time can be profitably spent, who have never heard the truth and the message of this last dispensation.

THEY RISE AND THEY FALL. There are many apostates who profess to have claims which they wish to maintain, and they cry loudly for investigation. The Church of God, they say, has fallen into transgression and gone astray, and they, since their apostasy, have been able to ascertain the causes of this and have found the remedy. This has been the cry of every apostate of note from the beginning of the work of God in these days until the present time. One after another has risen, in countless numbers, denouncing the servants of God as having fallen and gone astray and professing to have the power to correct the evils of which they complained. One after another they have passed away into oblivion, after fully exposing their folly and imbecility, while the men whom they have denounced and attempted to ruin have continued to increase in knowledge and in power with God and man. (August 1, 1863, MS 25:489)

OPPOSITION TO AUTHORITIES CAUSES APOSTASY. A friend . . . wished to know whether we . . . considered an honest difference of opinion between a member of the Church and the Authorities of the Church was apostasy. . . . We replied that we had not stated that an honest difference of opinion between a member of the Church and the Authorities constituted apostasy, for we could conceive of a man honestly differing in opinion from the Authorities of the Church and yet not be an apostate;

but we could not conceive of a man publishing these differences of opinion and seeking by arguments, sophistry and special pleading to enforce them upon the people to produce division and strife and to place the acts and counsels of the Authorities of the Church, if possible, in a wrong light, and not be an apostate, for such conduct was apostasy as we understood the term.

We further said that while a man might honestly differ in opinion from the Authorities through a want of understanding, he had to be exceedingly careful how he acted in relation to such differences, or the adversary would take advantage of him, and he would soon become imbued with the spirit of apostasy and be found fighting against God and the authority which He had placed here to govern His Church. (DEN, November 3, 1869)

SATAN SEEKS TO UNDERMINE AUTHORITIES. Though men may deny the faith, in one sense, and turn away from the path of righteousness and dissolve their connection with the Church, yet they will cling, in most instances, to what we term the first principles of the Gospel of Christ; and it is a very rare thing to see those who have been members of The Church of Jesus Christ of Latter-day Saints turning away and joining what we call sectarian churches. If they leave this Church, it is an exceedingly difficult thing for them to connect themselves with other denominations. . . .

But there are other principles more advanced with which the people are not so familiar, and of this the adversary seeks to take advantage, and when men deny the faith, they are apt to deny these principles; when they get into the dark, there is probably no point upon which they differ more frequently than that which relates to the authority that is exercised in presiding. This is a point that the adversary always aims at. . . .

It seems as though the adversary, in the day in which we live, seeks, by every means in his power, to undermine the influence and the authority of the man whom God has called to preside over His people. (December 5, 1869, JD 13:44)

CLEANSING PROCESS WEEDS OUT IMPURE. We are setting an example in regard to virtue. Yet, I feel there is secret sin practiced among us. There is this, however, for our protection; God is cleansing this people and purging those who practice sin from their midst. Those who commit sin gradually leave the Church. They get into the dark, and they become cold and indifferent and finally leave the Church. If it were not for God's power in this respect, we would soon become corrupt, doubtless, as other people.

God in His wonderful providence has so arranged matters that impurity cannot live in this Church for any length of time. There is a cleansing process going on. God is cleansing His Church, and He is purging out the wicked and the ungodly, and He is leaving the residue. No man can be confident of standing in this Church unless he is pure in heart, for the Holy Ghost will not dwell in unholy tabernacles.

Men may deceive their fellowmen; women may deceive their sisters; but they cannot deceive God. They cannot commit sin and retain the Spirit of God. It will leave them sooner or later. It will decrease within them and finally leave them, unless they repent of their sin. And this is our safety and the safety of this Church; God is cleansing it and removing from the midst of the people the corrupt.

Those who practice secret sin may hide it from their fellows, as some do, and think it is not known; but God will make it known. His Spirit will leave them, unless they repent with all their hearts and turn from their sins. God will have an honest people. He will have a pure people; He will have a virtuous people. He will cleanse us and keep cleansing us until we shall be pure, and there will be a people found that are not hypocrites. The hypocrite will be cleansed from the midst of the Saints. In this way we will be built up and the Church will increase. (October 6, 1895, DW 51:643)

Tell me the individual history of a member of this Church, and I will tell you his fate. Why? Because I know that certain causes will produce certain effects. And as with the individual so with the entire community. As a community we can only stand by doing right. Any man of experience in this Church can write the fate of members of the Church, so far as they know their course of life. Prophesy? Why, yes; predict it easily, because it has all been worked out thousands of times before. (DEN, September 15, 1900)

SIMILARITY OF PAST AND PRESENT APOSTASY. An examination of all the apostate schemes which have been concocted for the division and overthrow of the Church of Jesus Christ of Latter-day Saints reveals the curious fact that they all bear the marks of a common origin. The lapse of years and the change of men make no difference in this respect. If the programme of the apostates from the Church in Kirtland, and that of the apostates in Nauvoo, and that of those in later days be compared, the similarity is most striking. If they were the production of one brain, they could not be more alike. Even the language in some points is almost identical.

In Kirtland the doctrine which Joseph had taught, the organization which he had perfected, and the ordinances which he had administered were all divine, so said the apostates; but he had fallen, and was no longer a Prophet. He had transgressed, they said, and because of this his power and authority were taken from him.

The Nauvoo apostates took precisely the same ground. Everything that Joseph had taught and done up to a certain point, even including the acts and policy which their predecessors, the apostates at Kirtland, had objected to, was correct; but they affirmed that he had fallen, because of something which he had just then done. He began to teach false doctrine, they said; the possession of power had spoiled him; he had become so intoxicated by it that he did not yield that respect to others which was justly their due; in fact, instead of being a Prophet of God which he once had been, they declared he had become a tyrant. . . .

We never look for consistency in apostates from this Church; for of all people, they are the most illogical and inconsistent. . . . In one breath calling Joseph a Prophet, the doctrine and religion which he taught the immutable and eternal principles of heaven, and in the next denouncing him as guilty of everything that is low and vile, and clamouring for his blood. Napoleon, we believe, it was who said that there was only one step from the sublime to the ridiculous. We never knew an apostate from this Church to undertake to defend his own course and to assail the presiding authority in the Church who did not take this step. (January 11, 1870, MS 32:17-18)

PECULIAR FEATURE OF APOSTATES. There is a peculiar feature attending those who apostatize, of which the parallel cannot be found among any other people, except we go back to the primitive Christians—the immediate disciples of Jesus. Men may belong to any of the so-called Christian sects of the day, and they may renounce their belief or dissolve their connection with the religious bodies of which they are members, and we do not see that virulence, that spirit and disposition to seek for the blood of those with whom they were formerly connected, manifested on their part, which are manifested by those who have been members of The Church of Jesus Christ of Latter-day Saints and have apostatized therefrom. . . .

IMPURITY CAUSES LOSS OF SPIRIT. We who are connected with this Church and retain our membership with this people must be pure in our thoughts, in our words and in our actions; we must take a course to retain the Spirit of God in our hearts; and if we do not take a course of this kind, the Spirit of God will inevitably leave us and that light which had illumined our understandings, that joy and peace which have filled our souls and caused us to rejoice exceedingly before the Lord, will depart from us, and we shall be left in a worse condition than we were before we obeyed the Gospel. (May 6, 1866, JD 11:226-27)

HATRED OF APOSTATES. The instruments most effective in the hands of Satan in carrying out his designs are those who, having enjoyed the truth and the spirit which accompanies it, take a course to stifle its increase and abandon themselves to do evil. They can enter more devotedly into his feelings and wishes than strangers to the truth and its influences, because they follow in his footsteps.

Satan was at one time in the possession of truth and, doubtless, rejoiced in the sunshine of God's favor; but having taken a course to forfeit his claim to this glory and to check the further development of truth in himself, he became wholly abandoned to evil and has since sought with all his power to deprive others of that which he himself cannot enjoy. The intensity with which his followers exhibit this same hatred to the truth and its believers is in proportion to the progress they have made in its knowledge and the extent to which they abandon themselves to the influences which he exercises.

Every apostate from the truth, Judas-like, indulges in this same feeling; and the hatred which they bear to the principles they once rejoiced in and its believers, their former brethren, is varied in intensity by the progress they made in the knowledge of truth when they loved it and the extent to which they abandon themselves to the influence which their master exercises. . . . This is a natural consequence of the influence to which they give heed. They quench the Spirit of the Lord, and it deserts them; they become fully possessed with the Evil One, and then, like their master, nothing will satiate them but the blood of the just. Like the Gospel in ancient days, "Mormonism" draws out these feelings in a man at the present time. . . .

When a man obeys the truth, or the Gospel of Jesus Christ, which comprehends all truth, he receives a spirit of light and intelligence, of peace and joy; he has a foretaste, as it were, of heaven. If he cherish it, it will increase within him and continually afford him the purest happiness, will fill him with peace and good-will to men and gradually lead him into all truth. But if he grieve and quench it after having once enjoyed it, it will decrease within him, until he will be entirely destitute of it and a prey to exactly the opposite feelings to those produced by its presence. He will hate the truth as strongly as he formerly loved it, and he will wonder how he could ever see anything about it that was lovely or attractive. Hence, Satan does not have the power over men who never knew the truth that he does over those who apostatize therefrom. (December 27, 1856, WS 289-91)

APOSTATES FILLED WITH SPIRIT OF FEAR. In speaking about apostasy, it is a remarkable feature connected with it and with those who favor apostates and consort with them that they are filled with the spirit of fear. . . . The moment a man loses the Spirit of God and the spirit of the adversary takes possession of him, he is filled with fear; for "the sinners in Zion are afraid; fearfulness hath surprised the hypocrites." [Isaiah 33:14.]

They say their lives are in danger. . . . No honest man or woman need fear; indeed they never fear. What are they afraid of? They have done nothing to cause the spirit of fear to come upon them. It is only when a man does that which is wrong that he receives the spirit of fear. . . .

Those who have the Spirit of God and love their religion have nothing to fear; they can meet their brethren and sisters, the angels of God, and even the Lord himself, without having that dastard fear with them. In the knowledge of their weakness, and their ignorance, and doing many things unintentionally, they feel sorry; but still they are sustained with a consciousness of doing no intentional wrong. (May 6, 1866, JD 11:232-33)

APOSTATES ALWAYS CONSIDERED MORMONS. There is one peculiarity about the "Mormons," and the opinions men have in relation to them, that is not perceivable in any other denomination. Men may be born and raised in Presbyterianism, Methodism, or any of the numerous isms by which we are surrounded, and afterwards dissolve the connection with them and forsake the practice of their doctrines, and they will no longer be known by the name of the people to whom they formerly belonged; but this is not the case with those who have once been "Mormons." "Mormons" they were, and "Mormons" they will continue to be; the name will stick to them, however much they endeavor to get rid of it.

Although every action of their lives may be at complete variance with the doctrines of the Church and the practice of its members who are in good standing, yet, in too many instances, they are saddled onto the whole people, and they have to bear the reproach of the acts of men who have no more claim to the name of Latter-day Saint, or "Mormon," than Satan has to the title he was known by before he was cast out of heaven. (May 24, 1856, WS 116)

Wickedness may be committed by men who are members of the popular sects of Christendom, but the society of which they are members is rarely, if ever, charged with their wickedness; the opposite to this is too frequently the case when the offending party has been a Latter-day Saint—the Church must bear off all his transgressions, though he may have been excommunicated for years. "Mormonism" and its believers are despised; yet, men evidence, by their actions, that they expect more from it as a system and from its followers as practicers of its precepts than they do from any other system or society extant. (October 11, 1856, WS 223)

ALL SINNERS TO BE CUT OFF. "Mormonism" does not countenance wickedness of any kind; however loud a man may protest about being a "Mormon" and believing in "Mormonism," unless he endeavors to live holy and pure and to set a good example unto all by whom he is surrounded, he is not one with the Church of Jesus Christ of Latter-day Saints. A man who commits sin cannot have the presence of the Spirit of the Lord; and, though an official action may not have been taken in his case, yet he has virtually cut himself off from all participation in the blessings of his religion, has ceased to bring forth good fruit and becomes a withered and dried branch only fit for the burning. (March 20, 1857, WS 365)

Chapter 22

Evil Spirits and Secret Combinations

TRY THE SPIRITS. The Apostle John has written these words, "Beloved, believe not every spirit, but try the spirits whether they are of God." [1 John 4:1.]

This counsel applies to Saints in these days as it did in those unto whom the Apostle John wrote. It is right that Latter-day Saints should try every spirit which manifests itself or seeks to obtrude itself among them, not by seeking after it, but when it makes its appearance to see and understand by its fruits whether it be of God or not. It is necessary that we who live in these days should be careful not to be deceived. . . .

The Latter-day Saints should be careful not to entertain spirits which are not of God—spirits of delusion, spirits which lead men into darkness and error and which, if they follow, will lead them to destruction.

The adversary is very busy endeavoring to lead astray the children of men. In every possible way he seeks to seduce them from the path that the Lord has marked out. He appeals to them in the manner most likely to deceive them and brings influences of various kinds to bear upon them. If our eyes could be opened to see agencies he employs to effect his ends, we would be astonished. These agencies are invisible, but mankind are surrounded by them.

When we think that one-third of the hosts of heaven were cast out with Lucifer and fell with him and still are his angels, we can form an idea how numerous they are. Their punishment was like his, that they could not have a tabernacle of flesh and blood. Filled with anger and hatred, like their leader Lucifer, they have ever striven to destroy the family of God, to destroy those who, through obedience to Him, retained their first estate and had the privilege of entering upon their second estate, the probation which we now have. They operate upon the Latter-day Saints when they can, and by all their cunning arts seek to destroy the purposes of God. (August 1, 1889, JI 24:360)

MANY EVIL SPIRITS AT WORK. The Saints, at least, should understand that there are many spirits which are exerting their power among men and seeking to obtain an influence over them and that if they would escape from their effects, they must be upon their guard. But how many are there who are sufficiently careful upon this point? How many of those who have embraced the Gospel are jealously watching every avenue of their hearts lest a spirit which is not of God should enter therein and obtain power over them?

Does the man who finds fault with his brother in the Priesthood and grumbles against and condemns the President understand that when he does so he is giving place to a spirit which is not of God and which, if not expelled, will obtain such power over him that he will be led by it out of the Church and far from the path of righteousness? Or does the woman who scandalizes and talks about her sister know that in so doing she is giving utterance to the thoughts and feelings of a subtle, untruthful and delusive spirit which, if she retains it, will lead her to destruction? When men and women give utterance to such expressions and feelings, the evil influence is at work; they are being operated upon by it, though they themselves may not be aware of it; indeed, the great danger to the individual lies in he or she not being aware of the character of the spirit that is operating upon and leading him or her to commit the evil which it cannot accomplish itself, without the aid of human agency.

So long as evil spirits can obtain possession of living, human beings and influence them according to their wishes, so long has evil a tangible existence upon the earth. If there were no tabernacles for them to operate through—no men and women who would allow them to use their bodies (the great object of their desire, because of their own great lack of earthly attributes)—evil and sin would have no existence upon the earth. . . .

THE SHOCKING CHARACTER OF EVIL SPIRITS. If those who allow such spirits to possess and influence and speak and act through them were to behold them, with their eyes enlightened by the Spirit of God, in all their repulsiveness, they would be shocked at the character of the visitors they had entertained. But the first approaches of such influences are so insidious and insinuating that those to whom they introduce themselves are not aware of their character and the hideous train that they will call to their assistance and encourage to follow them, when once they have obtained an entrance into the human heart.

When an Elder or a Saint (through being off his guard and not suspecting the nature of the influence that is operating upon him) suffers himself, by any of the numerous temptations and fascinations which such spirits know so well how to use, to be diverted from attending to the duties of his ministry and religion with a perfect heart and an eye single to the glory of God, he has but little idea of the wicked troop which will follow the entrance of this unsuspected visitor at the avenue which he has left unguarded unless he instantly expel it and bid it begone. . . .

A LAW PERTAINING TO SPIRITUAL INFLUENCES. The day is fast approaching when the nature of spiritual influences will be fully recognized and understood and when man, by listening to the teachings of God's Spirit and Priesthood and obtaining a correct knowledge of the laws which govern them, will be freed from the power which in the days of his ignorance they have wielded over him. . . .

There is one law pertaining to spiritual influences which should be clearly understood by every Saint and that is, the Spirit of God will not dwell in unholy temples; there must be absolute purity, either existing or being cultivated, in every tabernacle where the Spirit of the Lord dwells constantly. It will plead with man as long as there is any disposition left within him to do right and he does not, by gross transgression, drive it entirely away from him; but it will "not always strive with man." [D&C 1:33.] If he would cultivate its acquaintance and cherish and seek to be governed by it, he would have it as an unfailing source of revelation and knowledge and peace and union and love, until he would be filled with the power of God and all the Divine attributes. But if he gives heed to and encourages other spirits, it will be grieved and forsake him; it will not divide its power nor share its sceptre with such as they. (April 9, 1864, MS 26:233-34.)

THE RISE OF SPIRITUALISM. Not only has faith in spiritual manifestations grown in the hearts of the Latter-day Saints, but something of a similar character has grown up in the midst of the world. The pendulum which had swung in one direction, in the direction of extreme unbelief, of extreme incredulity, concerning everything of a spiritual character, after the organization of this Church, after the restoration of the everlasting Gospel in its ancient purity and power . . . began to swing in the other direction, in the direction of a credulity, and willingness to have something that might be traced, or that could be attributed to a spiritual origin.

Some fifteen or sixteen years after this Church was organized spiritualism began to make its appearance, and thousands upon thousands of people were ready to receive anything that any charlatan chose to bring before them as the result of spiritual manifestations, until the whole nation of the United States, as well as some nations in Europe, were humbugged by the most extraordinary statements and ideas set forth by those charlatans. . . . But the same unwillingness to receive the truth, the same unwillingness to receive the Gospel and the blessings and gifts of God has continued to be manifested, and this belief or credulity concerning spiritualism has not had any favorable effect upon the people in causing them to receive the truth as it is.

Now, there is one power and one power alone . . . through which godliness and the power of God and the gifts of God can be made manifest with any degree of safety—that is, through the Priesthood of the Son of God. Take that authority away from the midst of men, and they would be left precisely in the same condition that the world was in at the time of . . . Joseph Smith. (October 7, 1883, JD 24:341-42)

INCREASED POWER OF SATAN. Satan has always had great power among those who have rejected the Gospel. Men do not come under condemnation until they hear the truth and the testimony of the servants of God and reject them. That portion of the Spirit of the Almighty which they have previously possessed then leaves them, the light which they have had gives place to darkness, and the adversary has great influence over them for they become his servants. This is one reason why he has more power among wicked and corrupt persons when the Gospel is upon the earth than at other times.

SPIRITUALISM SATAN'S PLAN TO DECEIVE. Soon

after the Prophet Joseph's death "spiritualism," as it is called, was made manifest; men and women began to receive revelations, not from the Lord Jesus but from spirits, and great wonders began to be shown. . . .

What a cunning plan this is of the devil to deceive people and prevent men and women from obeying the teachings of Jesus! He will give them power to do these things without believing in Jesus, without repenting of their sins and being baptized or having hands laid upon them. He makes it very easy for them and tries to lead the world down to destruction by this means. "Broad is the gate and wide the way that leadeth to the deaths; and many there are that go in thereat. . . ," but "strait is the gate, and narrow the way that leadeth unto the exaltation and continuation of the lives, and few there be that find it." [D&C 132:22, 25.] . . .

If we obey God, He will prepare us to dwell eternally in His presence; for, by obeying Him we will be made pure and holy and be free from sin, and He will give unto us His Holy Spirit and the gifts of the Spirit. These gifts are not like the power of Satan. Of what use or benefit is it to a person to see a table tip, to hear music played, to be carried out of one window into another? Is a man any better for all this? Or, are those who see it profited? Satan gives this power to mankind to delude them and lead them from the true path; but they are not benefited by it.

When a man or woman, or a boy or girl receives the Holy Ghost, it brings peace, joy, love and happiness; and the person who is in possession of this Spirit has a feeling of kindness and charity towards all mankind. His mind is enlightened and the things of God are made plain unto him. Society is benefited and the world is purified by its bestowal. (October 8, 1869, JI 4:164)

STRONG DELUSION AND LYING SPIRITS. There is one thing worthy of note in this connection and that is that when Joseph Smith first proclaimed to the people that God had spoken from the heavens and sent His holy angels to minister to him and bestowed upon him the knowledge and authority necessary to build up the Church, he met with opposition and ridicule on every hand. . . . He said the time would come when there would be strong delusion and lying spirits permitted to come forth among the people. He declared that God had restored the Priesthood to the earth and the ordinances of the Gospel and had established His Church in its purity and that those who did not believe the testimony of the servants of God and obey it would be given over to hardness of heart and become subject to evil influences that were known nothing of previous to the establishing of the Church and the restoration of the Priesthood.

Years elapsed before this prediction was fulfilled, but it was eventually verified. . . . What has produced this change? Why, it is the very thing which Paul said would come. The people in his day would not receive the love of the truth that they might be saved; "Therefore," said he, "for this cause God shall send them strong delusion, that they should believe a lie; that they all might be damned who believe not the truth, but had pleasure in unrighteousness." [2 Thessalonians 2:11-12.] They would not believe the testimony of the servants of God; therefore, they were given up to hardness of heart and spiritual blindness. When these things overtake them, they are ready to fall in with any spirit of influence that will manifest itself amongst them in an extraordinary manner. . . .

A WICKED AND ADULTEROUS GENERATION. The Elders of this Church have proved the truth of the words of Jesus that it is a wicked and adulterous generation that seek for a sign. You will generally find that they are wicked men who ask for this kind of evidence. A wicked man is not satisfied with the truth or with the testimony of the servants of God nor with the calm, heavenly influence of the Spirit of God which rests down upon those who receive the truth in honesty. No, such a man wants a sign; he wants to hear somebody speak in tongues or to see the eyes of the blind opened or the deaf made to hear, the dumb to speak, the lame to walk or the dead raised to life. Something of this kind he must have; the testimony of truth, though borne with angel's power, has no effect on such a heart. He wants something to convince his outward senses.

Thousands of such have rejected the Gospel of life and salvation as they did in the days of Jesus. They then rejected the testimony of the servants of God, and they hardened their hearts against it. But as soon as something came along that gratified them in the way they wanted—something that could tip a table or give some other singular manifestation of power, such as feeling invisible hands laid upon them or hearing music played by invisible performers or something of this character—they were convinced immediately that it was possible for spiritual beings to communicate with mortals, and now the Spiritualists number their converts by millions; they probably number more than any other denomination, if they can be called a denomination. They boast of their success.

A BOGUS OR COUNTERFEIT PRIESTHOOD. In this manner the nations of the earth are being subjected to strong delusions; and you will find that as the Kingdom of God increases and as the work spreads abroad and the Priesthood gains power and influence in the earth, these systems will gain power and influence in the earth . . . and strong delusion will increase and spread among the inhabitants of the earth. They did not make their appearance until this Church was organized and the testimony of its truth had been borne. As soon as the genuine Priesthood was restored the bogus or counterfeit made its appearance, and as this work increases in strength and potency in the earth, so will these delusions of which I speak, until those who reject the truth will be bound up in a strong delusion and delivered over to hardness of heart. It is written that the Spirit of God "shall not always strive with man" [D&C 1:33], and when the truth is offered to men and they reject it, that spirit will be withdrawn and another influence and spirit will take possession of them, and they will be led captive by the adversary. (January 31, 1869, JD 12:368-70)

SPIRITUALISM COUNTERACTS GOSPEL. Spiritualism professed to make it easy for all to obtain spiritual manifestations. No faith in Jesus, no repentance, no baptism, no laying on of hands needed to obtain them. Purity of life was not essential. The wicked and the reprobate, as well as those of better lives, could receive spiritual communications. In this way Satan used spiritualism to counteract the influence of the Gospel. If the servants of God held out the promise that the Holy Ghost and the gifts promised by the Savior would follow obedience to the ordinances, spiritualism could be pointed to as a means of obtaining signs without the use of ordinances.

The prevalence of spiritualism has had the effect to remove many of the objections which were urged against inspiration; and though the world has not been disposed to accept the Gospel, the force of the attacks upon the Latter-day Saints because they believed that the Lord did inspire men and that the gifts of the Spirit were bestowed in our day has been greatly weakened through the widespread acceptance of spiritualism. (March 1, 1893, JI 28:162)

A RULE FOR DETECTING SPIRIT OF EVIL. I will tell you a rule by which you may know the Spirit of God from the spirit of evil. The Spirit of God always produces joy and satisfaction of mind. When you have the Spirit you are happy; when you have another spirit you are not happy. The spirit of doubt is the spirit of the evil one; it produces uneasiness and other feelings that interfere with happiness and peace. . . .

When you awake in the morning and your spirits are disturbed, you may know there is some spirit or influence that is not right. You should never leave your bed chambers until you get that calm, serene and happy influence that flows from the presence of the Spirit of God and that is the fruit of that Spirit. So, during the day you are apt to get disturbed, angry and irritated about something. You should stop and not allow that influence to prevail or have place in your heart. (March 23, 1873, JD 15:375-76)

ASTROLOGY AND ITS EVILS. Man is prompted by an innate disposition to seek for a knowledge of the future. When properly controlled, this desire results in good to himself and his fellow-creatures. When he has a correct knowledge of God and his laws, he is prompted to seek for the Holy Spirit, and when he obtains that, the anxiety of his soul is legitimately and fully gratified. But when he is ignorant of God, he is liable to have recourse to practices which bring him under the bondage of superstition, and he is debased and rendered unhappy thereby.

Astrology is one of the means which has been used by men

from the earliest ages to pry into futurity and obtain its secrets. Before Abraham emigrated from Chaldea, that country was famous for its astrologers. It is called the mother-country of diviners, and especially of judicial astrologers—that is, those who pretended to foretell moral events, as if they were directed by the stars. To such a degree of power did this class of men attain in that country, that they formed the highest caste and enjoyed a place at court. So indispensable were they in Chaldean society, that we are informed no step could be taken, not a relation could be formed, a house built, a journey undertaken, a campaign began, until they had ascertained the lucky day and promised a happy issue. Some have claimed Egypt as the land where astrology had its origin. But, be that as it may, the people of that country, at a very early age, encouraged its practice as well as other arts of divination.

We find frequent allusions in the Bible to astrologers. Isaiah, in foretelling God's judgments upon Babylon, says in relation to them—"Let now the astrologers, the stargazers, the monthly prognosticators, stand up, and save thee from these things that shall come upon thee. Behold, they shall be as stubble; the fire shall burn them; they shall not deliver themselves from the power of the flame." [Isaiah 47:13-14.] With all their pretended knowledge, they could not save themselves, much less their city and nation. They perished, miserably perished with their countrymen, despite all their figures and horoscopes and arts of divination. Every nation which fostered or trusted in them has similarly perished. Assyrians, Egyptians, Grecians, and Romans, were all numbered among their believers. Through their agency, those people sought the knowledge of the future. But their knowledge was only partial; just enough of it mingled with the falsehood which they revealed to deceive their credulous victims, and lure them on to destruction.

Our object in alluding to this subject at the present time is, to put our people on their guard against this system. . . . Our words are addressed to those who patronize them, who in their credulity imagine that they can be benefited by what they tell them. If we could have influence with them, we would warn them of their danger. They tread on slippery ground. Those who practice this system are either complete apostates, or are on the verge of apostasy. Those who patronize it, if they persist in doing so, will go the same way. No man who practices astrology, or seeks to obtain knowledge through its agency, can retain his confidence in the means which God has appointed, by which the knowledge of the future can be imparted. He will, sooner or later, deny the faith. Like table-rapping, writing mediums, etc., it is a means which God does not acknowledge, but which he has condemned.

There may be some truth in the system. The hold it has retained of the human mind for so many ages could not have been, probably, had it not possessed some correct principles. But it is that truth which makes it the more dangerous. The devil will, at any time, tell nineteen truths, if by so doing he can make the people believe one lie. Under such circumstances the nineteen truths strengthen him, and are of far more use to him than lies would be. But such knowledge as Daniel possessed, obtained by him through the proper channel, was of far more avail in the day of need, in revealing the Lord's purposes, than all the astrology of Chaldea. (1868, MS 30:166-67)

DIVINATION. "And the magicians did so with their enchantments." [Exodus 8:7.] No doubt of it; those were palmy days for diviners; Egypt was in all her glory, had attained to an intellectuality which, if it did take a different direction to that of our day, will certainly bear comparison with it. It was in the direction of divination that the current of mind ran; nothing of importance was undertaken either by king, priests or people, without first obtaining information respecting results. To satisfy the requirements of the age, a class of men arose who made it their business to gratify the public taste by cultivating their powers of mind with a view to get an insight into the future.

It is not fair to assume that these men were mercenary in their motives, although some may have been so; they seem to have devoted themselves to study with a determination and disinterestedness such as usually characterize the earnest inquirer after truth; they were temperate in their lives, and even mortified their bodies by an abstemiousness which would have been trying to the sensualist; and this was all done with a desire to find favor with the gods "to whom all secrets are known."

Men of this stamp are likely to get information from the unseen world; and, in their researches after truth, as they understood it, they could hardly fail to stumble upon some of the principles which influence, if they do not control, human actions, and arrive at a knowledge of some of the great, but simple, natural laws which lie at the foundation of things. No stone was left unturned by them in their pursuit of that kind of knowledge they sought after—magic in the use of numbers and cabalistic characters, divining by omens, as the flight of birds, traces of which practice remain with us in the old saying: "One crow, good luck; two crows, sorrow," there is luck in odd numbers, etc. . . . Many very curious things were discovered by the magicians, as they were called, the memory of the some of which has been preserved to this day by tradition and in the "learned books" by those who dabble in the same "sciences." But it appears to have been more by communications with the unseen world that they obtained intelligence concerning things about to transpire on the earth.

Not that such kind of intelligence was at all times reliable; it was not so; but that a great many things were revealed which did prove true, there is abundant evidence on record. This was, indeed, the secret of the success of the "soothsayer," or, as the word implies, truth teller, for by an infatuation which appears natural to man, that which really occurred was believed to be the result of the prediction, and that which did not happen was attributed to a lack of faith in the people.

But that great wonders were wrought by the skill of the ancients in divination there can be but little doubt; it could not all have been deception any more than it is now. They may have had, as they have now in Asiatic countries, their sleight-of-hand conjurors of the "Wizard of the North" genus. Still, the fact of their having deceivers or imitators shows that the popular belief was in favor of those things being possible, and it is strong evidence that real miracles were performed. Not that there were then, any more than there are now, miracles in that impossible sense believed in by the ignorant, something done without a cause; but there were acts performed which were the result of natural operations not then understood by the masses. There is strong presumptive evidence of the fact that the prophets of Baal, for instance, did at times obtain fire from some supernatural source to consume their sacrifices, or it is not reasonable to suppose that four hundred and fifty men would have been so unwise as to expect such a thing. It was in the presence of Elijah that they failed, for which there must have been a reason; the sequel informs us what the reason was.

It is not logical, then, to deny to those ancient magicians the powers which both sacred and profane history ascribe to them; neither is it charitable to attribute it to venal or corrupt motives. As a class they were kept about the courts of kings and great men; great things were expected of them, and no doubt were realized; and it appears that they did not fail except when they were in the presence of beings who had higher power than themselves.

By taking this view we get rid of many difficulties which present themselves to the reader of ancient history; we can understand how it happened that in the Court of Babylon "the magicians, astrologers, sorcerers and Chaldeans," were baffled in the presence of Daniel, and to come nearer to our own times, the powerlessness of such men in the presence of Jesus and His disciples.

As to our denying the existence of great powers of divination in ancient times, because we cannot understand how they were attained to, it would be quite as just to deny the existence of these things now for the same reason. If the ancients had their soothsayers and astrologers, the moderns have their fortune tellers and Zadkiels; if the former had their necromancers, who held communion with the spirits of the departed, so have the latter—millions of them—in the "spiritualists." If they believed in sorcery, many now believe that their cattle or themselves can be "bewitched." If they had those who by their incantations could command the sick to be healed, in these days there are "Zouaves" and mesmerisers. If they had their witch of Endor to call up the shade of Samuel, there are those now who claim to call up Moses, Julius Caesar, or any one else when wanted. If they shut up their mediums in the secret recesses of the "adytum" to commune with the dead, there are in our day "seances" in which [men] are shut up in a cabinet, certainly for a less laudable purpose than the ancients sought in the secret chamber, which was to get information.

Now it is reasonable to believe that all these things are by the same spirit, for the works are the same. Never did this spirit shine forth more conspicuously than when the authority of the living God was upon the earth. With that authority, if the spirit of divination is not co-eval in the heavens, it appears to have always been contemporaneous on the earth, and it has always been antagonistic to that authority. Fifty years ago there was a great lack of faith in the supernatural; it is not so now. Men had by science endeavored to explain away all the phenomena ascribed to spiritual influence; nobody, comparatively, believed in the spirit of prophecy, either in a good or bad sense. There were no mediums, no "seances," no spirit-rapping and table turnings, no "interior revelations," no divination in its many forms.

Now these things are fashionable. How is it that this spirit which has slept for ages is again evoked? "Like causes produce like effects." It is the antagonism brought to bear against the authority of God which calls forth these manifestations; when that is not on the earth, the spirit of divination slumbers. It is only when Prophets and Apostles are among men with a view to bring about the Government of God, when this power as well as this authority are made manifest, the power of the opposite is needed to deceive. (June 26, 1869, MS 31:414-16)

ORACLES. Truth in astrology? There may be; probably if there were not nobody would believe it. . . . Now, what are the facts? A man believes in astrology, or planchette, or "intuition," or magic, or clairvoyance, or mesmerism, or any other "ism"—it is his oracle. He bows before it, and it becomes his oracle. He bows before it, and it becomes his idol; the more he will reverence it. Will he seek the true God? No. He will be weaned from any former attachment, when he ceases to drink of "the sincere milk of the world." To him there is no prophet but his prophet; no God but his. He may not have descended to this depth today, but it is only a question of time. Who consults any of these oracles to do good? What are the motives which actuate men to seek for information? "I want to be great, to be rich, to know who loves me," or, "who hates me," or "who wrongs me." Do any consult them with a view to be more useful members of society, to enable them to become better men and women socially, intellectually, morally? None.

Where, then, is the good of such "sciences falsely so-called"? If you are afraid to go to law unless the planets are propitious, it is because your course is unjust; if you are afraid to marry for the reason that "Venus is not well aspected" in the heavens, it is because you have doubts concerning the Venus you have chosen on earth; if you are afraid to plant today, because the configuration of the planets says no, it shows you lack confidence in the Being who causes the plants to grow.

But have the planets no influence on earth? Yes. The stream of light which flows upon this earth from countless myriads of suns, centers of other solar systems, help to sustain life both in animals and vegetable. The sun is by no means the only luminary which is engaged in ministering to man, and it is highly probable that the light derived from those planets circulating in this solar system, although only reflected light, may bring with it some of the qualities of the planet from which it is reflected. Perhaps those "hot and dry" and "watery and cold" qualities which the ancients noticed as qualities of certain planets, are really necessary to the perpetuation of this planet. At all events we may be assured of this: He who "made all things well," and pronounced everything "very good," did not create, and certainly would not perpetuate, any withering, pernicious influences, such as are ascribed to the rays of light which innocently fall upon the earth from the planets of our solar system. (July 3, 1869, MS 31:437-39)

THE PATH OF SAFETY. Now, the only safe course for you and all mankind to pursue is to obey the Priesthood, to listen to the teachings of the servants of God and never murmur against them. Then God's power will increase with you, and you will add knowledge to knowledge, light to light and be brought back into the presence of God. Then, when false prophets arise and wonderful works are performed by them through the power of the evil one, you will not be deceived; for you will know that they are not of God. Though they may call fire down from Heaven, you will still cling to the Priesthood of God. Apostates and all who fight against the Priesthood are liable to be led astray by the miracles and wonders which are performed by wicked men, for they have no guide; they have forsaken the true path and the authority which God has bestowed. (October 8, 1869, JI 4:164)

Chapter 23

The Law of Tithing—A Law of God

THE EARTH IS THE LORD'S. All who have any faith in the existence of a Supreme Being will acknowledge that the Lord has given man the earth to dwell upon, has furnished it with animals, vegetables and every element necessary for man's existence, comfort and happiness, that He can bestow upon man few or many of these blessings, as seemeth good in His sight, that, in fact, we and the earth and the fulness thereof are His, and that there is nothing that we call ours that is not in reality His. So, He can not only claim a tenth of the earth, and its contents and products, but even the whole. The Latter-day Saints think, therefore, that in paying a tenth they only pay a slight interest for all they enjoy. (July 15, 1863, MS 25:473)

LAW OF TITHING FOR MAN'S BENEFIT. The law of tithing does not, when obeyed by man, add to God's comfort, contribute to His wealth, increase his happiness or furnish Him with that of which He would be destitute if it were not obeyed; but it is given to man, and he is required to obey it that he may receive the reward and that he may acknowledge by this act—by this payment of the tenth of his increase—that all he obtains is the gift and comes from the beneficent hand of God and that he is dependent upon God. . . .

A NEGLECT OF TITHING LED TO ISRAEL'S DISASTER. When Israel served God, and were strict in observing this law, He blessed and prospered them, and His favor was shown towards them; but when they neglected this law, His anger and indignation were kindled against them, and one of the most fruitful causes of disaster to Israel was their neglect in this particular. . . .

There is something connected with the law of tithing that, when men do not have faith in God, appeals to their selfishness; and for a people to be wholehearted in its observance, they need faith in God. When Israel began to decline in faith in God, their selfishness increased, and their determination became stronger and stronger to grasp everything within their reach and to retain everything they gained possession of; and as this feeling grew, tithing and freewill offerings were withheld from the house of God, and in consequence of this the blessing of God was also withheld. . . .

NON-TITHE PAYERS UNWORTHY MEMBERS. I thank God for the revelation of this principle. I do for this reason—it appeals directly to man's selfishness. It makes men sacrifice their selfish feelings and causes them to show faith in God. If a man has not faith in God, he is not very likely to pay tithing or make many offerings. To use a common expression, he looks after "number one" and self-interest rules him. Such a man is an unworthy member of the Church of Christ.

TITHING BENEFITS ALL. When every man pays his tithing and witnesses unto God that that law is honorable in his sight, what is the result? Is anybody impoverished by it? No! Are we as Latter-day Saints any poorer because of the tithing we have paid? Not one cent. When that tithing is properly appropriated, it is expended in works which add to the wealth of the entire community. It contributes to the erection of public edifices; it adorns those edifices and creates a fund that is exclusively devoted to the work of God and that helps to build up and to make the community prosperous and respectable in the earth. It is a mighty engine, or would be if properly wielded, in establishing righteousness and truth in the earth. . . .

LANDS TO BE MADE FRUITFUL. I honestly believe, if the people of the United States would observe this law of tithing, devoting a tenth of their substance to the service of the the Most High, that . . . the fertility which formerly prevailed there would be restored. And when the day shall come, as come it will when we shall go back—and we expect to go back to Jackson County, Missouri, and to lay the foundation of a temple, and to build a great city to be called the Centre Stake of Zion, as much as we expect to see the sun rise tomorrow—I say, when that day shall come it will be found that that country will have its old fertility restored, and that and all the lands that the people of God will occupy will be healthy and fruitful; the land of any people who will honor God by obeying this law of tithing will be made fruitful to them; God will bless their industry, and they will rejoice and prosper therein. . . .

Those who have prospered most are they who paid their tithing honestly. And I have noticed it, as an individual, that when men close up their hearts in this direction and neglect their tithing and their offerings on fast days for the benefit of the poor, they lose their faith. This is one evidence of the loss of faith and confidence in the work. (September 8, 1872, JD 15: 146-55)

A PROTECTION AGAINST APOSTASY. The liberal tithe payer binds himself and his family more firmly to the Church. This of itself is an extremely desirable result. Whatever a man or a family can do to bind themselves more closely to the work of God is a great advantage in times of trial and temptation. Being thus bound by the interest they have taken in affairs, they are more likely to withstand temptation.

I remember having a conversation with President Young, at the time of the apostasy a number of years ago of certain prominent merchants from the Church, concerning their apostasy. There was one merchant who was approached by the others and solicited to join them in their attack upon President Young and the Authorities of the Church, but he resisted their approaches. There was no apparent reason why he should not have yielded as much as they did to those influences that prevailed with them. In speaking of this President Young said he had had occasion to examine the tithing record of the merchants, and he had found that this man of whom we were speaking had paid more tithing than all the rest together. He attributed his escape from apostasy to this fact, and said that the Lord had blessed him with power to withstand temptation and remain true to Zion. This is an interesting fact, and one full of meaning and instruction. I think that the faithful tithe-payer will not be found among apostates. (October 1, 1899, JI 34:599-600)

When people neglect this duty, it is evident they are losing their faith and their zeal in the work of God, and are in a position to grow cold and indifferent concerning it, and to lose the Spirit of the Lord. . . .

Men and women who pay their tithing attach themselves more firmly to the work of the Lord by so doing, and Satan has less power over them than he would have if they neglected this important duty. (February 1, 1898, JI 33:125)

PAYMENT OF TITHING NECESSARY. I say to you that in your non-payment of tithing you have stopped your progress and you have disobeyed a command of God just as much as if you had refused, after you had been baptized, to have hands laid upon you, just as much as you would have done, after having received the Gospel, had you refused to go into the temple and have saving ordinances administered to you there, such as the ordinance of marriage for time and eternity and other things. You may or may not think as I do, but I know I have taken the correct position in this matter. (April 1900, CR 57)

A PROFITABLE PRINCIPLE. I pay tithing because I think it is a profitable thing in every direction. I regard it as a good investment. But I do not do it for that alone. I do it because God has commanded it. I have always known it to be a correct principle since I was old enough to reflect upon it. I have paid tithing, therefore, from principle, believing that it not only benefits me spiritually (which is the most important of all) but that it enables me to go to the Lord in faith and ask Him for that which I need.

Many years ago I was in a very tight place financially, and I determined to put aside all I could as tithing. One day the Bishop of the Ward met me on the street and said: "Brother George, you are paying a pretty good tithing." "No, Bishop," said I, "I am not paying the tithing of that which I have received; I am paying the tithing of that which I would like to receive." And sure enough the next year I had as much income as I had paid tithing on the previous year.

Now, men will say that merely happened so. Well, all these things happen, don't they? I was relieved from my difficulty, and I had my faith confirmed. I have tried to follow that principle a good deal since. (DEN, August 18, 1899)

Chapter 24

Temporal Affairs and Economic Prosperity

THE PARABLE OF THE "UNJUST STEWARD." The parable of the "unjust steward" is to be found in the 16th chapter of Luke, and according to our opinion it conveys an exceedingly important lesson.

To begin with, it should be understood that the Lord has entrusted us all with a stewardship. He has placed under the control of man the elements of the earth, to do with them as seemeth good to him. This stewardship—that is, its extent or its value—may vary and does vary in each individual case. Some of us as stewards have large possessions and a large share of the elements which belong to the earth. Others have a smaller share. But we are all stewards, and undoubtedly will be required at some time in the future to account for the manner in which we use these stewardships.

In the parable referred to [Luke 16] our attention is directed to the case of one who was about to be deprived of his stewardship by his master. He was accused of having handled his master's goods in a wasteful or perhaps dishonest manner, and he was thereupon required by the master to give an account of his stewardship. Then he felt himself driven to the necessity of doing something that would be of benefit to him when he should lose his position. He argues to himself: "What shall I do? for my lord taketh away from me the stewardship: I cannot dig; to beg I am ashamed. I am resolved what to do, that, when I am put out of the stewardship, they may receive me into their houses." [Luke 16:3-4.]

Then he proceeds to exercise his authority as a steward, for he had not yet been deprived of it, to make himself friends out of the debtors of his master. He calls them all before him and says to one: "How much owest thou unto my Lord?" And upon being told, he reduces the amount one-half, giving what would appear to be a receipt or an amended bill to the debtor. The obligation of the next debtor he reduces twenty per cent; and while the record does not expressly say so, the inference is that he proceeded in like manner through the whole list of debtors—

the presumption is that he made similar settlements with all of them.

Everyone will be able to understand that in this manner he could accomplish that which he had set out to do—make to himself friends; by virtue of the stewardship which he still held he had used his master's property to gain favor for himself with his master's debtors. And he was commended for this, "because he had done wisely." [Luke 16:8.]

FRIENDS OF MAMMON OF UNRIGHTEOUSNESS. The Savior, concluding the parable, enjoined upon those who were listening to Him: "Make to yourselves friends of the mammon of unrighteousness; that, when ye fail, they may receive you into everlasting habitation." [Luke 16:9.]. . . The book of Doctrine and Covenants uses the words: "Make unto yourselves friends with the mammon of unrighteousness" [D&C 82:22], which in meaning is the same as the language used in the New Testament.

Now, herein is a great principle and a great lesson. Men have received stewardships, and some are entrusted by our Father with much of the "mammon of unrighteousness"—in other words, with worldly possessions and perhaps wealth. Being only stewards, and having in their hands or under their control the possessions with which the Lord has entrusted them, they can, if they are wise men, employ these possessions in doing great good to themselves by assisting and befriending those who by virtue of works of righteousness may not fail in attaining unto "everlasting habitation." They can by conferring earthly benefits make to themselves friends who may be in a position to receive them into everlasting habitations in case they themselves should fail in reaching that which they desired.

This may seem like strange doctrine, but it is nevertheless true. For instance: Those who conferred favors upon the Savior when He was upon the earth would certainly not be forgotten by Him in the eternal world. After His resurrection He was restored to the full power which He possessed before He took on a mortal tabernacle; and He was in a position so exalted as to be able to confer benefits on those who had shown kindness to Him. Abraham, the father of the faithful, "hath entered into his exaltation," the Lord tells us in the Doctrine and Covenants, "and sitteth upon his throne." [D&C 132:29.] A similar statement is made as to others. It applies to Prophets and Saints of both former and later time. Shall not these worthy persons be in a position to reward by some favor, or friendship, or intercession, or benefit, those who befriended them with the "mammon of unrighteousness" (in whatsoever sense the term may be used) when they were upon the earth? And if they are in a position to do this, is it likely that they will fail to make return for kindness previously shown them?

No doubt, if the full history of all the Prophets could be read, it would be found that in all ages when men of God were on the earth there were persons who used the wealth or the other means in their possession to benefit and assist these servants of the Lord in the labors that devolved upon them. It was surely so in the case of the Prophet Joseph Smith. Sometimes the people who have been thus moved to act in a friendly manner or to extend material aid have not had much faith in the Gospel; sometimes they have been total unbelievers and have not been strict in living according to the precepts laid down for the guidance and salvation of the children of men; yet they have been moved upon to render assistance to the servants of God.

We have many instances of this character in mind in the case of the Prophet Joseph. Those who acted toward him in this manner made a friend of him with the means or the "mammon of unrighteousness" which they held in their possession; and there can be no doubt that in the great future, when he will have attained to his exaltation and received the power that will be conferred upon him, he will be in a position to extend favor unto those who had conferred benefits upon him in the exercise of their stewardship in this life. It will be reckoned unto them for good, and not for evil; they will be commended because they "had done wisely," and thus in many instances will it be shown that the "children of this world are in their generation wiser than the children of light." [Luke 16:8.] (April 1, 1900, JI 35:219-20)

INHERITANCES IN ZION SHOULD BE PRIZED. One beautiful feature in the teachings of the servants of God in the early days of the Church, and one which has been repeated more or less all through our history, is the importance of having an inheritance in Zion, which really means the possession of a portion of land upon which to live either in a city or in the country. The teachings of the Prophet Joseph and of the Prophet Brigham, and in fact of all the first Elders of the Church, have been of a character to impress upon the people the value and sacredness of inheritances.

When mobs drove the people from their homes, they still looked upon the land which they had received, or which had been set apart to them as inheritances, as land that ought not to be sold or in any manner alienated; and to this day there are thousands of acres in Missouri, and probably in Illinois, that have never been sold by the Saints who owned them, and their present occupants have only a tax title to show for them.

I have fancied, however, that in latter times there has not been that feeling of reverence for inheritances, neither have they been esteemed as of so sacred a character, as was the case in the earlier days of the Church. Men part with them more lightly and for more trivial causes than they did in former days. A money consideration has seemed to have great weight in some of the people's eyes, and they have not looked upon their inheritances as something that should not be parted with but on the contrary as any other property, to be sold or bartered whenever it might suit the convenience of the owner or might inure to his profit. This, it seems to me, is a wrong conception, and wherever it prevails, it is likely to be followed by bad consequences. Of course there may be, and doubtless are, occasions when it may be wisdom to part with land; but the Latter-day Saints, of all people, should attach value to that which they have obtained as an inheritance in Zion. They should not look upon their possessions as the ordinary man does upon his, but should feel that there is an obligation connected with the ownership which ought to be observed. . . .

AVOID LIVING BY SPECULATION. Our children should be taught not to live by speculation, not to live by the various devices which are too common in the world, but to live in an honest, legitimate and healthful way, and seek to draw from the elements with which God has furnished the earth all that is necessary for support. The earth was created as a habitation for man. We should love it as our birthplace, and put a high value on any portion of it that we may possess; and when a boy or a girl obtains a portion of it, he or she should be taught to cling to it and not part with it lightly. This feeling should be cultivated among us as a people, and the effect upon the character of the people will be very healthful. (February 15, 1895, JI 30:107-109)

WASTEFULNESS A GREAT SIN OF THIS AGE. Wastefulness is one of the great sins of the age and above all of the land we live in. God has so abundantly blessed this continent with the precious things of the earth that its inhabitants do not rightly value His rich gifts to them, but use them with careless hands, thoughtless heads and ungrateful hearts. This is sinful; the Lord did not make anything to be wasted, and He is angry with those who thus abuse His gifts.

In the works of God nothing is wasted or without its use. What is not good for man is often good for beasts, and what is no use to either man or beast supports vegetable life. That which is poison to the animal creation is the food of the trees and the shrubs, and the refuse of our food is the richest element for those plants which, when grown to ripeness, become our most choice and health-giving viands—the grain and fruits we so much delight in.

But because God is so economical in the works of nature, and makes everything count for good for the whole, it is no reason that we should be wasteful and careless with those things that are of use to us. Neither can we urge as an excuse that we have plenty and to spare, when so many thousands have not enough.

TEACH CHILDREN THRIFT AND ECONOMY. Every wise parent will strive to teach his children true thrift and economy. True economy is using the right thing for the right purpose, and using just enough to accomplish the work, and no more. "He who is taught to live upon little, owes more to his father's wisdom, than he who has a great deal left him does to his father's care." The teachings of the wise father will be remembered through life; the riches of the careful father will probably be squandered more rapidly than they were acquired, if the riches be unaccompanied by wise teaching.

Boys and girls are often reminded that "wilful waste makes woeful want." This is a truth. Wastefulness is the mother of poverty. If we would be rich in the things of this world, which are all the gifts of our Eternal Father, we must use that which is placed in our charge with care and wisdom. If we do not, His blessing will be withheld from us. But some of us do not know how to put our time, our talents and our property to the best possible use. We waste our time, hide our talents and let our possessions go to ruin. Therefore, we must be taught. (May 23, 1874, JI 9:126)

LEARN TO SAVE. The habit of saving should be taught children at an early age. They should in youth receive lessons of self-denial. In this view the habit of tithe-paying, apart from the blessings which follow obedience to the law itself, is most excellent. It teaches economy; it inculcates self-denial; it enforces the necessity of saving. To be sure, it is a law of God to be observed and obeyed for its own sake. But its value, in adding to the inclination to be thrifty and careful and saving, is also very great; and it cannot be taught to children too early or too earnestly.

They should be impressed, as an inducement to saving, with the importance of making provision for the future. It is a very humiliating thing for a man or a family who may have been in the possession of means to be compelled to depend upon neighbors or friends or public charity for support. It is a most pitiful sight to see persons, when advanced in years or for other reasons incapable of performing much labor, destitute of the means of livelihood and forced to depend upon others for their living. In many cases such a condition may be unavoidable; but there are many other cases where it is simply the result of improvidence.

It is most unwise for persons or families to fall into the habit of consuming their entire income. A portion of the earnings should be regularly laid aside so that if sickness, want of employment or old age should throw them upon their own resources, they will have something other than charity to depend upon. Young couples in marrying should repress the inclination for display. They should learn to live within their means—not to consume all that they earn—and to commence in the beginning of their career to lay aside a portion of their income each week or month. Then, they should guard against any idle fancy which might prompt them to draw out and expend the means which they have saved. By cultivating the habit of saving they will, without becoming avaricious, find pleasure in self-denial, and have pleasure without being miserly in seeing their savings gradually increase. Men and women who pursue such a course as this can feel an independence and a consequent happiness that they cannot enjoy if they follow the contrary course. (March 15, 1900, JI 35:190-91)

STAY OUT OF DEBT. The man who borrows and puts himself under obligations to his fellow-man is to that extent the slave of his creditor; and when short of funds and unable to meet his engagements, he is often compelled to submit to humiliation and be goaded by those whom he owes. It is a most painful position for a sensitive man to occupy to be in debt without the ability to meet his obligations when they are due. The Latter-day Saints have been taught that when they borrowed they should be sure that, when the time came for the payment of the debt, they would be in a position to liquidate it. (September 1, 1893, JI 28:536)

DEBTS OF HONOR. A man's verbal promise should be as good as his written obligation, and it would indeed be a happy condition if we were in a position where we would need to make so few promises concerning financial obligations that we would not forget them, but promptly meet everything that is due. . . .

Debts of honor are just as binding as are legal obligations. Doubtless our readers have heard of the case of the impecunious English statesman who would dodge corners to avoid meeting his creditors. One day a man who held his note saw a sum of money paid to him, and immediately thereafter stepped up to the debtor and presented his note for payment. "I cannot pay that," replied the statesman, "for the money I just received I must pay on a debt of honor. You have my note and that will hold good until my other obligations are discharged."

The creditor looked at him for a moment and then said, "I will make my debt one of honor," and immediately destroyed the note.

"That being the case," was the response, "I must pay yours first, as it is of longer standing."

THE BURDEN OF DEBT. We advise our young people to avoid the distresses of debt, to live within their means and to economize to such an extent that from their incomes they can save some little against a time of need. If you would only talk with some men whose credit has been strained because of indebtedness, we believe the lesson would be impressed upon your minds never to be forgotten, that debt is a burden which prevents peaceful, restful nights and fills the mind with anguish during the day time, thus preventing the development of those finer sensibilities with which every creature is endowed, retarding also the growth in spirit which is possible to those who owe no man anything. (February 1, 1896, JI 31:81)

PLAN OF SALVATION EMBRACES BOTH TEMPORAL AND SPIRITUAL. The plan of salvation embraces everything that belongs to men in the flesh on the earth. In the mind of our God there is no distinction between that which is spiritual and that which is temporal. He uses this phrase in revelations to us because He adapts Himself to our condition and to our mode of looking at affairs; but with Him there is no distinction between temporal and spiritual things.

There is no distinction between spiritual salvation—of course, with some qualifications—and temporal salvation. Our bodies are as dear in the sight of God as our spirits. Our spirits cannot be separated from our bodies, to have us perfect. The body and the spirit are the soul of man—not the spirit alone, not the body alone, but the body and the spirit. And God gives revelations for the temporal salvation of His children—that is, for the salvation of their bodies—and they are as important in their place as His revelations concerning their spirits.

Hence it is that the Latter-day Saints are a practical people. We have offended the religious world because we deal so much in temporal things and speak so much about them, as though they were a part of salvation. Well, we view them as being a part of salvation. But, it gives offense to many, and they think that it is improper for men who are ministers of religion to meddle with such things. We have had that to contend with from the beginning, especially since we gathered together.

It has been necessary that there should be care bestowed upon the temporal salvation of the people, and the leaders of the Church of Jesus Christ of Latter-day Saints have been animated by the Spirit of God to do this, and to provide by counseling in the greatest wisdom that they could obtain, for the deliverance of the people from evils which threatened them. . . . There was a time when it was absolutely necessary that the people should be counseled upon many points which affected their temporal salvation. (December 31, 1893, DW 48:163)

DIRECTION IN TEMPORAL MATTERS. The policy of directing the Latter-day Saints in the management of their temporal business has been a duty which the Authorities of the Church have never failed to discharge from the days of its organization until the present. The Prophet, Joseph Smith, wise leader as he was, knew what would be for the good of the people, and, during his life-time, he urged his views upon them with all his energy and influence. It was his province to teach the people upon every subject connected with life here and hereafter. There was nothing that pertained to their welfare and elevation, and redemption from evil, that he considered outside of his Priesthood. . . .

He found it necessary at times to give very stringent counsel to the Saints, and to threaten with excommunication from the Church those who did not deal with the people on the plan that he prescribed. (February 1, 1870, MS 32:66-67)

LABOR A BLESSING TO MANKIND. It has been argued that labor and toil are the consequences of God's curse, and that they who have to labor for their daily bread are accursed also. But is it so? When man was immortal, before Adam fell, God placed him in the Garden of Eden to dress it and to keep it. No curse had then fallen on this fair earth; all thereon had been pronounced by the Great Creator "very good." [Genesis 1:31.] Yet, Adam had to dress and cultivate the garden; for though the earth then did not bring forth weeds and thorns and thistles, yet it required man's watchcare and superintendence to keep it in order.

When Adam first disobeyed God's command, and sin and death were brought into the world thereby, God told Adam that He would curse the ground for his sake, and that he should eat his bread by the sweat of his brow. Yet, we do not read that God cursed his labor, or made it dishonorable. True, the ground was to bring forth thorns and thistles, but labor was to subdue the earth and cover the place where these thorns and thistles grew with fruit trees, flowers and grain.

Labor, instead of a curse, has been a blessing to mankind. No bread is so sweet as that earned by honest toil. Labor is happiness; no heart is more joyful than the one busy with the works of love and duty. Labor is health; none are more vigorous than the laborer. Labor is life; without it we should stagnate, and the generations of man would soon cease upon the earth. Without it arts, science and civilization must perish; in fact, all human life, except that of the rudest and most savage kind, must perish also.

GOD HAS SET THE EXAMPLE. Labor is eternal and divine. In six days the Lord made heaven and earth. The labor of this earth's redemption will occupy the Millennium and stretch into eternity. The world, with all its fellows, is the handiwork of God; and the worlds yet to be will manifest the wisdom and creative power, the skill and labor of divine beings, and worlds will multiply and systems grow. . . .

That in which God has set us the example cannot be ignoble or degrading. It was He who made this world with all its wonders. Can we, for very shame, call our fellow men vile, vulgar or contemptible because they help to beautify this same earth that our Heavenly Father has framed? Shall they who build the cities, till the soil, or in any other way help to make this earth habitable and glorious, be esteemed less than they who simply partake of the blessings without aiding in the struggle to obtain them? . . .

No young man or young woman should be ashamed of useful labor. . . . It is one of the greatest lessons taught by the Gospel that all must be workers. Let us so strive that our labor shall not be in vain, but that our every effort shall count for good, and that our knowledge of some trade, profession or art, while developing our own powers and talents, shall benefit to the uttermost the people and the work of the most high God. (March 14, 1874, JI 9:66)

ALL NEEDFUL LABOR HONORABLE. All work that the world needs doing is honorable, and all men who do it, and do it well, are honorable also. . . .

No trade that men are called to engage in for the happiness of the world is disreputable. It is the way in which the man supplies the world's needs that makes him what he is, honorable or dishonorable. He who does what he has to do, and does it aright, is the peer of every other son of Adam, be he prince or peasant. Honor and honesty are confined to no class or caste. He who decries any necessary labor because he is engaged in some other branch of this world's industry, or belongs to some other station in life, is short-sighted and slow of understanding.

The rich and poor are needed, as the world at present exists, but the rich should not oppress the poor, nor the poor wrong the rich. The day will come in the history of God's Kingdom when there will be no poor in the midst of the Saints, as the time will also come when there will be none sinful nor corrupt therein. (February 28, 1874, JI 9:54)

GOSPEL OPPOSED TO IDLENESS. Connected with our temporal labors there is probably no point of more importance than the providing of employment for our people. The spirit of the Gospel of the Lord Jesus Christ is opposed to idleness. We do not believe that a man who has the spirit can rest content if he is not busily employed. (April 8, 1887, MS 49:291-92)

HALF-HEARTEDNESS NOT A VIRTUE. It is a safe rule of life for us all and as wise as it is safe to never do or say anything except that upon which we can honestly ask the approval and blessing of God. . . . Furthermore, that upon which we can ask the blessing of God, we should do with our might. Half-heartedness is not a virtue, especially in serving the Lord; nor is it a recommendation in our daily contact with our fellow man. . . .

We all should have something useful to do, and we all should do it well. Each of us should choose an honest calling and then endeavor to be perfect in the calling we have chosen. To do this we must esteem no detail too trifling that has a bearing upon our success. It is not wise to despise small things, for "trifles make the sum of human things"; and little by little, step by step, seldom by giant strides, we progress towards the perfection of goodness or retrocede towards its sad opposite.

THE KEY TO SUCCESS IN BUSINESS. All true business principles are based on justice and the rights of every party to a transaction. Success in business does not so often arise from that inclination to overreach, by some miscalled smartness, as in the prompt use of opportunities. There is more in the use of opportunities than in the measure or amount of them; however bright the sun may shine we cannot see the path we should take if we keep our eyes shut. Promptness, punctuality, honesty, industry and civility are key words to success in the labors, the duties and business of life.

Be prompt; then you will be first in the market. Be punctual; then others will put confidence in your word. Be honest; there is no excuse to be otherwise; it wears the best and triumphs in the end. Be economical; wastefulness is one of the great sins of the age; it should be remembered that a gain usually requires effort and outlay—that which we save is clear. Be polite; nothing valuable is lost by civility and kindness. Be industrious. . . .

Withal, trust in God and keep His laws. None of us can afford to omit this whatever our rank or occupation. It will add lustre to our talents and give strength to every action of our lives and shape our course to the greatest usefulness here and to the brightest happiness hereafter. (January 9, 1875, JI 10:6)

POSSESSION OF WEALTH NOT PURPOSE OF EXISTENCE. The Lord has sent us here for a wise purpose. He has given us these glorious tabernacles, complete in all their parts, and given unto us laws which are necessary that we should obey to redeem these bodies and pass safely into His presence, to dwell there in the midst of eternal burnings. This is the mission He has given unto us to perform on the earth, and a more glorious mission could not be given to the sons and daughters of God.

The possession of prosperity, boundless wealth in gold and silver, fine raiment, magnificent dwellings, horses and carriages, and all these things attainable on the earth, are but secondary matters compared with it. They are merely auxiliaries to aid us in accomplishing our destiny and are not given unto us to set our hearts upon, or for us to consider our time well spent in looking after them and nothing else. We ought to value riches no more than we do the earth on which we tread, the air we breathe or the water we drink.

The man who seeks after the perishable things of this life and allows his mind to dwell upon them to the exclusion of the things of God which pertain to his eternal salvation has failed to comprehend the mission God has assigned him. (October 23, 1864, JI 10:347-48)

Is it right that we should be prudent, that we should take care of those gifts and blessings which God has given unto us, that we should take care of those gifts and blessings which God has given unto us, that we should husband our resources, that we should be economical and not extravagant? Certainly, this is right; this is proper; we should be culpable if we were not so. But with this there is also something else required, and that is to keep constantly in view that the management and care of these things is not the object that God had in sending us here; that is not the object of our probation. (July 25, 1880, JD 22:100)

God has made us all stewards. He has placed means in our hands. What better use can we make of this substance than to build up His Kingdom upon the earth, to help establish His righteousness, and to devote everything that we have to the advancement of His cause? And He will reward us. He will receive us into everlasting habitation, and He will increase His glory, honor and power upon us. (March 26, 1893, DW 46:484)

THE CHURCH OUR GREATEST INTEREST. Now, there should be no interests outside of this Church that to us are of greater importance than the interests of the Work of God. We should have no interest separate from it, and all that we have and are should belong to that Work. We should use every faculty that we have for the advancement of the interests of the Church of God, and never feel that we have separate and distinct interests from it. We will find this the best and safest preventative against apostasy.

So long as a man feels that all he has, and all that he ever hopes to possess, belong to the Kingdom of God, and he feels to use all for the advancement thereof, there is less danger of his apostatizing than there otherwise would be. He is identified with the Work—he forms a part of the great structure—and there is no distinction between the man and the Kingdom, because he is completely absorbed in it; therefore, such an individual—so long as he retains that spirit and feeling—is very unlikely to forsake the Church of God. (January 5, 1863, MS 26:212)

LOVE OF GOD MUST PREDOMINATE. The Lord has bestowed upon us the temporal blessings which we have for a wise purpose. We should use them aright and not set our hearts upon these perishable things. We should hold them as the gifts of God, subject to His counsel. The man who sets his heart upon riches cannot serve the God of Israel. No man can serve two masters, Jesus said. He said it 1800 years ago; it is true to-day.

Whenever you see a man serving mammon, you may know he cannot serve God as well. There cannot be a division in these services; half-hearted service cannot be acceptable to the Lord. We must serve God with all our hearts, our love and affections reaching after Him, and the things of this world must be looked upon by us as secondary considerations. They are good enough in their place, right enough to be attended to, but subordinate always to the love of God. That should be the first love, greater than every other love.

A man that loves a wife, a man that loves a child, a man that loves anything upon the earth more than God, is not a true Latter-day Saint. . . . He cannot serve God and mammon together. One love must predominate; it must be superior to every other love, and that is the love of our Heavenly Father, the keeping of His commandments and attending to the ordinances of salvation which He has revealed to us. (June 27, 1881, JD 22:288-89)

SEEK FOR TRUE RICHES. One of the most remarkable things in human life is the love which mankind have for the things of the world. Take, for instance, money. Men will risk their lives and their salvation, they will commit the most cruel and wicked acts, even murder itself, and trample upon all affection and do the vilest things for the sake of money. Yet, when they get money in this way, it can only be kept, at the longest, until death, and, in many instances, even while they are living it slips out of their hands as water does when a man tries to grasp it. However rich a man may be, even if he had the wealth of a nation in his hands, when he dies he leaves it all behind.

Is it not strange, this being the case, and everybody knowing it to be so, that people will love money and frequently do such wicked things to obtain it?

This love of money is one of the great agencies through which the devil strives to destroy the work of God and to ruin the souls of men.

The love of the world and the love of God cannot exist at the same time in the same bosom. A true Latter-day Saint loves God and His work more than he does the world. . . . He strives to conquer the love for the perishable things of the world that seem a part of fallen human nature. He looks forward to a higher, a purer and a more eternal life than that which he now possesses. (June 1, 1881, JI 16:126)

THE KEY TO PERFECT HAPPINESS. There is no person living, however rich he or she may be, who is entirely satisfied. There is something that he or she does not have that he or she would like to have. It is not given to men and women on the earth to be entirely satisfied, if they seek for satisfaction and happiness in worldly things. There is only one way in which perfect happiness can be obtained, and that is by having the Spirit of God. Whoever has that, whether rich or poor, whether old or young, whether honored or obscure, whether in adverse or in prosperous circumstances, is happy; for it produces joy and peace in the bosom of the one who possesses it. But without it a person cannot be truly happy, even if he or she should have the wealth of the world at command. Give such a person a palace to live in, and every luxury that money can procure, with carriages and horses, and servants to perform every service, and yet he or she will not be happy as the poor man or woman who has the Spirit of the Lord.

LOVE FOR WORLDLY THINGS A GREAT EVIL. The love of worldly substances is an evil which has always troubled mankind. People always have sought to obtain this substance; they still seek for it, because they think it desirable and that it brings happiness and gratification. . . . One of the greatest causes of the downfall of young women is their fondness for dress and display. . . . Statistics . . . show that more women are led astray by this cause in this country than by any other. How horrible to think of that women would part with virtue for the sake of fine dress! And it is the same with men. To gratify lust, to wear fine clothes, to have money to spend, men will sacrifice virtue and every manly quality.

CORRUPTING INFLUENCE OF WEALTH. We dread the increase of wealth among the Latter-day Saints, for the reason that it has a corrupting effect upon men and women. If we could be organized as God designs we shall be, we should not have these fears; but at the present time our society is in the same condition as all society is in Babylon. Each man works for himself and for his family. If he is a good money-maker, his own family alone, in the most of instances, gets the benefit of it; and as wealth increases among us, we are divided into classes as the people are in Babylon.

Should this continue to be the condition of the Church of Jesus Christ of Latter-day Saints, it could not fill its mission on the earth, for sooner or later it would become like the society of the earth from which its members have been gathered. The corrupting influences of riches has destroyed many nations; it would have a bad effect upon us. . . .

Wealth is a blessing when properly used. It adds to comfort; it contributes to happiness, and it enlarges usefulness. But when it is improperly used, it becomes an injury. When people set their affections upon it, are made vain and proud by it, think themselves a little better than their neighbor because of it, then it becomes a curse. When men and women and their children can dress better than their neighbors, can live in finer and more elegantly furnished houses, can have better education and finer horses and carriages and, because of their advantages, look down upon others who do not have them, they are in an unfortunate position and are to be pitied. With such feelings wealth does not bring happiness. (June 1, 1882, JI 17:168)

ALL TO BENEFIT FROM TALENT OF BUSINESS MEN. The time must come when the talent of men of business shall be used for the benefit of this whole people, just as the talent of President Taylor, just as the talent of President Joseph F. Smith and that of President Wilford Woodruff, and that of the Twelve Apostles, and that of the leading Elders of this Church; as their talent is used for the benefit of Zion, so must the talent of men who are gifted with business capacity be used in like manner—not for individual benefit alone, not for individual aggrandizement alone, but for the benefit of the whole people, to uplift the masses, to rescue them from their poverty. That is one of the objects in establishing Zion, and anything short of that . . . is not Zion. (October 8, 1882, JD 23:281-82)

THE TRIAL OF PROSPERITY. We are to be tried in all things, and sooner or later we must be tested by prosperity and plenty. Many people who remained faithful Latter-day Saints while they were poor may be unable to stand when they are rich. Riches has a very corrupting effect upon the human heart, and it requires a very pure people to be as honest, virtuous, humble and upright when surrounded by luxury and wealth as when they are in poor and destitute circumstances.

Yet, the Lord has said that the riches of the earth are His; He has promised to give the earth and the dominion thereof to

His Saints. But He will not give these to His people to destroy them. No; they must learn to use but not to abuse these blessings. They must not put their hearts upon them or be corrupted by them.

But how can the Saints be saved from this? If other people and nations have been corrupted by wealth and luxury and gone to destruction, is there not danger of the Latter-day Saints meeting with a similar fate when they become rich? If they were to feel and act as many other people, there would be great danger of their going as they have gone and are going. But the Lord has revealed the Gospel to save them from this fate. . . .

WE ARE STEWARDS. If you always remember that your lives, your ability, the food you eat, the water you drink, the clothes you wear, the earth you tread, the air you breathe, are all the Lord's, you may be useful. Of course, if you know that all these things are the Lord's, and that He has placed His servants to teach you His will, you will do what He tells you, through those servants, with the means that you may have. Then, whether you are rich or poor will make no difference. All your property, whether much or little, will be disposed of by you as He may dictate. You will look upon yourselves as stewards, and if you have a hundred dollars in your hands, you will say, this is the Lord's, and if He wants it, He can have it. If you have a million dollars, you will feel the same. And where people have this feeling, riches cannot hurt them. Latter-day Saints must have this kind of faith and feeling, or they cannot build up Zion and be the people the Lord is desirous they should be. (April 15, 1871, JI 6:60)

MUST CLEAVE UNTO GOD. When we have an abundance of everything that is necessary for our comfort and convenience, we do not feel our dependence upon our God as we do under other circumstances. When times are pleasant, when there is no persecution, when there are no arrests made and no disposition to send the people to prison, or to commit other acts of infamy or outrage upon them, then there is not the same feeling of anxiety and the same desire to seek unto God and to beseech Him for His power to be extended to us that there would be or is when we are in peril. When in peril we feel that we must cleave unto God, that we must seek unto Him earnestly to receive His aid and deliverance. (May 26, 1889, DW 38:709)

PROSPERITY BRINGS GREAT DANGERS. Our Prophets have predicted that when the time should arrive for this people to be tried with prosperity, then they would be in great danger. I have heard this prediction uttered hundreds of times, until it has almost become like an old story with us. I heard the Prophet Joseph say, when he was living, that the time would come that this people would be tried with abundance; but he warned them to be careful of these things.

The Lord has told us, through the revelations which He gave to Joseph, that it must needs be that the riches of the earth were His to give to His people; "but," He said, "beware of pride, lest ye become as the Nephites of old." [D&C 38:39.] This was the warning God gave to us years ago, and it has been repeated in our ears from that time until the present, and still there is a great necessity that we should treasure it up in our hearts and often reflect upon it. . . .

Here we are, and the world are seeking to mingle with us, and they are becoming uncommonly gracious unto us, as a people; they can smile upon us and be kind unto us. They would have us believe that they welcome us warmly to their smiles and friendship.

FRIENDSHIP OF WORLD DREADED. There is danger in this; this is the danger that the Prophets have dreaded. It is an insidious danger that comes creeping like a snake through the grass and pounces upon us before we are aware of its proximity. But stir us up, as a people, by persecution and abuse, and there is no power on earth we would not unitedly stand against. Through the help of God we have successfully resisted every power that has been arrayed against us. Let the enemy come out against us as an open antagonist, and he finds us an impenetrable phalanx that cannot be moved.

Our danger is not in this; but it lies in our being found asleep and off our watch tower, unsuspecting and unprepared for the enemies' most subtle attacks. It is in scenes like these that we are required to be the more watchful, and in times like these that we are required the more to have the power of God upon us and the revelations of Jesus Christ in our hearts, or we are sure to be overcome. . . . There is danger, and there is a necessity for us to be up and have our eyes open to the signs of the times and the danger that menaces us and that threatens to ensnare our feet.

INDIFFERENCE WEAKENS RESISTANCE TO EVIL. I have no fears if we will only obey the counsel of God's servants, if we will only listen diligently to those things which they impart unto us and honor their teachings and be attentive to our duties. But when I see Saints indifferent about their meetings, passing their Sundays without caring whether they hear instructions or not, and their religion becomes a secondary consideration with them, then I am afraid for such individuals, because they are not in a position to resist the attacks of that tempter, who is continually watching to destroy us and the Work of God from off the face of the earth.

MUST MEET AND OVERCOME TRIALS IN ALL THINGS. The Lord our God is working with us; He is trying us, probably with trials of a new sort that He may approve of us in every respect. If we have set out to obtain celestial glory, the precious and inestimable gift of eternal lives, there is no trial necessary for our purification and perfection as Saints of God that we will not have to meet, contend with and overcome. Such trials will come in various shapes, on the right hand and on the left, whether they be in having everything move on prosperously, or in adversity, hardship and the laying down of our lives for the truth, until the design is fully accomplished and the dross of our natures is purified and these earthly tabernacles are redeemed from everything that is groveling and low and brought into entire subjection to the mind and will of God. (October 23, 1864, JD 10:346-47)

PROVIDE GOOD HOUSES. A woman looks upon a house as a matter of much more importance than a man does. It is her home. And when I see wives in houses of a poor class when their husbands might build better, I think their husbands do not understand woman's nature as they should do. Women with families should have good houses, and husbands should labor to get them, and then leave them to adorn them and make them comfortable and desirable. Children like to have a nice house, because they can invite their companions to it. Men should strive to make their families comfortable in this way. It is their duty to do so. (June 20, 1883, JD 24:225)

LORD WATCHES OVER TREASURES OF EARTH. Unless the Lord is willing to grant us wealth, it will be impossible for us to get it. He can lock up or unlock the treasures of the earth at His will. Years before any gold or silver mines were discovered in this region, President Young used to say publicly that he could stand in his doorway and see localities where there were the richest kind of mineral deposits. Yet, he did not seek to obtain these treasures. He doubtless knew it would be useless for him to attempt it. The time had not come for the Saints to possess them. In a sermon which President Young delivered June 17, 1877, he said:

> These treasures that are in the earth are carefully watched, they can be removed from place to place according to the good pleasure of Him who made them and owns them. He has His messengers at His service, and it is just as easy for an angel to remove the minerals from any part of one of these mountains to another, as it is for you and me to walk up and down this hall. This, however, is not understood by the Christian world, nor by us as a people. There are certain circumstances that a number of my brethren and sisters have heard me relate, that will demonstrate this so positively, that none need doubt the truth of what I say. [JD 19:36-37.] (February 1, 1880, JI 15:30)

Chapter 25

America—A God-Inspired Nation

AMERICA KEPT HIDDEN BY LORD. This is a sacred land. It is a land choice above all other lands upon the face of the earth. It was kept hidden from the nations for long centuries, and the reason for this has been given to us; it was that the land might not be overrun by the nations of the earth, and that it might be reserved for the great drama of the last days. It is a remarkable thing, and we would be incapable of understanding the reason why this land had been hidden for so many centuries from the knowledge of the nations of the earth if the Lord had not revealed it. . . .

The knowledge of it was completely hidden, as completely as if it did not belong to our globe. Navigators sailed to and fro; but through the long centuries that elapsed from the confusion of tongues at the Tower of Babel, when the inhabitants of the earth were scattered, until the time that Columbus, inspired of God, went from court to court, pleading with the governments of nations to give him the means to penetrate the ocean and find what he supposed was the Indies—during all that time the knowledge of this land was kept from all the nations of the earth.

Is not this wonderful? How can we account for it? There is only one way, and that is the way the Lord accounts for it; He tells us through His servant that the knowledge of this land should be kept from all the nations of the earth, because if it were not they would overrun the land. It was a land too choice to be left unoccupied, possessed of too many of those elements that enrich individuals and peoples. The nations of the earth would have swarmed here by the hundreds of thousands, and there would have been no place found upon the land for the people who now possess the land. There would have been no room for the Church of Christ, no room for the Kingdom of God, no room for the gathering of the millions that will yet come to Zion, to build up the Kingdom of God on this land and to prepare the way for the establishment of the New Jerusalem; for this is the favored land upon which the New Jerusalem will be established.

We, therefore, can see today how the Lord has prepared the way for the gathering of the people from all the nations of the earth, and how His providence has been over this choice land above all other lands. There is plenty of room here, not crowding upon anybody, not compelled to come as conquerors have in other ages who have overrun other lands and driven out or destroyed the people who occupied the land, in order that they might possess it. No necessity for this, for God has made abundant provisions.

THIS LAND RESERVED FOR RESTORATION OF GOSPEL. He has kept in reserve this glorious land, in order that in the last days His Kingdom could be established, and that under the inspiration which He should give a government might be founded—a government of liberty, a government of freedom, giving to all the utmost liberty they could desire, and promising to those who should possess the land many precious things; for He has told us that none should be brought here except they should come by His permission. Therefore, the emigration that has come from the beginning, and that is still coming, comes by the permission of the Almighty. He is watching over it, and He will control it and bring to pass His purposes in connection with it. He has told us that if we will only worship the God of this land, Jesus Christ, we cannot be brought into bondage or into captivity by any other nation.

AMERICA'S FUTURE DEPENDS ON RIGHTEOUSNESS. The powers of Europe may band together and indulge in hopes of conquering this nation; but the Lord has said—and it will be fulfilled if we do right—that they will be defeated in all their schemes, and this shall be a land of liberty unto the righteous. This nation of ours, so glorious in its past, so glorious in its prospects of the future, will stand and never be overthrown, unless the inhabitants of the land reject Jesus Christ, the King and the God of the land.

Now, we know the conditions upon which victory will be assured to us as a nation. If this nation had listened to Joseph Smith, the Prophet of God, if they had been counseled by him, God would have adopted this nation and its government, and made it His, for the promises are to that effect. Now, what the future will be depends upon the conduct of those who possess the land and upon the administration of affairs in the land. (April 10, 1898, CR 84-85)

A BLESSED LAND. This land is a blessed land unto all the inhabitants of the earth who will act righteously, but is and will be cursed to those who will not. There is a curse and a blessing upon the land. No nation can prosper in this land that works unrighteousness, and it is a painful thing to say that our own nation, unless it repents, will meet with disasters sooner or later. It pains us to say this, but it is true. God has said it. It will be true about us. This land can only be blessed to us if we work righteously. Let us turn round and oppress the weak and do wrong, and God will curse the land to us. There will be trouble in the land among the inhabitants of the earth as long as they work wickedness, just as sure as God has spoken.

A GOD-INSPIRED NATION. There has been no nation prospered as our nation has. No government was ever framed by man that is so strong and so good and well adapted to the happiness of human beings as our government is. There never was a better instrument framed for the happiness of man than the Constitution of the United States. The men who framed it were inspired of God. The men who fought the battles of the Revolution were the same. Washington was inspired of God; he was sustained by the almighty arm of God; and the defeats that the mother country received were in accordance with the plan of God. This land was kept for this purpose. For centuries it was hidden from all the nations of the earth. . . .

Those who contended for liberty in early days were men who desired to serve the Lord. They may have been mistaken in many things, but they were zealous in this and devoted to it, and many of them were willing that every human being should have the rights that they contended for themselves. (November 20, 1881, JD 23:102)

CHRISTOPHER COLUMBUS—A GOD-INSPIRED MAN. It is an easy matter to talk now about the discovery of America and imagine how easy of accomplishment it was; but at the time the voyage of Columbus was performed it was the most daring adventure that could be thought of. It required the inspiration of the Almighty to enable Columbus to perform such a voyage. Attempts have been made to prove that Scandinavians discovered America long before the voyage of Columbus. Whether they did or not, it is of but little moment, so far as the nations of Europe are concerned. It was the voyage of Columbus that opened the new world, and that made clear the pathway by which this continent could be reached and be peopled by the white races of Europe.

The Book of Mormon thus speaks of the discovery of the continent in the description of the vision which Nephi had of the future:

> And I looked and beheld a man among the Gentiles, who was separated from the seed of my brethren by the many waters; and I beheld the Spirit of God that it came down and wrought upon the man; and he went forth upon the many waters, even unto the seed of my brethren, who were in the promised land. [1 Nephi 13:12.]

It is a remarkable fact that investigation has proved that Columbus declared that he was called of God to make this voyage. He professed to be the messenger of the Blessed Trinity, called by God to discover countries in the West. There were many ideas connected with this in his mind which were incorrect. He does not seem to have conceived the idea that he was to be the discoverer of a new continent; but he supposed, and probably during his life was never undeceived on that point, that the lands which he had discovered were the eastern part of Asia. Among the arguments which he used to convince Queen Isabella, who was a strong and ardent Catholic and zealous for the propagation of that faith, was that he was called by God to fulfill certain important prophecies before the destruction of the world. All the blessings of the "true faith" were to be brought from Spain to peoples not yet known, so that all nations might be gathered under the banner of Christianity.

Among his records is found the following statement:

> I have associated with scientific men, clerical and lay, and the Latin Church and the Greek, with the Jews and Moors, and many others. To that end the Lord gave me the spirit to understand. In the science of navigation he endowed me richly; of astronomy, and also geometry and arithmetic he gave me what was necessary.

On another occasion he wrote:

> I came to your Majesty as the Messenger of the Blessed Trinity. . . . Notwithstanding all the troubles that befel me I was certain that my undertaking would succeed, and I held firmly to this opinion for all else will perish, save only the word of God; and indeed God speaks very clearly of these lands by the mouth of Isaiah in many passages of holy writ, and He declares that the knowledge of His Holy name shall be spread through the lands from Spain.

It required such a man as Columbus, inspired of the Lord, to accomplish this great work. His ideas were ridiculed and scoffed at, but he never relinquished them. With that perseverance which the Lord gives to those whom He raises up to accomplish great works, he could not be discouraged.

King Ferdinand never took a warm interest in the scheme of Columbus; and the honor of aiding this man, upon whom Nephi saw the Spirit of God descend, belongs to Queen Isabella, a noble representative of her sex.

There is a story that the crew mutinied against Columbus and were determined to turn back. They were frightened at the distance they had sailed, and saw no prospect of discovering the land which Columbus assured them they would find. A compact, it is said, was entered into between Columbus and the mutineers, by the terms of which Columbus was given three days' grace. If in that time the ocean did not reveal its secrets, he was to turn back. It is stated that on October 7th, when the voyage had lasted a month, Columbus was induced to steer no longer due west, but to turn in a southwesterly direction. Columbus yielded reluctantly to his clamorous and faint-hearted crew in thus changing his course, and then signs of land near at hand began to multiply, and everyone was on the lookout, in the hope of being the first to see the shore, for the Queen had promised a reward of 10,000 maravedis (about $30 of our money) to the man who should first set eyes on the long-sought-for land. They landed on one of the islands of the Bahama group.

It is stated that if Columbus had been permitted to pursue his original due west course, he would have first reached the coast of North Carolina. But it was ordered otherwise. Had he done so, the present United States would have then been the heritage of Ferdinand and Isabella. There was a Providence undoubtedly in this, guiding his movements. . . .

In all these events the Latter-day Saints can see the hand of the Almighty. To them every step taken has a meaning. They can perceive how plainly the Lord guided this man and these nations in order to bring about the fulfillment of His purposes. No people on the earth can truly take greater interest in the celebration of Discovery Day [Columbus Day] than the Latter-day Saints. (October 15, 1892, JI 27:626-27)

A MOST GLORIOUS GOVERNMENT. It is true that it has not always been a land of liberty to the Latter-day Saints. We have suffered from wrongs and oppressions. The principles embodied in the Declaration of Independence—that glorious instrument which was proclaimed on July 4th, 1776—and afterwards embodied in the Constitution of the United States, are broad and liberal enough to satisfy every reasonable human being and, when carried out and maintained, make our government the most glorious for human freedom and the development of human beings of any government on the face of the earth. Under no other form of government could the Latter-day Saints have been protected by the organic law of the land as they have been in America. In assisting the fathers of our country it was the design of the Almighty Father to frame a form of government under which it would be possible for the Church to live and enjoy all those rights which were necessary for the accomplishment of His purposes. . . .

INSPIRED MEN RAISED UP. When the time came for the discovery of the land, the Lord moved upon Christopher Columbus and made him an instrument to bring to light the western hemisphere. In like manner the colonies which afterwards became the United States were formed under His direction, His providence was over them, and the seeds of religious freedom were sown by the men whom He led to this land as an asylum of refuge from the tyrannies of the old nations. The love of liberty was fostered until it brought forth the important fruits which were witnessed in the Declaration of Independence, in the Constitution of the United States and in the formation of a great nation.

The men who were the instruments in performing these

great works were inspired of the Lord to accomplish that which they did. This is easily perceived in reading the history of those times. In many instances, probably, they themselves were unconscious of the fact that the Lord had raised them up for that end. Thomas Paine, who is known throughout Christendom as an unbeliever in religion, was no doubt inspired to take the part he did in propagating the principles of liberty. If he had been told so, he might not have believed it; but undoubtedly the Lord was with him, and with Thomas Jefferson, who also was skeptical, and other men who had but little or no faith in God. They laid the foundation of this magnificent structure, this glorious form of government, the corner stone of which was religious freedom—freedom for all to believe as they please, and to carry that belief into practice, so long as it did not interfere with the rights of their fellowmen.

A CAUSE FOR REJOICING. Notwithstanding the wrongs we ourselves may have suffered, we of all people have the greatest cause to rejoice in Independence Day. We should always honor it and revere the memories of the men who "pledged their lives, their fortunes, and their sacred honor" on that memorable 4th of July, to maintain the cause of liberty. They made sacrifices for posterity, and they did so with true courage and unyielding determination. God was with them in their counsels and in their battles, and He gave them power to accomplish the purposes for which they started out. They were a poor people, destitute of resources, but they were sustained by the Lord, and were able to hold their own against the mightiest nation then on the earth, and to obtain from that proud power a recognition of their rights and of the government they had framed.

Our children should value the labors of the fathers of the country, and honor the day which they made so glorious by their Declaration of Independence. . . .

BLESSED ABOVE ALL OTHER LANDS. Again we have another mighty nation possessing this land. What nation can compare with ours in its growth, its prosperity, and in the power which God has given to it? The growth of this nation is simply marvelous. . . . Wealth has increased to an unexampled extent in a very brief period. Everything that could be desired to make a nation great and prosperous and happy has been bestowed upon this American Republic.

If the people would live righteously and serve the God of the land, there would be no limit to the blessings bestowed upon them; but if they turn to iniquity and yield to sin, the judgments of the Lord will assuredly fall upon them, and it will be with them as it was with the nations that have preceded them. . . .

A nation so favored of heaven as this is, a people inhabiting a land so greatly blessed above all other lands, cannot reject the Lord, who gives them these blessings, without incurring His displeasure. While He gives the most glorious promises to the righteous, on the other hand He threatens the severest judgments if the people turn to iniquity.

One advantage that we have is that we have been informed of these promises and these threats, and we can receive the fulfillment of the promises, if we live according to the conditions upon which they are based. If we are righteous, we must prosper. Nothing can prevent it. But should we be unrighteous, we shall be scourged.

We need have no fear as to the final results. Unrighteousness will bring its punishment, nor will it be deferred. The wrath of God will be poured out upon the ungodly. But, those who keep the commandments of God can rejoice in blessings present and prospective. (July 15, 1891, JI 26:445-47)

HAND OF PROVIDENCE MANIFESTED. In looking back on the past history of our race, there is to be discovered the hand of Providence very visibly manifested in every event that has taken place for centuries. We can see the providences of God leading and guiding the affairs of men to the grand consummation effected by the men of '76. He is a dull student of history who fails to recognize in all the events which have taken place the hand of an over-ruling Providence.

When we peruse the history of the nation from which our forefathers sprang, we can see how visibly God over-ruled circumstances to raise up a free people. From the days of Magna Charta down to the Revolution of 1688, events were shaped to bring to pass the emancipation of the human mind from the thraldom under which it had groaned.

The Reformation came in; men's minds were prepared for it. There seemed to be a peculiar combination of circumstances favorable to the development of religious inquiry. Men were disposed to throw off the shackles with which the human mind and intellect had been enthralled; they were disposed to examine and investigate and reject that which did not appeal to their reason and which was not sustained by their judgment. . . .

We believe that the Declaration of Independence was inspired by Almighty God, and that the men who framed and proclaimed it were raised up and inspired for this special purpose. This is the estimate which we place upon these documents; hence, it will be instantly perceived that we can do nought else than uphold them, carry out their principles, and hand them down to our children as the most precious legacy we can bequeath to them. . . .

EVERY NATION BENEFITTED BY THE REVOLUTION. It was not America alone which felt the benign influences resulting from the efforts of the Revolutionary Fathers. Every nation in Christendom and upon the face of the earth has been benefitted to a greater or less extent by their struggles, sacrifices and victories. . . . From the throes of our Revolution, from the sufferings and sacrifices of the Revolutionary Fathers, was begotten a spirit of liberty that has spread throughout the earth. Nations afar have felt it; its leaven has entered into their political systems, and has had a tendency to relieve the oppressed; and so long as this Republic endures, so long will the love of liberty be cherished in the hearts of the down-trodden of every land, and they will be benefitted to an extent they would not realize were this government not in existence. In fighting, therefore, the battles of American Independence the Revolutionary Fathers fought the battles of mankind; they fought for liberty in every land, and the example which they gave to the nations never has nor never will be forgotten. (July 24, 1871, MS 33:483-85)

The Declaration of Independence should be familiar to every child of our land, and the principles which it announced should be engrafted in the minds of all. They should be preserved by us in their original purity and transmitted to our children after us without being in the least impaired. (June 15, 1881, JI 16:138)

FOUNDING FATHERS NOT ORDINARY MEN. We reverence their memories and desire to emulate their great example in risking all for right. To our view they are more than ordinary men; we recognize in them the direct instruments of Heaven, chosen and inspired to raise aloft the standard of liberty under which men from every clime and of every creed could dwell in peace and security, so long as they did not interfere with the rights of their fellow-men. Others, while watching their struggles and progress, could see the foundation being laid of institutions to secure to mankind the largest possible amount of liberty and happiness; but we go beyond that. We know that the Almighty, through the agencies of the revolution, prepared the way for the establishment of His own Eternal Kingdom—that Kingdom in which the grandest prophecies of human freedom ever sung by angel, Prophet or inspired tongue will be realized. (July 4, 1870, DNW 19:259)

FOUNDATIONS FOR STABLE GOVERNMENT. The teachings from the platform and in the schools have been that the men who framed the Declaration of Independence and the Constitution, and who took part in the councils and battles of the Revolution, were especially inspired and sustained by the Almighty, and that those instruments are the foundations upon which stable government for all time, upon this continent, must rest. Joseph Smith, whom they look upon as a Prophet, taught this; and since his day others have constantly repeated the teaching. Persecution never weakened their attachment to the principles of free government, and, when they fled as religious exiles to the Rocky Mountains, they did not forget they were American citizens. They hoisted the Stars and Stripes, and announced their determination to live under the Constitution of their fathers. But they claimed for the Constitution powers which others did not think it possessed.

When expelled from a State under an exterminating order of its governor, they held that the Federal Government, by virtue of the Constitution, had the power to protect and re-instate its citizens in their rights. Martin Van Buren, when appealed to as the chief executive, thought differently. The State was sovereign and could not be reached; and he replied: "Your cause is just, but I can do nothing for you." [*History of the Church* 4:40, 80.] The people claimed then, as now, for the Constitution, that it was designed to protect the humblest citizen in every right of liberty and of worship that did not disturb good order or interfere with the peace and happiness of others. (October 24, 1881, MS 43:676)

Chapter 26

Constitutional Government and Politics

THE CONSTITUTION AND THE SAINTS. We cannot as a people close our eyes or our ears to that which is going on around us. No people on this continent are more interested in public movements than are the members of The Church of Jesus Christ of Latter-day Saints. So many predictions have been made concerning the future of our own nation that we would be a very stupid people if we were not deeply interested in the fulfillment of those predictions and in watching the signs which will precede or accompany them.

The Book of Mormon is a most precious record if for no other reason than this: it gives us a clear idea concerning the fate of the people of this land in their national capacity. Not only does the Book of Mormon furnish us with the most interesting and definite information, but the Book of Doctrine and Covenants also can be read by Latter-day Saints with the deepest interest because of the events which are foreshadowed in the revelations which it contains. (September 1, 1896, JI 31:522)

CONSTITUTION PROVIDES FOR PERFECT LIBERTY. The Constitution was an instrument devised by the highest human wisdom, and was admirably adapted for the purpose for which it was designed. No better instrument was ever framed by human intellect. Under its wise provisions and guarantees, the people of every section and of every creed on this great land could dwell in peace and in harmony, and enjoy the most extensive rights consistent with good order. And its benefits need not have been confined to this continent; but the people of every nation and of every land could become partakers of the blessings which are guaranteed, and dwell in peace and security under its aegis.

But the views of its framers have not been carried out. The love of place and of power has risen paramount to the love of country; and those who should have been the most faithful defenders of the Constitution have been its most deadly foes. . . .

While the Constitution was properly respected, and the wise admonitions of its framers were attended to, the nation became great, prosperous and happy without a parallel in history. But to have a people truly great and permanently prosperous, there is something more needed than a good constitution, a perfect form of government and liberal laws. With virtue and honesty in the people, and a disposition to strictly obey and comply with the laws, imperfect and faulty though they may be, an illiberal form of government, and an inferior constitution, do not check progress or entirely debar the subjects of such a government from enjoying much real happiness.

But that government which we have guaranteed unto us, under our Constitution, has never been excelled, if indeed it has ever been equalled, in the liberality of its provisions for the rights and enjoyment of its citizens. Under its benign working, when properly administered, man can enjoy the most perfect liberty compatible with his well-being, and progress to the highest point of excellence and greatness attainable in a state of mortality. There are no checks, no limits to his progress. His path is unobstructed by any obstacle which perseverance and energy cannot overcome. . . .

PEACE AND HAPPINESS OF WORLD CONSIDERED. Though their [the Founding Fathers] labors were confined to this land, and to the establishment of free government here, yet their great and philanthropic hearts beat high with hopes for the emancipation of the toiling and down-trodden millions of other lands, and they jealously watched and guarded every movement, knowing well that any misadventure on their part would injure the cause of liberty everywhere throughout the earth. The peace and happiness of the whole race of man were the objects for which they labored; and this was the aim which they kept constantly in view in the Declaration of Independence, in the framing of the Constitution and in all their acts in founding the government.

And had the people of these United States lived up to the Constitution, and the principles and precepts which the Fathers bequeathed to them, instead of there being division in our nation, and a deadly internecine war being waged between two sections [the Civil War], we would have gone on increasing in greatness and power until we would have annexed the world and extended the blessings of free government unto all people. . . .

THE DAY-STAR OF THE BRIGHTER DAY. They, with full confidence in the Divine Power, which had thrown protection around them like a wall of fire, gave that instrument to the world with the most sanguine hopes in the bright and glorious future which awaited our country. Yet, this work was but the forerunner to a greater. They reared a temple of liberty amid the noble pillars of which the infant Kingdom of God, then in the future, could gather strength and vigor and power to protect and perpetuate the edifice that gave it early shelter.

While all others throughout this wide-spread republic celebrate this day [July 4] because it is the anniversary of liberty and freedom to them, we doubly rejoice, for not only do we see in it the birth-day of civil and religious freedom, but the day-star of that glorious morn that would usher in light to chase away the night of ages, truth to drive error back to its dark bounds, and redemption for all mankind, till a regenerated world, emancipated from the slavery of sin and death, should bask in the eternal sunshine of salvation, exaltation and glory. They, through the dim vista of the future, saw faintly the dawning light of that bright day; we looking from the past to the future, nearer to the effulgence of its glory, can see with closer vision its brilliance, and feel already the heavenly warmth of its rays as they shine around our hearts.

If those to whom the sacred trust was committed should not prove true to their integrity, there is a people who revere the Hand by which the boon was bestowed, honor the men who were the chosen ones to usher in the birthday of freedom to the world, and will cling to the Constitution till its blessings are enjoyed by every land trodden by the foot of man. . . .

We celebrate the day and honor the memory of the Revolutionary Fathers because they were the men who pioneered the way for the work in which we are engaged—because it was the initial step, in these latter times, in the pathway of endless and universal freedom; and when the rising glories of our country shall shine with effulgent splendor, and the children of every land shall enjoy the blessings of liberty and freedom, we shall celebrate the day we have now assembled to commemorate and honor the memory of those who have made it notable and glorious for all time. (July 4, 1865, DNW 14:317)

A LAND OF LIBERTY. This land has been dedicated to liberty, dedicated by the Lord our God, and by men who have lived upon this land, to liberty, and as long as this land shall be a land of liberty, it will be a blessed land to the inhabitants thereof; but when it ceases to be a land of liberty, then as sure as God has spoken, this government will go down—that is, any government that will war against the principles of liberty. . . . (January 18, 1885, JD 26:142)

FORCES OF DESTRUCTION. No people or government can defy the sound principles of law which are essential to the correct administration of justice and to the maintenance of the rights of its citizens, without calling into existence forces which are calculated to lead to its destruction. (April 8, 1887, MS 49:293-96)

A government that lends itself to the oppression of its citizens will sooner or later receive punishment. That which it sows it will reap. It will be a harvest that will be most bitter and sorrowful for those who reap it. (November 20, 1884, JD 26:12-13)

THE PROPER ROLE OF GOVERNMENT. Government has the right, and owes it to its citizens, to protect them in their rights—to protect their lives, to protect their property, to protect them in all their civil rights, and in their religious rights also, and to prevent others from doing them violence. Beyond this it should not go. (June 25, 1882, JD 24:45)

THE FIRST AMENDMENT. The adoption of the first amendment to the Constitution was an intimation to the world that in free America the inquisition over the rights of conscience was forever ended. The States had been released from the political tyranny of the mother country; by this amendment they were released from the religious traditions, the soul-crushing, the body-destroying laws and practices in religious matters of the old world. The new Republic turned her back upon all these, and, led and inspired by the Almighty, she swept away every restriction and oppressive enactment that could in the least prevent her from becoming, as Washington said, "an asylum for the poor and oppressed of all nations and religions." This flag of political and universal religious liberty was unfurled to the world. (1879, *A Review* 24)

NO GOVERNMENT FORCE IN RELIGION. If our Government should attempt to use force in religion, it will find its power stop short at the conscience of man. No truthful, conscientious man can bend or deny his convictions at the bidding of King, President, Congress or Court. Congress and Court may say what they think is religion and what is not religion, and those who are of their way of thinking may accept their definitions, but no free man will allow them to prescribe what his religious duty shall be, and how it shall be rendered to his Creator. . . .

Grant to Congress and the Courts the power to define the rights of conscience, and the limit beyond which faith shall not be carried into action, and religious liberty is practically at an end. The battles for spiritual freedom, which have been so nobly fought in the generations past, and which have been gained by the sacrifice of so much precious blood, will, so far as we are concerned, have been fought in vain. We shall be remanded back to the days of Henry the VIII, when "the King's Majesty had as well the care of the souls of his subjects as their bodies; and might by the law of God, by his Parliament, make laws touching and concerning as well the one as the other." (1879, *A Review* 39)

THE SUPREME COURT. This Government cannot afford to punish the humblest of its citizens wrongfully. The Supreme Court, elevated as it is above all courts in the land and above all its citizens, is not so high that it can justly deny to the lowliest and most oppressed, even though accused of crime, his rights as a citizen, without a sacrifice of its own honor and dignity. It should be remembered that "one foul sentence does more harm than many foul examples; for the last do but corrupt the stream, while the former corrupteth the fountain." . . .

The Supreme Court of the United States is a tribunal towards which I have ever looked with respect and reverence. Its decisions are entitled to the greatest consideration. They carry with them the weight of great authority. Individually, the members of the Court occupy a high place in the public confidence and esteem. Their lives, and the events and actions of their lives, for many years, are before the world, and form a conspicuous part of the history of the country. United as they are in the capacity of a Supreme Court of this great nation, they form a judicial tribunal which is not surpassed, if equaled, in dignity by any other on earth. . . .

High as is my respect for the Supreme tribunal of the land, my respect for the Constitution and my reverence for God are higher. I cannot assume for human laws and human decisions that which I assume for God's laws—that they are beyond question. To do so would be to claim for their fallible authors an infallibility which belongs only to the Creator. I cannot exalt man to an equality with God. That the laws of Congress have not always been constitutional and perfect, that the decisions of the Supreme Court have not always been infallible, the history of the nation clearly establishes. It requires no great age, no venerable experience, to remind citizens of this fact; men of middle age have but to contrast the present with the past, which they can recollect, to convince themselves of it. (1879, *A Review* 2-4)

FUTURE DEPENDS ON INTEGRITY OF PEOPLE. Though the Fathers of the Republic were confident in the integrity of their own motives, and were satisfied as to the propriety of establishing such a form of government, yet they were fully aware that its success and perpetuity depended, altogether, on the integrity and correct deportment of the people. They fully realized that, by the indulgence in local prejudices and party animosities, under guidance of ambitious leaders, occasions might easily be found or created for the introduction of sectional agitation and strife that would result, unless checked, in the dismemberment of the Union.

They were not blind to the evils which monarchists predicted would attend the Republic; neither did they pass off the stage of action without lifting up their voices in solemn warning to guard the people against the dangers of disruption. They knew that the safety and preservation of the Union and all the blessings of a free government were dependent upon the integrity of the people—that so long as they abstained from local prejudices and attachments, from separate views and party animosities, and accorded unto all the same privileges they claimed for themselves, so long the Union would be preserved intact. (September 27, 1856, WS 210-11)

JOSEPH SMITH WOULD HAVE SAVED NATION. God intended, as has been predicted in the Book of Mormon, to make of these United States, if they would receive His Gospel, the mightiest nation on the face of the earth. It is the mightiest now, and if they would receive the message He has sent unto them, He would impart to them His power and acknowledge this nation as His own. But they murdered the Prophet of God, the man whom God had called and inspired. They were not satisfied till he was slain, thinking thereby to destroy the work which he had been the instrument in the hands of God of founding.

He would have saved the nation by the wisdom which God gave him, if the people had listened to him. There would have been no war of the rebellion if Joseph Smith's counsel had been listened to. If the principles he taught had been heeded, the nation would not have been rent asunder as it was during that bloody period. Instead, it would have gone on increasing in strength and power, the blessing of God being with it. (September 23, 1900, MS 62:772)

THE SAINTS AND THE CIVIL WAR. When the South raised the flag of rebellion, there was no well-informed Latter-day Saint who could approve in his heart of such conduct, however much we might have expected it. Joseph Smith had predicted, nearly thirty years before the rebellion broke out, that it would occur; however much this might be the case, there was nothing connected with the principle of secession or rebellion that met with the approval of the Latter-day Saints. And it is a remarkable fact that God, through the acts of our enemies, caused us to be placed in a position where, in the war of the rebellion, we should not be compelled to shed the blood of our fellow-men. . . .

We were here in the mountains, in a position where we could do nothing in the strife. President Lincoln asked for some men to guard the great highway, to preserve the mails and keep open communication, and these men were sent out. But they did not have to fight. . . .

THE MORMON BATTALION. When five hundred men—after we were driven from Illinois in 1846—were required to make up the Mormon Battalion for the Mexican War, the promise of God to these five hundred men was that they should not be compelled to shed blood during their absence, and in a remarkable manner this prediction was fulfilled. They never shrank from doing their duty as good, loyal citizens and soldiers, but there was no blood-shedding by the Mormon Battalion.

We have been in all our troubles preserved from shedding blood. We are not a blood-shedding people. Our garments are not stained with the blood of our fellow-men—I mean as a people. . . . We are at peace with all mankind. God has given unto us a law concerning this, that we must hoist the standard of peace and continue to proclaim it, and then if we are called upon to defend ourselves, we are told to leave our cause in the hands of God. We are a people who love peace, and in the turmoil, in the wars, in the confusion, in all the disorders that will eventually occur, not only in Europe, but in our own land—our own blessed land in many respects which shall become yet very unhappy in consequence of internal broils and disunion—when all this shall take place, we are the people who will present such an aspect to the world, that they will say, "here are the features we desire; they have the peace our souls long for." (October 9, 1881, JD 22:327-28)

CIVIL STRIFE COMING. The day will come, and it is not far distant, when in our own nation there will be civil strife, there will be domestic broils, there will be a withdrawal of peace, and men will yet have to come to the Latter-day Saints for that peace and that freedom from civil strife that cannot be found elsewhere. . . . We have been taught to believe that the time will come when constitutional government will be overthrown upon this land, and that it will be the province of the Latter-day Saints to uphold those principles which God inspired the founders of this government to embody in the Constitution; and it seems to be fast approaching. (August 31, 1884, JD 25:274)

DOWNFALL OF GOVERNMENT PREDICTED. Men are so ready and willing to be deceived in regard to that which will produce their destruction, that they put off the day of dread.

Although Joseph Smith and the Elders of this Church have proclaimed, both by their own voice and by publications, the downfall of this government, and set forth things so plainly to those that would look at them, yet the people have closed their eyes and have pressed forward in their own way; and they will so continue until every word shall be fulfilled. (September 9, 1860, JD 8:301)

We cannot look forward with any very bright hope for the future of this nation, unless there is heartfelt repentance on the part of the people. Affairs will grow worse and worse, and all the evils that have befallen and are befalling other nations will come upon this. (July 15, 1881, JI 16:162)

ANOTHER CIVIL WAR PREDICTED. The day will come when our own nation will be convulsed with intestine strife. The civil war that is past is not the only war that will take place in this land. It is a matter of regret to think it should be otherwise. But God has spoken. There will be intestine strife in our own nation. Already we can see, as it were, the seeds of this germinating and sprouting in the midst of neighborhoods and of communities, and it will break out after a while, and men will flee to Zion.

The prediction was made . . . by Joseph Smith that the time would come when those who would not take up their sword to fight against their neighbor in this blessed land . . . would be compelled to come here for protection, for we will be the only people that will be at peace on the continent. . . . It will be fulfilled just as sure as God has spoken it. (June 22, 1884, JD 25: 238-44)

TYRANNY OF A REPUBLIC. While the people are pure, while they are upright, while they are willing to observe law, the best results must follow the establishment and maintenance of a government like this: but, on the other hand, if the people become corrupt, if they give way to passion, if they disregard law, if they trample upon constitutional obligations, then a republican form of government like ours becomes the worst tyranny upon the face of the earth. An autocracy is a government of one man, and if he be a tyrant, it is the tyranny of one man; but the tyranny and the irresponsibility of a mob is one of the most grievous despotisms which can exist upon the face of the earth. . . .

INNOCENT BLOOD NOT ATONED FOR. Deeds of violence will become more common, whether the world believe it or not. The Lord inspired His servants to predict these things, if the spirit of mobocracy were permitted to reign unchecked and unpunished. Innocent blood has been shed in our land, the blood of innocent men, the blood, as we believe, of Prophets and Apostles and Saints of God; and their blood stains the escutcheon of the States where it was shed, and it has not been atoned for. There has been no voice of protest against those deeds. . . .

NATIONS HELD RESPONSIBLE. When men permit the spirit of mobocracy and violence to prevail, when they suffer crime to go unpunished, when innocent blood is shed and is not atoned for, the time must come sooner or later when the evil results will become widespread. As men sow, so will they reap. It is an eternal law and can only be avoided by deep repentance. Every nation which commits a crime must atone for that crime. God holds nations responsible as He does individuals. (July 3, 1881, JD 22:135-38)

A GREAT REVOLUTION COMING. It is not going to be a great while—and many of you will see it too—before there will be a great revolution in the earth. Just as sure as the Lord lives the day will come when there will be consternation not only in foreign nations but in our own nation. The people of this republic are actually treading upon a volcano, and they do not know how soon the fires may burst forth, how soon the governmental fabric of this nation, the most glorious the sun has ever shone upon, the best that man without the Priesthood has had upon the earth, shall tumble. And why? Through the corruption of the people.

The best government becomes the worst government when the people become corrupt, when bribery in high places rules, when political parties condescend to purchase votes. The power of a government is weakened when Senators, Representatives and Presidents get their places by the use of money. Woe to a nation when this becomes the case. It is doomed and sooner or later it must fall. (October 6, 1879, JD 20:339)

SAINTS SHOULD LIVE ABOVE NEED FOR LAWS. Now the Latter-day Saints, as far as they are personally concerned, ought to be perfectly indifferent as to prohibition; they ought to live above the necessity of such a clause in the Constitution of Utah. There should be no need of such a thing for them. But is this the case? No, it is not. Latter-day Saints, so-called, patronize saloons; Latter-day Saints, so-called, do other vicious things, and disgrace their name and their calling by their conduct.

Now, if we live as we should do, it would make no difference what the laws were concerning the sale of liquor; it would make no difference what the laws are concerning theft, slander, bearing false witness, fornication or adultery. We would live above all these laws. And we will not be the people of God till we do live above them. We shall not see the millennium, of which we speak and sing, and which we are looking forward to, unless we do live above the laws that are enacted to restrain and punish evil practices. (March 3, 1895, DEN March 4, 1895)

WE MUST MAINTAIN OUR RIGHTS. In our contention for liberty—for we to-day are the defenders of the Constitution, and we shall have Constitutional principles to maintain and defend in the courts of the nation, we are being forced into this duty and position—God will bless us and preserve us, and carry us off triumphantly, and the words of Joseph, which were inspired by the Almighty, will be fulfilled to the very letter, namely, that the Elders of this Church will be the men who will uphold and maintain the Constitution of the United States, when others are seeking to trample it in the dust, and to destroy it.

We are a free people—let others seek to bring us into

bondage as they may—we are a free people, with the perfect right to worship our God and to carry into effect the principles that He has revealed. And if the whole world array themselves against us, and the combined power of the nation puts itself against this work, they must go down in the struggle, because they are occupying a false position. If fifty hundred millions of people were to say to the contrary, no matter, the principle still remains true, that under the Constitution in this land, a man has a perfect right to do that which God requires at his hands as long as he does not intrude upon the rights of his neighbor.

If one man stood alone in this position, and millions of men were to say it is not so, that lone man would still be right. We have that right. God has given it to us under the Constitution of the land in which we dwell, and if men enact laws and pile one law upon another until they reach to the sky, it would not change this. It is an eternal principle, and it will stand—this principle of liberty, the liberty that God has given unto every human being—the right to do that which seemeth good in his own sight, to follow the dictates of his own conscience, as long as, in so doing, he does not trespass upon the rights of his fellow man. We stand by that fearlessly, and stand by it for ourselves, and for our children after us. I would not abate one iota, not a hair's breadth, myself, in this feeling. I would feel that I was a traitor to myself and to my posterity if I were to yield in the least upon this.

We must maintain our rights, not aggressively, not in any quarrelsome spirit, but in a spirit of quiet firmness, quiet determination to maintain our rights, to contend for them, and to never yield one hair's breadth in maintaining them. This is our duty as individuals and as a people. (January 18, 1885, JD 26: 142-43)

Let us guard well our franchise, and in one unbroken phalanx, maintain and sustain our political status, and, as patriots and freemen, operate together, in the defense of what few liberties are left us, in the defense of the Constitution, and in the defense of the inalienable rights of man, which rights always exist and are before and above all constitutions, and thus perpetuate to posterity the inestimable blessings of freedom, including the right to live, the right to be free, and the right to pursue happiness, unmolested by any influence, power, or combination. (August 29, 1882, MS 44:614)

SAVIORS OF LIBERTY. The days are fast approaching concerning which the Prophet Joseph Smith often spoke. He taught the Elders that the time would come when the Constitution of the United States would be treated with contempt and trampled upon as of no value. . . .

I was much impressed by a remark made to me lately by an eminent man. "It is very wonderful," said he, speaking of the Latter-day Saints, "that a colony of religious exiles in the heart of the continent should be contending to-day for precisely the same principles of liberty that the men of our American revolution battled for."

He could see our true position. It is the exact position that the Prophet Joseph Smith, in the spirit of prophecy, said we should occupy. He said that the day would come when it should devolve upon the people of this Church to uphold the Constitution and the liberty guaranteed by it upon this continent. That is being literally fulfilled before our eyes. We are struggling to maintain its principles and to preserve its liberties. We are assailed in our own persons. The Constitution is being trampled upon in the attempts which are being made to reach and destroy us. It becomes, therefore, an act of self-preservation on our own part to save it. We shall rescue and uphold it. The liberties it guarantees we shall preserve, not for ourselves alone but for all men.

It may seem at some times as if we must go down, the odds against us will be so great. But the Lord is on our side. He never has deserted, He never will desert, His people. All that we have to do is to go about the business He has assigned us without being disturbed, and He will take care of us. We must borrow no trouble, but trust Him. And His peace will flow unto us like a river and His salvation will surround us. (April 1, 1883, JI 18:99)

CHURCH ORGANIZATION TO STEM ANARCHY. As God lives the day will come that constitutional government and the rights of man will have to be maintained by the Latter-day Saints, and that at a time when there will be no other power upon this land that will be able to make headway against the tide of evil that will flood the country. And it will be due to our organization that is magnificent as our enemies freely admit. We are a consolidated power. And when anarchy reigns, as it will do, for it is coming, and every man that opens his eyes to see the evils that abound—if he does not persistently resist the truth—must have a secret dread of it in his heart, when that comes, there will be no power upon this continent that will be able to stem it, except the organization which God has given to us. . . .

We are gaining experience day by day. God is training us in this way. We are receiving a training such as no other people receive. Men are being made statesmen in spite of themselves. . . . The day will come when we will exercise this authority in a far wider sphere than in this limited territory. The same wisdom that has maintained the organization of this people, and that enables us to withstand attacks that would swamp any other people, will enable us to act in a far more extended sphere. (June 20, 1883, JD 24:222-23)

There will be trouble. You may look for it. God has said it, and it will come; and the day will come, just as sure as God has spoken it, when the Latter-day Saints will be the only people upon this North American continent that will have the power to uphold constitutional government. (May 20, 1894, DW 49:227)

EVILS OF MOB RULE. The case of many of the great evils under which our government suffers at the present time is that the mob rules. Men who are dependent upon votes for office bend to the wishes of the mob and comply with their most insolent demands, regardless of principles or of the question of right or wrong that may be involved in the demand. . . .

Now, there are thousands of men in these United States who are as much opposed to the evils under which the country suffers as are the Latter-day Saints—thousands of patriotic, liberty-loving men and women; but they are scattered throughout the country, without organization and without the power to act in concert. Amid the noisy clamors which prevail, their voices are unheard in the protest against these evils.

In this respect, though few in number, we have the advantage. We are organized. Through the union which God has given unto us we can bear the shock of conflict. It is the design of Providence that we shall stand in the gap, that we shall struggle for and maintain that liberty which was bought by the shedding of precious blood in the founding of this government. Those who understand the nature of the conflict now in progress perceive that we are contending for more than the superficial observer imagines. We are contending for the fullest civil and religious liberty of all men of every creed and of every nationality—a liberty that will permit every man to serve his God according to the dictates of his own conscience, and to perform all other matters to suit himself, so long as in doing so he does not intrude upon the rights and liberties of his fellow-men.

The occurrences of every day prove to us how necessary it is that some people should stand up for liberty and right, and endeavor to induce the nation to walk in the old paths, to put down mobocracy in every form, to befriend the friendless, to protect the unprotected, to defend the weak and the powerless, and to maintain justice and fair dealing in the land, and not suffer any combination of men to attempt to crush our individual or weaker people, because they are unpopular. . . .

The Latter-day Saints have been predicting . . . what the fate of this nation would be unless there should be repentance, and every day the significance of their predictions becomes more apparent. If liberty be preserved, we are the people to preserve it. If anarchy were to reign in these United States today, and our present form of government were to be broken up by civil strife, we, through the blessing of God, are the people, and, I may say, the only people on the continent, capable of self-government, and of maintaining order and every attribute of good government. When those days shall come, as come they undoubtedly will, then the superiority of our system will be made plain, and thousands will be glad to seek refuge in Zion, and protection for life and property from that people whom many of them, to-day, in their ignorance, would be willing to see destroyed. (January 11, 1886, MS 48:18-20)

THE PRIESTHOOD TO SAVE THE NATION. God has chosen this people with the express purpose of making them a great people. We shall be, if we fulfill the destiny that is assigned to us. We shall be the saviors of our nation, and we shall save the nation through the Priesthood that God has established in His Church. This may come in contact with some of your ideas. You may think it will be done through party conventions, through politics, or through political leaders. It will never be done in that way.

It will be done through the power of God, through the revelations of Jesus Christ. It will be done through the medium of that authority He has placed on the earth, and which He recognizes as His. That will be the way in which this will be brought about. It will be brought about in God's own time and God's own way, and these Latter-day Saints—you who are here today, with other Latter-day Saints throughout these valleys—will be the people that will accomplish this under the direction of the Almighty. . . . (January 1, 1897, DW 54:292)

THE NEED OF PATRIOTISM. Every day magnifies the importance of a saving, patriotic element which shall hold aloft the purity of American institutions. With each recurring campaign the opportunity for the labor of such an element becomes more apparent. Every year makes it a necessity nearer and more absolute. In various ways, and by almost imperceptible degrees, the Constitution is being assailed. Sometimes its plain provisions are distorted if not openly violated. . . . Sometimes it is evaded and undermined, and by gradual processes is made to cover proceedings at which the fathers of the country would have stared. Laws which are not in accord with its spirit are sometimes enacted, and very frequently proposed. Men are becoming strangers to patriotism, and are striving after position and pelf.

Every year, according to careful authorities on the subject, the evils and corrupt practices of politics are increasing, and each year the perils which menace the nation become more imminent. Of course there are thousands and tens of thousands of brave men and women who still love the institutions of our land and would maintain them in purity with their lives. But the elements of an opposite character are increasing with great rapidity, and thoughtful men, in even their most sanguine moments, cannot but view the future with some dread.

A DUTY OF PREPARATION. We have alluded to this condition and tendency, not to cause gloom or alarm, or to give rise to political fears or discussion, but to invite the attention of our young people to a duty which clearly rests upon them. They should study the history of the country we live in, not only since, but before the arrival of Columbus and the establishment of the American government. The lessons of the ancient people dwelling here abound in instruction and in comparisons with events occurring in our own days. The views and lives of the founders of American liberty, if examined with patriotic impartiality, will be found almost prophetic in many respects.

Predictions made since the foundation of the Church with reference to the part our people would enact in preserving the Constitution should also be studied prayerfully and in faith. We think, if this be done, every reader will reach the conclusion that perhaps in the past we have been, and in the present are, paying too little attention to our preparation for the work in hand and are but feebly conscious of the importance of the destiny in store. (September 15, 1896, JI 31:544)

SEEKING FOR POLITICAL OFFICE DESPICABLE. I want to say that whenever you see men aspiring for office and planning to get office do not encourage them. Let the office seek the man, and let us not be plotting and resorting to all sorts of dodges to secure success to our party, in order that some of us may get into office. Such arts are despicable. They are the arts of the low politician. We want to stand on a higher plane, and look at these things as men who have been enlightened by the Gospel of the Lord Jesus Christ. (April 8, 1894, DW 48:704)

Let men go into office free and untrammelled. Let them be elected because they are the men most suitable, and not because they want the office. Let us, as a people, endeavor to find men who do not seek for office, and who do not want it, but who take it because it is the wish of their fellow citizens. (November 20, 1884, JD 26:17)

POLITICAL CAMPAIGNS. I will not read a political paper. I will not allow one to come into my house. My children shall not read the misrepresentations and falsehoods that are circulated by men through papers. The atmosphere of my family shall not be defiled by their presence. I will not read the speeches which contain these attacks. If men cannot tell the truth, if they cannot speak truly of principles, I do not want to read their utterances; and if they do speak the truth, and then are assailed for it, I do not want to read the assaults made upon them. (October 14, 1894, MS 56:757)

POLITICS A NOBLE PROFESSION. A time is coming when the youth of these mountains will have to take part in governing the nation, and a greater or less knowledge of political history will be absolutely necessary to them. First of all, the general proposition may be laid down that such a thing as purity in politics is not impossible, though at present somewhat rare. The science or profession, as it may be called, is in its proper phase a noble one; and for a man who is conscientious, full of moral courage, able to resist the temptations which beset the politician's path in a thousand alluring forms, and can restrain his ambition within proper limits, no more inviting or more praiseworthy direction could be desired in which to exercise his talents than to study and solve questions of statesmanship and devise measures which shall be of lasting benefit of his race. Viewed in this light politics are worthy of the best endeavors of the brightest minds; and such a system would we wish to see introduced to and studied by our young men whose destiny is to uphold and sustain pure government, and be in this direction as the servants of God are in all others—benefactors of the world of mankind. (March 15, 1885, JI 20:87)

THE SAINTS AND POLITICS. It becomes a question of some importance in these days whether the Latter-day Saints can divide on politics and still be Latter-day Saints, still have fellowship for one another and still preserve that respect one for the other that the Gospel requires.

The discussion of politics has brought to the surface many strange exhibitions of feeling among members of the Church. . . . Many have yielded to a spirit that produces anything but harmony and love, and there is considerable danger that this agitation may almost prove too strong an ordeal for the faith of many men who have passed through a good many trials in the past and been undisturbed thereby.

Some of us can speak with the utmost confidence and say that it was not and is not contrary to the will of the Lord that this division on party lines should take place. This being the case, it necessarily follows that members of our Church can take sides in politics without doing anything that is inconsistent with their character as Saints of the Lord. Because evil passions arise, because men grow angry and contend, because men even descend to falsehood and defamation, and resort to tricks to gain their ends, this conduct does not prove that there is any defect in our religion, or that a division on party lines is not proper; it only shows the fallibility of men and their failure to practically apply the principles of their religion to the affairs in which they are engaged. . . . If men cannot retain the Spirit of God, and cannot treat each other as Latter-day Saints, then there is some failure in the men who place themselves in such a condition. . . .

We have been taught from the beginning to be governed by the principles of our religion in all the relations of life—in our buying, in our selling, in our trading, in fact, in every department of human transactions. The whole burden of the teachings of the leaders of this Church has been to this effect. We have been informed that our religion is a practical religion, an everyday religion, not to be put on with our Sunday clothes, nor to be laid off when we assume our working apparel. And these teachings will apply to politics as well as everything else.

If members of the Church should be guilty of conduct in politics that would not be justified in other transactions and in the ordinary affairs of life, then they step out of the path which as Saints they should walk in. Men can grieve the Spirit of God by overstepping the bounds of right in political matters as well as in other directions. Because a man is engaged in politics, he has no right to break the divine laws which have been given to us for the regulation of our lives as the children of God; and those who do this will lose His Holy Spirit. . . . (November 1, 1892, JI 27:645-46)

NO FAITH IN POLITICAL PARTIES. We do not place our faith in political parties, either Democrats or Republicans.

We believe one would be as willing as the other to crowd us to the wall if it could be sure of winning popular applause for the act. While we have warm friends in both parties, we cannot expect especial favor from either. The Lord is determined to have the glory for carrying on and consummating His own work, and to do this He is fully able. Therefore, to sum up the condition of the world in brief words, it may be stated that the only opposition to the Kingdom and power of God is found in the power of Satan. Those who are not for the one are for the other, and it is only a question of a short time as to which will be triumphant. (March 15, 1885, JI 20:87)

DISCIPLINE OF CHURCH OFFICERS. The Church asks that its principal officers, whose duties are of a character necessary for the maintenance of the Church and its perfect organization, should devote themselves to the ministry that is assigned to them and which they accept in taking office. The Church asks that if at any time they are invited to assume other duties, the Church, through its Authorities, shall be consulted as to the propriety of these officers accepting these or not. Is there anything improper in this? Is there any interference with the rights of free men? Not in the least. . . . If any officer should think that his rights are interfered with by this rule of discipline, he is at perfect liberty to resign his ecclesiastical office. But I am prepared to say that no man of any party would be refused permission to accept office if it were at all possible for him to hold it consistently with his ecclesiastical duties.

The Church of Jesus Christ of Latter-day Saints does not consider that it is wrong for its officers to hold civil office. It is a different organization in many of its features from any other religious organization, and there is nothing inconsistent in its ecclesiastical officers performing their full duty as citizens in or out of civil office. (June 15, 1896, JI 31:362)

INDEX

A

B

C

G

H

I

J

K

L

R

S

T